Practical Concurrent Haskell

With Big Data Applications

Stefania Loredana Nita
Marius Mihailescu

Apress®

Practical Concurrent Haskell: With Big Data Applications

Stefania Loredana Nita
Bucharest, Romania

Marius Mihailescu
Bucharest, Romania

ISBN-13 (pbk): 978-1-4842-2780-0
DOI 10.1007/978-1-4842-2781-7

ISBN-13 (electronic): 978-1-4842-2781-7

Library of Congress Control Number: 2017953873

Cover image by Freepik (`www.freepik.com`)

Managing Director: Welmoed Spahr
Editorial Director: Todd Green
Acquisitions Editor: Steve Anglin
Development Editor: Matthew Moodie
Technical Reviewer: Alejandro Serrano Mena
Coordinating Editor: Mark Powers
Copy Editor: Kim Burton-Weisman

Distributed to the book trade worldwide by Springer Science+Business Media New York, 233 Spring Street, 6th Floor, New York, NY 10013. Phone 1-800-SPRINGER, fax (201) 348-4505, e-mail `orders-ny@springer-sbm.com`, or visit `www.springeronline.com`. Apress Media, LLC is a California LLC and the sole member (owner) is Springer Science + Business Media Finance Inc (SSBM Finance Inc). SSBM Finance Inc is a **Delaware** corporation.

For information on translations, please e-mail `rights@apress.com`, or visit `http://www.apress.com/rights-permissions`.

Apress titles may be purchased in bulk for academic, corporate, or promotional use. eBook versions and licenses are also available for most titles. For more information, reference our Print and eBook Bulk Sales web page at `http://www.apress.com/bulk-sales`.

Any source code or other supplementary material referenced by the author in this book is available to readers on GitHub via the book's product page, located at `www.apress.com/9781484227800`. For more detailed information, please visit `http://www.apress.com/source-code`.

Printed on acid-free paper

Contents at a Glance

Contents

v

About the Authors

Stefania Loredana Nita holds two bachelor of science degrees from the University of Bucharest: one in mathematics (2013) and one in computer science (2016). She received her master of science degree in software engineering in 2016, also from the University of Bucharest. She has worked as a developer for an insurance company (Gothaer Insurance) and as a teacher of mathematics and computer science in private education. Currently, she is a computer science PhD student at the University of Bucharest. She is also a teaching assistant at the same university. She has been a researcher and developer at the Institute for Computers in Bucharest, Romania, since 2015. Her domains of interest are cryptography applied in cloud computing and big data, parallel computing and distributed systems, software engineering.

Marius Mihailescu received Bachelor's degrees in science and information technology (2008) and in computer engineering (2009) from the University of Southern Denmark. He holds two master of science degrees: one in software engineering (2010) from the University of Bucharest and one in information security technology (2011) from the Military Technical Academy. His PhD in computer science (2015) is from the University of Bucharest. His thesis was on security of biometrics authentication protocols. From 2005 to 2011, he worked as a software developer and researcher at several well-known companies (Softwin, NetBridge Investments, and Declic) in Bucharest, Romania (in the areas of software and web development, business analysis, parallel computing, cryptography researching, distributed systems). From 2012 to 2015, he was an assistant in the Informatics Department at University of Titu Maiorescu and in the Computer Science Department at the University of Bucharest. He has been a lecturer at the University of South-East Lumina since 2015.

About the Technical Reviewer

Alejandro Serrano Mena is working towards his PhD thesis in software technology at Utrecht University. He is passionate about functional programming: he codes Haskell for personal and professional projects, and lectures on functional paradigm at academic and industrial conferences. He is the author of *Beginning Haskell* (Apress, 2014). He has taken part in the Google Summer of Code program, enhancing his Haskell development experience. His current position involves research in improving the way in which developers get feedback and interact with strong type systems such as Haskell's.

Haskell Foundations. General Introductory Notions

CHAPTER 1

■ ■ ■

Introduction

The general goal of this book, *Practical Concurrent Haskell: With Big Data Applications,* is to give professionals, academics, and students comprehensive tips, hands-on examples, and case studies on the Haskell programming language, which is used to develop professional software solutions for business environments, such as cloud computing and big data. This book is not an introduction to programming in general. You should be familiar with your operating system and have a text editor.

To fully understand Haskell and its applications in modern technologies, such as cloud computing and big data, it's important to know where Haskell came from.

When we are discussing Haskell for the cloud, we have to look at it from an Erlang-style point of view. Concurrent and distributed programming in Haskell could be a challenging task, but once it has been accomplished and well integrated with a cloud environment, you will have a strong, reliable, efficient, secure, and portable platform for software applications.

Programming for the cloud with Haskell requires a generic network transportation API, importing and using libraries for sending static closure to remote nodes, and the power of API for distributed programming.

Generic network transport back-ends are developed for TCP (Transmission Control Protocol - represents one of the most used Internet communication protocols) and message of type in-memory, and several other implementations that are available for Windows Azure.

What Is Haskell?

Haskell is a lazy, purely functional programming language. The reason that it is called "lazy" is because only the expressions to determine the right answer to a specific problem are used. We can observe by specifying that the opposite of lazy is *strict*, which means that the evaluation strategy and mechanisms describe very common programming languages, such as C, C++, and Java.

In general, an evaluation strategy is used for argument(s) evaluation for a call or the invocation of a function with any kind of values that pass to the function. Let's take, for example, a call by a value using the reference that specifies the function that evaluates the argument before it proceeds to the evaluation of the function's body and content. Two capabilities are passed to the function: first, the ability to look up the current value of the argument, and, second, the ability to modify it through the assignment statement. A second type of strategy, called *reduction strategy*, is specific for lambda calculus; it is similar to an evaluation strategy.

The goal of a reduction strategy is to show how a complex expression is reduced to a simple expression using successive reduction steps. In practice, a reduction strategy is a function that maps a lambda calculus term with expressions that will be reduced to one particular reducible expression. For decades, mathematical logicians have studied the properties of this system. The shallow similarities between the description of evaluation strategies has led programming language researchers to speculate that the two strategies are identical—a belief that can be observed in popular books from the early 1980s; but as we have stated, they are different concepts. Lambda calculus is not the objective of this book, but lambda calculus represents a formal system in mathematical logic used to express computation based on function abstractions and applications that use variable binding and substitution.

© Stefania Loredana Nita and Marius Mihailescu 2017
S. L. Nita and M. Mihailescu, *Practical Concurrent Haskell*, DOI 10.1007/978-1-4842-2781-7_1

In practice, most programming languages use the call-by-value and call-by-reference evaluation strategy for function strategies (C# and Java). The C++ programming language, as a lower-level language, combines different notions of parameter passing. Haskell, a pure functional language, and non-purely functional languages such as R, use call when needed.

To illustrate how the evaluation strategy is working, we have two examples: one in C++ and one in Haskell.

Here is the first simple example in C++ that simulates the call by reference, provided by wikipedia (https://en.wikipedia.org/wiki/Evaluation_strategy).

```
void modify(int p, int* q, int* r) {
    p = 27;      // passed by value: only the local parameter is modified
    *q = 27;     // passed by value or reference, check call site to determine which
    *r = 27;     // passed by value or reference, check call site to determine which
}

int main() {
    int a = 1;
    int b = 1;
    int x = 1;
    int* c = &x;
    modify(a, &b, c);    // a is passed by value, b is passed by reference by creating a
                         //     pointer (call by value),
                         // c is a pointer passed by value
                         // b and x are changed
    return 0;
}
```

The second example uses Haskell. You can see the evaluation strategy by using call by need, which represents a memorized version of call by name, where, if the argument that sends to the function is evaluated, that value is stored for different subsequent uses.

```
cond p x y = if p then x else y
loop n = loop n
z = cond True 42 (loop 0)
```

Haskell is known as a pure functional language because it does not allow side effects; by working with different examples, we can observe that Haskell is using a set as a system of monads to isolate all the impure computations from the rest of the program. For more information about monads, please see Chapter 2.

Side effects in Haskell are hidden, such that a generic over any type of monad may or may not incur side effects at runtime, depending on the monad that is used. In short, "side effects" mean that after every IO operation, the status of the system could be changed. Since a function can change the state—for example, change the contents of a variable, we can say that the function has side effects.

Haskell is a functional language because the evaluation process of a program is equal to the evaluation of a function in the purest and natural mathematical way. This is different from standard languages, such as C and Java, in which the evaluation process is taking place as a sequence with statements, one after other— known as an *imperative language/paradigm*. In the last few years, impure and functional languages like F# or Swift, have been adopted more and more.

When creating applications for cloud computing, it is very important to understand the structure of the Haskell program and to follow some basic steps, which are described in Chapter 2. Let's overview these steps.

- At the topmost level, Haskell software is a set of modules. The modules allow the possibility to control all the code included and to reuse software in large and distributed software in the cloud.

- The top level of a model is compounded from a collection of declarations. Declarations are used to define things such as ordinary values, data types, type classes, and some fixed information.

- At a lower level are expressions. The way that expressions are defined in a software application written in Haskell is very important. Expressions denote values that have a static type. Expressions represent the heart of Haskell programming.

- At the last level, there is lexical structure, which captures the concrete representation of a software in text files.

A Little Bit of Haskell History

To discuss the full history of Haskell would be a laborious task. The following is from *The Haskell 98 Report* (https://www.haskell.org/onlinereport/).

> *In September of 1987, a meeting was held at the conference on Functional Programming Languages and Computer Architecture (FPCA '87) in Portland, Oregon, to discuss an unfortunate situation in the functional programming community: there had come into being more than a dozen non-strict, purely functional programming languages, all similar in expressive power and semantic underpinnings. There was a strong consensus at this meeting that more widespread use of this class of functional languages was being hampered by the lack of a common language. It was decided that a committee should be formed to design such a language, providing faster communication of new ideas, a stable foundation for real applications development, and a vehicle through which others would be encouraged to use functional languages. This document describes the result of that committee's efforts: a purely functional programming language called Haskell, named after the logician Haskell B. Curry whose work provides the logical basis for much of ours.*

Because of the huge impact that cloud computing and big data has on developing technologies, Haskell continues to evolve every day. The focus is on the following.

- Syntactic *elements*: patterns guards, recursive do notation, lexically scoped type variables, metaprogramming facilities

- Innovations *on type systems*: multiparameter type classes, functional dependencies, existential types, local universal polymorphism, and arbitrary rank-types

- Extensions *for control*: monadic state, exceptions, and concurrency

As we mentioned, this book is not an introduction to Haskell. We remind you that there are two standards: 98 and 2010. The main complier, GHC, extends these languages in different ways. You are encouraged to read *The Haskell 98 Report* and the *Haskell 2010 Language Report* (https://www.haskell.org/onlinereport/haskell2010/); both are freely available on the Internet.

The Cloud and Haskell

This section discusses the problem of designing distributed processes and implementation processes for cloud environments. Compared with other initial implementations, the aim isn't to change the API. The API, such as the efforts to combine Erlang-style concurrent and distributed programming in Haskell to provide generic network transport API, libraries intended to send static closures to remote nodes, or a very rich API for distributed programming API, are and represents couple of examples of what we can use in the process of developing applications in Haskell for cloud environments. The real aim is to gain more flexibility in the network layer and transport layer, such as shared memory, IP and HPC interconnects, and configuration (i.e., neighbor discovery startup and tuning network parameters). When designing and implementing software applications with Haskell for the cloud, it's better to consider both schemes, as shown in Figure 1-1 and Figure 1-2.

Figure 1-1 points outsome dependencies between different modules for the initial startup implementation in Cloud Haskell. The arrows indicate the direction of the dependencies.

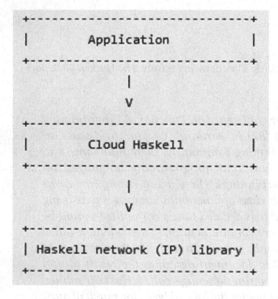

Figure 1-1. *Haskell for cloud module dependencies (figure from* http://haskell-distributed.github.io/wiki/newdesign.html*)*

Figure 1-1 indicates the initial implementation uses a single specific transport, based on TCP/IP (Haskell network (IP) Library).

Figure 1-2 shows the various modules that are provided in the new design. We divided a generic system into two layers: the Cloud Haskell layer and the Network Transport layer. Each layer has a back-end package that can be used with different transports.

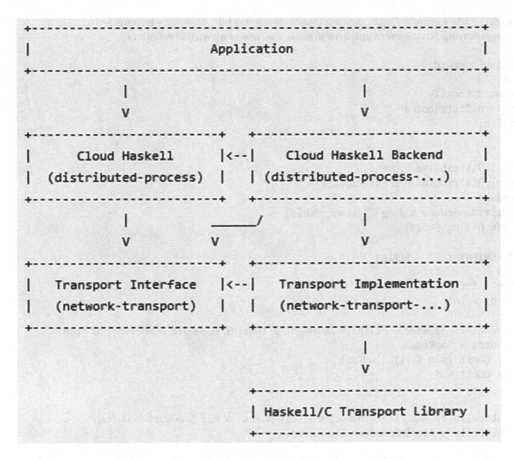

Figure 1-2. Designing the modules (figure from http://haskell-distributed.github.io/wiki/ newdesign.html)

According to the official documentation (http://haskell-distributed.github.io/wiki/newdesign. html), applications designed and developed with Haskell are encouraged to use the Cloud Haskell Layer.

> *Complete applications will necessarily depend on a specific Cloud Haskell backend and would require (hopefully minor) code changes to switch backend. However, libraries of reusable distributed algorithms could be written that depend only on the Cloud Haskell package.*

The following code example, CountingSomeWords, illustrates how necessary imports are used in a distributed programming environment and how to make them to work with MapReduce.

```
module CountingSomeWords
  ( Document
  , countingWordsLocally
  , countingWordsDistributed
  , __remoteTable
  ) where

import Control.Distributed.Process
import Control.Distributed.Process.Closure
import MapReduce
import MonoDistrMapReduce hiding (__remoteTable)
import Prelude hiding (Word)

type DocumentsWithWords  = String
type SomeWord        = String
type HowOften = Int
type countWords = Int

countingSomeWords :: MapReduce FilePath DocumentsWithWords SomeWord HowOften HowOften
countingSomeWords = MapReduce {
    aMap     = const (map (, 1) . words)
  , aReduce = const sum
  }

countingWordsLocally :: Map FilePath DocumentsWithWords -> Map SomeWord HowOften
countingWordsLocally = localMapReduce countWords

countingSomeWords_ :: () -> MapReduce FilePath DocumentsWithWords SomeWord HowOften HowOften
countingSomeWords_ () = countingSomeWords

remotable ['countWords_]

countingWordsDistributed :: [NodeId] -> Map FilePath DocumentsWithWords -> Process
                            (Map SomeWord HowOften)
countingWordsDistributed = distrMapReduce ($(mkClosure 'countWords_) ())
```

The next example will show how to use one of the most important characteristic of cloud computing within Haskell.

```
module MapReduce
  ( -- * Map-reduce skeleton and implementation
    MapReduce(..)
  , localMapReduce
    -- * Map-reduce algorithmic components
  , reducePerKey
  , groupByKey
    -- * Re-exports from Data.Map
  , Map
  ) where
```

```haskell
import Data.Typeable (Typeable)
import Data.Map (Map)
import qualified Data.Map as Map (mapWithKey, fromListWith, toList)
import Control.Arrow (second)

-- | MapReduce skeleton
data MapReduce k1 v1 k2 v2 v3 = MapReduce {
    mrMap    :: k1 -> v1 -> [(k2, v2)]
  , mrReduce :: k2 -> [v2] -> v3
  } deriving (Typeable)

-- | Local (non-distributed) implementation of the map-reduce algorithm
--
-- This can be regarded as the specification of map-reduce; see
-- /Google's MapReduce Programming Model---Revisited/ by Ralf Laemmel
-- (<http://userpages.uni-koblenz.de/~laemmel/MapReduce/>).
localMapReduce :: forall k1 k2 v1 v2 v3. Ord k2 =>
                  MapReduce k1 v1 k2 v2 v3
               -> Map k1 v1
               -> Map k2 v3
localMapReduce mr = reducePerKey mr . groupByKey . mapPerKey mr

reducePerKey :: MapReduce k1 v1 k2 v2 v3 -> Map k2 [v2] -> Map k2 v3
reducePerKey mr = Map.mapWithKey (mrReduce mr)

groupByKey :: Ord k2 => [(k2, v2)] -> Map k2 [v2]
groupByKey = Map.fromListWith (++) . map (second return)

mapPerKey :: MapReduce k1 v1 k2 v2 v3 -> Map k1 v1 -> [(k2, v2)]
mapPerKey mr = concatMap (uncurry (mrMap mr)) . Map.toList
```

Book Structure

This book has two parts.

- Part I is covers eight chapters on the basics of Haskell, including what you need know to develop and move applications in cloud computing and big data environments.

  - Chapter 1 outlines the most important goals of this book and it guides you through the entire structure of the book.

  - Chapter 2 presents medium-advanced examples of source code that help you understand the difference between creating a software application for local use and a software application used for a cloud-computing environment.

  - Chapter 3 brings all the elements for developing software applications using parallelism concurrent techniques. Threads, distributed programming, and EVAL monad for parallelism represent the most important topics.

  - Chapter 4 goes through the different strategies used in the evaluation process during code execution. The strategies described in this section provide the most important steps needed to integrate within applications.

- Chapter 5 focuses on the importance of using exceptions thrown by different situations of using a monad in order to integrate I/O operations within a purely functional context.

- Chapter 6 covers the importance of cancellation conditions as a major component for developing an application using parallelism.

- Chapter 7 discusses some powerful tools for resolving important issues that could appear in the process of developing distributed applications. These problems include race conditions due to forgotten locks, deadlocks, corruption, and lost wakeups.

- Chapter 8 covers debugging, which plays an important role in the process of developing and updating software applications. Sometimes the debugging process is problematic because Haskell does not have a good debugger for advanced software applications. Some modern techniques that could be used in debugging process are discussed.

- Part 2 is focused on developing advanced software applications using big data and cloud computing environments.

  - Chapter 9 covers the most important methods for processes and messages, and techniques used for matching messages. The section will present a domain-specific language for developing programs for a distributed computing environment.

  - Chapter 10 covers the most comprehensive techniques and methods for calling and using big data in Haskell by providing case studies and examples of different tasks.

  - Chapter 11 goes through concurrency design patterns with the goal to understand how to use them for applications based on big data.

  - Chapter 12 presents the steps necessary for designing large-scale programs in such a manner that there are no issues when ported in a big data or cloud environment.

  - Chapter 13 looks at Hadoop algorithms and finds the most suitable environment for running different data sets of varying sizes. The experiments in this chapter are executed on a multicore shared memory machine.

  - Chapter 14 covers the necessary tools and methods for obtaining an interactive debugger.

  - Chapter 15 presents MapReduce for cloud computing and big data, together with all the elements that can be used for developing professional applications based on data sets and for creating an efficient portability environment.

  - Chapter 16 offers original ideas for serving applications on data mining, web ranking, analysis of different graphs, and so on. Elements for improving efficiency by creating and developing caching mechanisms are provided.

  - Chapter 17 presents case studies that demonstrate the running process on large clusters. Parallelization of programs are provided and executed on large clusters.

Summary

This chapter introduced the main ideas behind cloud for Haskell, such as

- the main concepts behind developing Haskell applications for cloud computing environments.

- dependencies and how they are used to gain the greatest performance.

- designing modules and setting the new layers necessary for every application developed with Haskell for the cloud.

It also covered the book's structure and provided an overview.

CHAPTER 2

■ ■ ■

Programming with Haskell

Haskell represents a purely functional programming language that provides many advantages and the latest innovations in the design of programming languages. The most recent standard of Haskell is Haskell 2010; but in May 2016, the Haskell community started working on the next version, Haskell 2020.

The Haskell platform is available for download at https://www.haskell.org/platform/, where there are other versions of installers and an installation guide. After downloading of the appropriate version, just follow the steps. In this book, we will use version 8.0.1.

This chapter focuses on some of the basic elements that you need to understand before continuing to the next chapters. The information is intended for the users and programmers who already have some experience in Haskell programming.

Functional vs. Object-Oriented Programming

Before starting programming with Haskell, it is important to understand the principles of functional programming (FP), and the similarities and the differences between it and object-oriented programming (OOP). We assume that you have (at least) a basic knowledge of object-oriented programming.

The purpose of OOP and FP is to create programs that are easy to understand, flexible, and have no bugs; but each paradigm has its own approach.

Broadly, the similarities between the two programming paradigms are in the levels of expressive power and the capabilities of encapsulating programs into more compact pieces that could be (re)combined. The main difference is the connection between data and the way operations are applied on that data.

The most important principle of OOP is that the data and the operations applied on that data are closely linked: an object contains its own data and the specific implementation of the operations on the owned data. Thereby, the main model to be abstracted is the data itself. OOP allows you to compose new objects, but also to extend the existing classes through the addition of new methods.

Conversely, the main principle of FP is that functions represent the primary model that should be abstracted, not the data. The implementations of the functions are also hidden (as in OOP), and the abstractions of language are given by the functions and the way they could be combined or expressed. As its name suggests, writing new functions represents the main activity of functional programming.

© Stefania Loredana Nita and Marius Mihailescu 2017
S. L. Nita and M. Mihailescu, *Practical Concurrent Haskell*, DOI 10.1007/978-1-4842-2781-7_2

Language Basics

This section discusses Haskell programming basics, but first you need to understand the components of a Haskell program.

- The most important level of a Haskell program is a set of *modules* that allow you to control namespaces and reuse software in big programs.

- At the top of a module, there are the *declarations* that define different elements (for example, values, or data types).

- The next level is represented by *expressions*, which is static and designates a value. These are the most important elements of Haskell programming.

- The last level is represented by the *lexical structure*, which catches the concrete frame of Haskell programs in the text files.

A *value* is evaluated by an expression, which has a static *type*. The type system permits defining new data types and more types of *polymorphism* (parametric or ad hoc).

In Haskell, there are several categories of names.

- *Values*. The names for variables and constructors

- *Elements associated with the type system*. The names for type constructors, type variables, and type classes

- *Modules*. The names for modules

You need to pay attention when naming variables and type variables. These names represent identifiers, which should start with a lowercase letter or an underscore. Other names should begin with an uppercase letter.

As in every programming language, comments are allowed. To comment on a single line, use -- before the comment. A multiline comment begins with {- and ends with -}. The following are examples.

```
-- This is a single line comment.
{- This is
a multi-line commnet. -}
```

It is recommended that you already have the WinGHCi window open. The following examples can be implemented and tested in WinGHCi or by opening the command prompt or terminal, depending on your operating system (Windows or Linux). Figure 2-1 and Figure 2-2 show examples of what the windows look like when GHCi is launched. When you open the GHCi (or WinGHCi, for Windows users), you can see two lines of text, as shown in Figure 2-1. The first line gives the module version of GHCi. In the second line, there is Prelude>. What is it about? Prelude represents the standard; it is imported by default in all modules. You can stop importing the Prelude module by enabling the NoImplicitPrelude extension, or by writing a specific import statement for it. The structure and the internal content of the Prelude module can be found at https://www.haskell.org/onlinereport/standard-prelude.html and https://hackage.haskell.org/package/base-4.9.1.0/docs/Prelude.html.

Figure 2-1. *WinGHCi window*

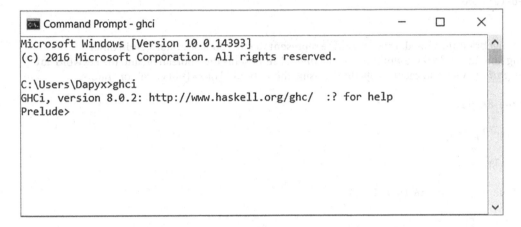

Figure 2-2. *Launching GHCi from command prompt*

Arithmetic

Now that you know a few things about Haskell language programming, let's do some arithmetic. The following are examples of using the arithmetic operators +, -, *, and /.

```
Prelude> 5 + 3
8
Prelude> 175 - 23
152
Prelude> 55 * 256
14080
Prelude> 351 / 3
117.0
Prelude> 5 + 3
8
Prelude> 175 - 23
152
Prelude> 55 * 256
14080
Prelude> 351 / 3
117.0
```

You can combine these operators by using parenthesis. If you want to operate with a negative number, you should use the parenthesis—for example 5 * (-3); otherwise, you will get an error message. Also, there are mathematical functions such sqrt, abs, min, max, and succ.

```
Prelude> 133 * 18 + 5
2399
Prelude> 133 * (18 + 5)
3059
Prelude> 374 / (20 - 31)
-34.0
Prelude> 3 + sqrt(9)
6.0
Prelude> abs(25-100)
75
```

Boolean algebra is permitted. True and False represent the two Boolean values. As in other programming languages, && represent the Boolean *and*, || represents the Boolean *or*, and the keyword not represents *negation*. Also, you can test equality by using the == (equal) or /= (not equal) operators.

```
Prelude> True && False
False
Prelude> False || True
True
Prelude> not True
False
Prelude> (True || False) && (not True)
False
Prelude> 100 == 100
True
Prelude> 100 /= 100
False
```

■ **Note**   The True and False values begin with an uppercase letter.

When you use arithmetic operators or Boolean operators, the left side and the right side of the operator should have the same type; otherwise, you will get an error message.

```
Prelude> 2 + 2
4
Prelude> "xy" == "xy"
True
Prelude> 2 + "xyz"
<interactive>:26:1: error:
    • No instance for (Num [Char]) arising from a use of '+'
    • In the expression: 2 + "xyz"
      In an equation for 'it': it = 2 + "xyz"
Prelude> True && 5
<interactive>:29:9: error:
    • No instance for (Num Bool) arising from the literal '5'
```

- In the second argument of '(&&)', namely '5'
  In the expression: True && 5
  In an equation for 'it': it = True && 5
```
Prelude> 3 == "xy"
<interactive>:30:1: error:
```
  - No instance for (Num [Char]) arising from the literal '3'
  - In the first argument of '(==)', namely '3'
    In the expression: 3 == "xy"
    In an equation for 'it': it = 3 == "xy"

In the preceding example, the + operator also expects a number on the right side, and the && operator expects a Boolean value on the right side. The equality can be verified only between two items of the same type. The example tests the equality between two strings, which is successful, and between a number and a string, which are different types, so there is an error message. Still, there are some exceptions when you operate with items of different types. This is when implicit conversion occurs. For example, addition using an integer value and a floating-point value is allowed because the integer can be converted to a floating-point number. The following is an example.

```
Prelude> 3 + 2.5
5.5
```

Pairs, Triples, and Much More

If you want to set a specific value or expression to a variable, use the keyword let. You do not need to declare the variable before setting a value. In Haskell, once you set a value to a variable, you cannot change that value in the same program. It is similar to a problem in mathematics—a variable cannot change its value in the same problem. The variables in Haskell are *immutable*. The following advanced example shows that if you set two values to a variable, you will get an error.

```
Prelude> let x = 4
Prelude> x
4
Prelude> let y = "abc"
Prelude> y
"abc"
```

Tuples are useful when you know the number of values to be combined. Tuples are marked by parenthesis. Its elements are separated by commas; they are not homogenous and they can contain different types.

```
Prelude> let pair = (2, "orange")
Prelude> pair
(2,"orange")
```

As you can see in the preceding example, our tuple is a pair with two elements of different types: a number and a string. Tuples are inflexible, because every tuple with its own size and types actually represents a type itself. Thus, general functions for tuples cannot be written. For example, if you want to add an element to a tuple, you should write a function for a tuple with two elements, a function for a tuple with three elements, and so on. You can make comparisons between tuples only if their components can be compared.

```
Prelude> let fstTuple = ("apple", 2, True)
Prelude> let sndTuple = ("orange", 3, True)
Prelude> fstTuple == sndTuple
False
Prelude> let trdTuple = ("green", False)
Prelude> fstTuple == trdTuple
<interactive>:53:13: error:
    • Couldn't match expected type '([Char], Integer, Bool)'
                    with actual type '([Char], Bool)'
    • In the second argument of '(==)', namely 'trdTuple'
      In the expression: fstTuple == trdTuple
      In an equation for 'it': it = fstTuple == trdTuple
```

There are two important functions, which are applied on a particular type of tuples, namely the pair: fst and snd. Intuitively, fst returns the first element of the pair and snd returns the second element of the pair. In Haskell, you call a function by writing its name, followed by parameters divided by spaces.

```
Prelude> fst trdTuple
"green"
Prelude> snd trdTuple
False
Prelude> fst (5, True)
5
```

Lists

Lists are similar to tuples. The main difference between them is that the lists are homogenous data structures; thus, all elements are of the same type. For example, you can have a list of integers, or a list of characters, but you cannot mix them in the same list. Lists are marked by brackets, and the elements are separated by commas. The strings are a list of characters, so the "Haskell" string is actually the list ['H', 'a', 's', 'k', 'e', 'l', 'l']. You can apply different functions on lists. Thus, because strings are lists of characters, you can apply many functions on them.

```
Prelude> [1, 2, 3] ++ [4, 5]
[1,2,3,4,5]
Prelude> "functional" ++ " programming"
"functional programming"
```

The ++ represents the concatenation of the left-side list with the right-side list (with elements of the same type). When two lists are concatenated, the left-side list is traversed entirely, and the elements of the right-side list are added at the end of the first list. This could take a while if the left-side list has many elements. Intuitively, adding an element to the beginning of a list is much faster. To add an element at the beginning of the list, use the cons operator (:).

```
Prelude> 1:[2,3,4]
[1,2,3,4]
Prelude> 'A':" flower"
"A flower"
```

■ **Note**   In the second example, the character is between single quotes, and the string is between double quotes.

If you want to extract an element on a particular index, use ! !. Pay attention to the chosen index: if it is greater than the number of elements, or if it is negative, you will get an error message. The first index in a list is 0. A list can contain other lists, with the following rule: the lists can have different sizes, but they cannot contain different types.

```
Prelude> [2,4,6,8,10] !! 4
10
Prelude> [2,4,6,8,10] !! 6
*** Exception: Prelude.!!: index too large
Prelude> [2,4,6,8,10] !! -5
<interactive>:64:1: error:
    Precedence parsing error
        cannot mix '!!' [infixl 9] and prefix `-' [infixl 6] in the same infix expression
Prelude> [[1,2], [3], [4,5,6]]
[[1,2],[3],[4,5,6]]
```

Lists can be compared if they contain elements that can be compared. The first element of the left-side list is compared with the first element of the right-side list. If they are equal, then the second elements are compared, and so on.

```
Prelude> [1,2,3] < [5,6,7]
True
Prelude> [1,2] < [-1,6,7]
False
Prelude> [1,2,3] < [-1,6,7]
False
```

There are many useful functions in lists, such as length, head, tail, init, last, maximum, minimum, sum, product, reverse, take, drop, elem, null, and much more. Figure 2-3 is an intuitive representation of the results of the functions head, tail, init, and last.

```
Prelude> length [1,2,3,4,5]
5
Prelude> head [1,2,3,4,5]
1
Prelude> tail [1,2,3,4,5]
[2,3,4,5]
Prelude> init [1,2,3,4,5]
[1,2,3,4]
Prelude> last [1,2,3,4,5]
5
Prelude> minimum [1,2,3,4,5]
1
Prelude> maximum [1,2,3,4,5]
5
Prelude> reverse [1,2,3,4,5]
[5,4,3,2,1]
Prelude> sum [1,2,3,4,5]
15
Prelude> drop 3 [1,2,3,4,5]
[4,5]
Prelude> take 2 [1,2,3,4,5]
[1,2]
Prelude> elem 6 [1,2,3,4,5]
False
```

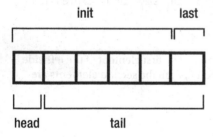

Figure 2-3. *A visual representation of the results of functions head, tail, init and last*

■ **Note**   The empty list is [ ]. It is widely used in almost all recursive functions that work with lists. Note that [ ] and [[ ]] are distinct things, because the first is an empty list and the second is a non-empty list with one empty list as an element.

Source Code Files

In practice, source code is not written in GHCi; instead, source code files are used. Haskell source code files have the extension .hs. Let's suppose that you have a file named Main.hs with the following source code.

```
main = print (fibo 5)

fibo 0 = 1
fibo 1 = 1
fibo n = fibo (n-1) + fibo (n-2)
```

This source code represents a function that computes the Fibonacci number on a specific index. For the moment, take the function as it is; we will explain it in the next subsection. Let's recall how to compute the Fibonacci numbers: $F(0) = 0$, $F(1) = 1$, $F(n) = F(n-1) + F(n-2)$, where $n > 1$.

Now, let's return to the source code files. The file could be saved anywhere, but if the work directory is different from the current directory, you need to change it to that directory in GHCi, using the :cd command, as follows.

```
Prelude> :cd C:\Users
```

To load a file into GHCi, use the :load command.

```
Prelude> :load Main
```

After loading the module, you can observe that the prompt was changed into *Main> to indicate that the current context for expression is the Main module. Now, you can write expressions that include functions defined in Main.hs.

```
*Main> fibo 17
2584
```

When loading a module, GHC discovers the file name, which contains, for example, a module M, by looking for the file M.hs or M.lhs. Thus, usually, the name of a module should be the same as the file; otherwise, GHCi will not find it. Still, there is an exception: when you use the :load command for loading a file, or when it is specified invoking ghci, you can provide the file name instead of a module name. The specified file will be loaded if it exists, and it could comprise any number of modules. If you are trying to use multiple modules in a single file, you will get errors and consider it a bug. This is good, if there are more modules with the same M name, in the same directory; you cannot call them all M.hs.

If you forget the path where you saved a source code file, you can find it, as follows.

```
ghci -idir1:...:dirn
```

If you make changes in the current source code file, you need to recompile it. The command for recompilation is :reload, followed by the name of the file.

Functions

You have used functions since the beginning of this section; for example, all arithmetic operators are functions with two parameters or the functions applied to lists. Now, it's time to define our functions. Let's take the function from the previous subsection. To run a function, you need to write the function's name, followed by the arguments, which are separated by spaces. Parentheses for arguments are not needed.

You haven't used the return keyword. This is because Haskell does not have a return keyword; a function represents a single expression, not a succession of statements. The outcome of the function is the worth of the expression. Still, Haskell has a function called return, but it has a different meaning than in other programming languages.

Let's write a simple function that computes a power.

```
Prelude> pow a b = a ^ b
Prelude> pow 2 10
1024
```

A function has a type, which could be discovered using the :type command.

```
Prelude> :type pow
pow :: (Num a, Integral b) => a -> b -> a
```

As secondary effect, a dependence on the global state and the comportment of a function is introduced. For example, let's think about a function that works with a global parameter, without changing its value and returning it. When a piece of code changes the value of the variable, it affects the function in a particular way, which has a secondary effect; although our function does not change the value of the global variable, which is treated as a constant. If a variable is mentioned out of scope, the value of the variable is obtained when the function is defined.

The secondary effects are usually invisible outcomes for functions. In Haskell, the functions do not have secondary effects, because they are depending only on explicit arguments. These functions are called *pure*. A function with side effects is called *impure*.

```
Prelude> :type writeFile
writeFile :: FilePath -> String -> IO ()
```

The Haskell type system does not allow combining pure and impure code.

if-else

As in other programming languages, Haskell also has the if-else statement. Its syntax is very simple. Let's write a function that returns the maximum between two values.

```
Prelude> maximum a b = if a > b then a else b
maximum :: Ord t => t -> t -> t
Prelude> maximum 5 6
6
```

An important aspect of Haskell is indentation. You need to pay attention to how you organize your code. For example, if you write the maximum function in an .hs file, then it should look like the following.

```
maximum a b = if a > b
                        then a else b
```

Now, let's return to our function. The word maximum represents the name of the function, and a and b are the parameters. The = after the parameters suggests that the implementation of the function is next. Then, you compare the two parameters and return the greatest of them.

The if-else statement has three elements:

- A *predicate*, which represents the Bool expression which follows the if keyword

- The then keyword, which is followed by an expression, and evaluated if the expression that follows the if statement is True

- The else keyword, which is followed by another expression, and evaluated if the expression that follows the if statement is False

The two expressions that follow then and else are called *branches*. They should be the same type; otherwise, it will be cancelled by the compiler/interpreter. The following example is wrong because 10 and abc have different types.

```
If expression then 10
        Else "abc"
```

In Haskell, the if-else statement without an else statement is not allowed, because it is a programming language based on expressions.

RECURSION

The recursion is very important because many functions are recursive, and it represents a manner in which a function is called by itself. Let's remember a previous example: the function that computes Fibonacci numbers. For example, if you call

```
fibo(4) = fibo(3) + fibo(2) = (fibo(2) + fibo(1)) + (fibo(1) + fibo(0)) = ((fibo(1) +
fibo(0)) + 1) + (1 + 0) = ((1 + 0) + 1) + 1 = (1 + 1) + 1 = 2 + 1 = 3
```

As you can see, fibo(4) calls fibo(3) and fibo(2), and so on. The elements of the function that are not defined recursively are called *edge condition*. They are extremely important because they represent the conditions needed to escape from recursion.

The recursion represents one of the base elements of Haskell, because it shows us what something is, rather than how it is computed. Also, it replaces for and while loops.

Types

Variables represent names for expressions. When a variable is linked to an expression, the expression cannot be changed into the current scope, but you are allowed to use the variable, instead of the linked expression. In other word, a variable identifies a location of memory, which could have different values at different times.

Simple vs. Polymorphic Types

A *simple value* is a value that has only one type. This is discussed more about types in the "Data Types" section.

A polymorphic value is that value which could have multiple types. It is a very useful and used feature of Haskell. There two main types of polymorphism: *parametric* and *ad hoc*.

Parametric Polymorphism

Parametric polymorphism occurs if the variable has more than one type, such that the its value could have any type resulted from replacing the variable with explicit types. This means that there are no constraints regarding type variables. The simplest and the easiest example is the identity function.

```
Identity :: a -> a
```

The a can be replaced with any type, whether it is a simple type, such as `Int`, `Double`, `Char`, or a list, for example. So, for a, there is no constraint regarding the type.

The value of a parametrically polymorphic type has no knowledge of type variables without constraints, so it should act in the same way regardless of its type. This fact is known as *parametricity*, and it is very useful, even if it is limiting.

Ad hoc Polymorphism

Ad **hoc polymorphism** occurs when a variable chooses its type according to its behavior at a particular moment, because it is an implementation for every type. A simple example is the + function. The compiler should know if it is used to add integers, or two floating-point numbers.

In Haskell, ambiguity is avoided through the system of type classes or class instances. For example, to compare two objects, you need to specify how the == operator behaves. In Haskell, the overloading is extended to values; for example, a `lowerLimit` variable could have different values according to its use. If it refers to an `Int`, its value cloud is –2147483648, and if it refers to Char, its value could be '\NUL'.

Type Classes

In Haskell, you identify the following aspects of type: *strong*, *static*, and *automatically inferred*.

The *strong* type system of Haskell assures the fact that a program does not contain errors obtained from expressions without a meaning for compiler.

When a program is compiled, the compiler knows the value of every type before the code is executed. This is assured by the *static type system*. Also, when you write expressions of different types, you will get an error message. By combining the strong type and the static type, the type errors will not occur at runtime.

```
Prelude> 2 + "5"
<interactive>:28:1: error:
    • No instance for (Num [Char]) arising from a use of '+'
    • In the expression: 2 + "5"
      In an equation for 'it': it = 2 + "5"
```

At *compilation*, each expression's type is known. If you write an addition symbol between a number and a Boolean value, you will get an error message. In Haskell, each thing has a type. A benefit of Haskell is that it has the *type inference*, through which the type is implicitly inferred. So, if you write a number, you do not need to specify that it is a number.

Strong and static types bring security, while inference makes Haskell concise, so you have a safe and an expressive programming language.

Function Types

In Haskell, the functions have types. When you write functions, you can give them an explicit declaration, a fact that is helpful when you deal with complex functions. If you want to declare a function, you proceed as follows.

```
getMax :: [Int] -> Int
```

The meaning is intuitive. In the preceding example, the getMax function returns the maximum value from a list of integers. The :: symbol is followed by the domain of the definition of the function, and the -> shows the type of the result.

If you have a function with more parameters, you proceed as follows.

```
addition :: Int -> Int -> Int
```

Here, you have the addition function, which computes the sum of the two integers. The first two Ints show the type of the parameters, and they are divided by the -> symbol, and the last Int shows the result type.

It is recommended that functions be written with the explicit declaration; but if you are not sure about that, you can just write the function, and then check its type using the :t or :type commands.

Data Types

The following are some basic data types.

- Int: Integer numbers, which are signed and have fixed width. The range of values is not actually fixed; it depends on the system (32/64 bits), but Haskell assures that an Int is larger than 28 bits.

- Integer: Integer numbers with unbounded dimensions. The Integer type consumes more space and is less performant than Int, but it brings more dependably correct answers. In practice, it is used less than Int.

- Double: Floating-point numbers. Usually, the double value is represented in 64 bits, using the natural floating-point representation of the system.

- Char: Unicode character.

- Bool: A value from Boolean algebra. There are only two possible values: True and False.

Different from other programming languages, Haskell does not explicitly have the data type string. Strings are actually lists of characters.

If you want to check the type of value or an expression, you simply use the :t command, followed by the value or expression, as follows.

```
Prelude> :t 5.3
5.3 :: Fractional t => t
Prelude> :t "abcd"
"abcd" :: [Char]
Prelude> :t (5 < 2)
(5 < 2) :: Bool
```

Input/Output (IO) Mechanisms

GHCi accomplishes more things than evaluating straightforward expressions. When an expression has the type IO a, for some a, GHCi is executing it like an IO computation. Basically, a value which has type (IO a) represents an action that when it is executed, its result has type a.

```
Prelude> length "Haskell"
7
Prelude> 100/2
50.0
```

When an expression's type is general, it is instantiated to IO a.

```
Prelude> return True
True
```

The result of an expression's evaluation is printed if

- It represents an instance of Show

- Its type is not ()

In order to understand the following example, it is necessary to understand do notation. By using do, the notation (instruction) represents an alternative to the monad syntax.

The following example implies IO and you refer to the computation's values as actions. It's important to mention that do is applied with success with any monad.

The >> operator works in the same way as in do notation. Let's consider the following example, which is formed from a chain of different actions.

```
putStr "How" >>
putStr " " >>
putStr "is with programming in Haskell?" >>
putStr "\n"
```

The following example can be rewritten using do notation.

```
do putStr "How"
        putStr " "
        putStr "is with programming in Haskell?"
        putStr "\n"
```

As you can see, the sequence of instructions almost matches in any imperative language. In Haskell, you can connect any actions if all of them are in the same monad. In the context of the IO monad, the actions that you are implementing could include writing to a file, opening a network connection, and so forth.

The following is a step-by-step translation in Haskell code.

```
do action1
       action 2
       action 3
```

becomes

```
action1 >>
do action2
       action3
```

and so on, until the do block is empty.

Besides expressions, GHCi takes also statements, but they must be in the IO monad. Thus, a name could be bounded to values or a function for further use in different expressions or statements. The syntax of a statement is the same as the syntax of do expressions.

```
Prelude> x <- return "abc"
Prelude> print x
"abc"
```

The preceding statement, x<-return "abc" could be "translated," so *execute return "abc" and link the outcome to variable x.* Later, the variable could be used in other statements; for example, for printing.

When -fprint-bind-result is enabled, the outcome of a statement is typed if

- the statement does not represent a binding, or it is a binding to a single variable (v <- e).

- the type of the variable does not represent polymorphism, or (), but it represents a Show instance.

The binding could also be done using the let statement.

```
Prelude> let y = 10
Prelude> y
10
```

A characteristic of the monadic bind is that it is strict; namely, the expression e is evaluated. When using let, the expression is not instantly evaluated.

```
Prelude> let z = error "This is an error message."
Prelude> print z
*** Exception: This is an error message.
CallStack (from HasCallStack):
  error, called at <interactive>:18:9 in interactive:Ghci8
```

Another important thing is that you can write functions directly at the prompt.

```
Prelude> f x a b = a*x + b
Prelude> f 3 5 2
17
```

Nevertheless, this will be a little awkward when you are dealing with complex functions, because the implementation of the function should be on a single line.

```
Prelude> f a | a == 0 = 0 | a < 0 = - a | a > 0 = a
Prelude> f 100
100
Prelude> f (-324)
324
Prelude> f 0
0
```

But Haskell comes with a solution. The implementation could be divided into multiple lines, using the :{ and :} commands.

```
Prelude> :{
Prelude| f a
Prelude| | a == 0 = 0
Prelude| | a < 0 = -a
Prelude| | a > 0 = a
Prelude| :}
```

If an exception occurs while evaluating or executing statements, they are caught and their message is typed, as you have seen in previous examples.

The temporary binds can be used the next time you load or reload a file, because they will be missed after (re)loading, but can be used after the :module: command (discussed in the next section) when it goes to another location. If you need to know all of the binds, you can use the following command.

```
Prelude> :show bindings
x :: [Char] = "abc"
y :: Num t => t = _
it :: Num t => t = _
z :: a = _
```

If +t is enabled, you can find every variable's type.

```
Prelude> :set +t
Prelude> let (x:xs) = [1..]
x :: Integer
xs :: [Integer]
```

There is another possibility that GHCi identifies when a statement is not terminated, and permits writing on multiple lines. It is enabled by the :set +m command. The last line is empty to mark the end of multiple line statement.

```
Prelude> :set +m
Prelude> let a = 100
Prelude|
```

If you want to bind values to more variables in the same let command, you should proceed as follows:

```
Prelude> :set +m
Prelude> let a = 154887
Prelude|        b = 547
Prelude|
```

For multiple line statements, you can use do. The individual statements are separated by semicolons. The right brace marks the end of the multiline statement.

```
Prelude> do {
Prelude| print b
Prelude| ;print b^ 2
Prelude| }
547
299209
Prelude>
```

The multiple-line statements could be interrupted as follows.

```
Prelude> do
Prelude| print a
Prelude| ^C
Prelude>
```

Haskell has a special variable, called it, which receives the value of an expression typed in GHCi (of course, the expression should not be a binding statement).

```
Prelude> 2*3
6
Prelude> it+5
11
```

You need to remember that an expression must have a type, instantiated from Show; otherwise, you will get an error message.

```
Prelude> head

<interactive>:14:1: error:
    • No instance for (Show ([a0] -> a0)) arising from a use of 'print'
        (maybe you haven't applied a function to enough arguments?)
    • In a stmt of an interactive GHCi command: print it
```

Note that the it variable changes its value every time a new expression evaluation occurs, and the previous value is missed.

Haskell permits the use of command-line arguments through the getArgs function, which is passed to the main using the :main command.

```
Prelude> main = System.Environment.getArgs >>= print
Prelude> :main abc xyz
["abc","xyz"]

Prelude> :main abc "xyz pq"
["abc","xyz pq"]
Prelude> :main ["abc", " xyz pq "]
["abc","xyz pq"]
```

Any function could be called using -main-is or the :run commands.

```
Prelude> abc = putStrLn "abc" >> System.Environment.getArgs >>= print
Prelude> xyc = putStrLn "xyz" >> System.Environment.getArgs >>= print
Prelude> :set -main-is abc
Prelude> :main abc "xyz pq"
abc
["abc","xyz pq"]
Prelude> :run xyz ["abc","xyz pq"]
xyz
["abc","xyz pq"]
```

Modules

This section introduces the notations and information necessary for understanding the rest of the book.

It's important to acknowledge the fact that a module in Haskell serve in two directions with a specific purpose: controlling namespaces and creating abstract data types. This aspect is very important in understanding complex applications that are developed in a cloud and big data environment.

If you are looking at a module from a technical perspective, a module is a very big declaration that starts with module keyword. Consider the following example, which presents a module called Tree.

```
module Tree (Tree(Leaf, Branch), fringe) where

data Tree a                     = Leaf a | Branch (Tree a) (Tree a)

fringe :: Tree a -> [a]
fringe (Leaf x)    = [x]
fringe (Branch left right) = fringe left ++ fringe right
```

The following example is presented from official documentation available at https://www.haskell.org/tutorial/modules.html, which has the best explanation. It can be used as a prototype for different tasks that can be implemented into a distributed environment. An important operation in the preceding example is the ++ infix operator, which concatenate the two lists, left and right. In order for the Tree module to be imported into another module, follow this code snippet.

```
module Main (main) where
import Tree (Tree((Leaf, Branch), fringe)

main = print(fringe(Branch(Leaf 1)(Leaf 2)))
```

The various items that are imported into and exported outside of the module are called *entities*. Observe the explicit import list in the declaration of the import. If you omit this, it would cause all the entities that are exported from Tree to be imported.

:load/:reload

As you already know, the default module of Haskell is Prelude. You can change it by importing another module using the :load command. When it is appended, it automatically imports into the scope corresponding to the last loaded module. To be certain that GHCi imports the interpreted version of a module, you can add an asterisk when you load it, such as :load *modulename.

```
Prelude> :load Main.hs
Compiling Main              ( Main.hs, interpreted )
*Main>
```

Now, you can use expressions that involve elements from the loaded module. The star that accompanies the name of the module shows that the module represents the full top-level scope of the expressions from the prompt. In the absence of the asterisk, only the module's exports are observable.

:module

The :module command also permits scope manipulation. If the module keyword is accompanied by +, then the modules are added; if it is accompanied by -, then the modules are removed. If there is no + or -, the actual scope is substituted by the modules after the :module command.

The use of module brings more benefits than using the import command. The main facilities are

- the full top-level of a scope is opened through the * operator.

- the unneeded modules can be removed.

:import

The :import command is used to add modules.

```
Prelude> import Data.Char
Prelude> toUpper 'a'
'A'
```

To see all imported modules, use the :show imports command.

```
Prelude> import System.IO
Prelude> :show imports
import Prelude -- implicit
import Data.Char
import System.IO
```

As you can see, Prelude is imported implicitly, but it could be replaced with the explicit Prelude import. When there are more modules in the scope, it name conflicts could rise. In this case, Haskell will alert you.

As you have seen, there are two ways to get a module in the scope: by using `:module`/`import` or by using `:load`/`:reload`. Still, there are significant differences between the two approaches in the collection of the modules.

- *The collection of modules that are loaded.* changed using `:load`/`:reload` and viewed using `:show` modules.

- *The collection of modules in the scope at the prompt.* changed using `:module`/`import`, and instantaneous after `:load`/`:reload`, and viewed using `:show imports`.

A module can be added into the scope (through `:module`/`import`) if

- the module is loaded.

- the module belongs to a package known by GHCi.

In any other cases, it will be an error message.

Operators Used as Sections and Infix

In Haskell, there are two types of notations used for function calling: *prefix notation* and *infix notation*. Usually, prefix notation is used: the name of the function, followed by the arguments. The infix notation is where the name of the function stands between its arguments. Note that the infix notation can be used for functions with two parameters. If the function has more than two parameters, then the infix notation becomes inconvenient and difficult to follow.

The best-known infix functions are operators. As you well know, the arithmetic operators take two arguments, so they are by default infix. However, if you begin the line with an arithmetic operator in parenthesis, followed by the two arguments, then it becomes a prefix function.

```
Prelude> (+) 4 5
9
Prelude> (*) 10 10
100
```

Anyway, there is a way to use infix notation for an ordinary function. This is done by putting the name of the function between the ` symbol, as follows.

```
Prelude> let concatPrint x y = putStrLn $ (++) x y
 Prelude> concatPrint "a" "b"
 ab
 Prelude> "a" `concatPrint` "b"
 ab
```

There is a particular language structure for an incomplete application on infix operators. Broadly, when you use an operator, it behaves like a function that receives one of the arguments, and the other is put in the place of the misplaced side of the operator.

- `(4^)`: the left side is the same to `(^)` 4, or more formal `\a -> 4 ^ a`

- `(^4)`: the right side is the same to flip `(^)` 4, or more formal `\a -> a ^ 4`

Sectioning a function is very useful because it allows you to write a function, without giving a particular name to that function; for example:

- (1+): the function which increments by one a value

- (2*): the function which doubles a value

- ('\t':): the "tab" function

The minus operator cannot make a right section, since it would be deciphered as unary invalidation in the Haskell language. The Prelude capacity "subtract" is accommodated this reason.

Local Declarations

In Haskell, local declarations can be used. This is done by using the let keyword, which binds a particular value to a variable; for example:

```
Prelude> let a = -5 + 1 in a + 10
6
```

This is equivalent to

```
{
 int a = -5 + 1;
 ... a + 10 ... ;
}
```

In Haskell, the variable receives a value that cannot be changed.

Partial Application

When a function is called with some arguments missing, you actually obtain another function. This can be seen as something like "underloading," but the specific term is *partial application*. For example, let's think about the power function. It takes two arguments: namely, the base and the exponent. If you have a program in which only the irrational number e is used as a base, you could define a new function that takes one argument— namely, the exponent, as follows.

```
Prelude> powE x = (exp 1) ^ x
powE :: (Integral b, Floating a) => b -> a
Prelude> powE 5
148.41315910257657
```

This is very useful when you have complex functions with many parameters, but most of the time, you do not use all parameters.

You need to pay attention to an important aspect: the functions are not partial; you only partially apply a function.

Pattern Matching

In pattern matching, you need to specify patterns in which the data could fit, then check which patterns fit, and then manipulate the data as the pattern indicates. A function could have many implementations for various patterns, an approach that leads to organized, clean, and easy-to-read code. Pattern matching could be used with any data type. The following is an example of a function that tests if a number is zero (it was written in a file called Main.hs).

```
main = testInteger 5

testInteger 0 = print "zero"
testInteger x = print "not zero"
```

And in GHCi, after changing the work directory.

```
Prelude> :load Main
[1 of 1] Compiling Main              ( Main.hs, interpreted )
Ok, modules loaded: Main.
Prelude> testInteger 0
"zero"
Prelude> testInteger 6
"not zero"
```

When a function contains patterns, they are checked from top to bottom. When a match is found, the corresponding implementation is chosen. The "-5" argument fits in the second pattern, so a corresponding message is printed. You could use the if-else statement, but let's think about how a function would look if it contains a branched if-else. Let's say that you write a function that prints the name of a color according to a number as an argument, as shown in the following. If you did not use patterns, the branched if-else would become difficult to follow.

```
color 1 = print "green"
color 2 = print "blue"
color 3 = print "red"
color 4 = print "orange"
color x = print "any color"
```

Here are some arguments.

```
Prelude> color 1
"green"
Prelude> color 5
"any color"
Prelude> color (-100)
"any color"
```

You need to pay attention to the order of patterns. If you put the last pattern on the first place, then, always would be typed "any color", because any number would fit in x.

If the function does not contain a general pattern, and you call it with an argument that does not fit in any pattern, then you will get an error message (after removing the last line of the function).

```
Prelude> color (-100)
*** Exception: Main.hs:(3,1)-(6,24): Non-exhaustive patterns in function color
```

You can use patterns in function that have tuples as parameters; for example, you have two points in the xOy axis system and you want to compute the distance between them. First, let's remember the formula for the Euclidean distance: given two points, $A(x_1, y_1)$, $B(x_2, y_2)$, the distance AB is given by the formula $AB = \sqrt{(x_1 - x_2)^2 + (y_1 - y_2)^2}$. You would do it like this:

```
distance x y = sqrt((fst x - fst y)^2 + (snd x - snd y)^2)
```

Or, if involving patterns, it would be

```
distance2 (x1,y1) (x2, y2) = sqrt((x1 - x2)^2 + (y1 - y2)^2)
```

In Haskell, there are already defined functions that return the first or the second component of a pair. But what if you would work with triples? You can write your own functions.

```
firstElement :: (a, b, c) -> a
firstElement (x, _, _) = x
secondElement :: (a, b, c) -> b
secondElement (_, y, _) = y
thirdElement :: (a, b, c) -> c
thirdElement (_, _, z) = z
```

The underscore (_) means that you can put anything on that index.

Guards

You use guards when you want to test if a property for one or more values is true or false. Of course, you could use the if statement, which is similar to guards, but guards are easy to read and they fit well with patterns. The following is an example in which the name of the weekday is typed according to a number as parameter.

```
dayOfWeek day
 | day == 1 = print "Monday"
 | day == 2 = print "Tuesday"
 | day == 3 = print "Wednesday"
 | day == 4 = print "Thurday"
 | day == 5 = print "Friday"
 | day == 6 = print "Saturday"
 | day == 7 = print "Sunday"
 | otherwise = print "The week has only 7 days. Please, choose an integer between [1, 7]."
```

The guard is represented by the pipes symbol (|). In essence, it is a Boolean expression. The expressions are evaluated one at a time, in order of appearance. If the result is True, then the corresponding instructions are used; else, the next expression follows, until it finds the expression whose result is True. For example, if you call the preceding function with 3, first, it is evaluated as day == 1 (which is False); then, day == 2 (also False); then, day == 3 (which is True), so the corresponding instruction is used.

The guards are useful when there is a long-branched if-else statement. Imagine how the code would look if you used if-else. Usually, the end guard is otherwise, which covers all the possibilities that are not found explicitly in the previous guard. For example, what if you gave the number 8 as a parameter to our function? Of course, an eighth day of the week does not exist, so the result is "The week has only 7 days. Please choose an integer between [1, 7]." What about 100 as an argument? Or 0? Or –5? Of course, they are included in the last guard. If all guards are evaluated as False (this is the case when you do not include otherwise), then you will get an error message (after removing the last line).

```
Prelude> dayOfWeek 10
*** Exception: Main.hs:(7,1)-(14,28): Non-exhaustive patterns in function dayOfWeek
```

The guard could be written on the same line, but it would be difficult to follow. Also, a function that uses a guard could have as many parameters as you want.

Instance Declarations

A declaration of an instance has the following form.

```
instance (asserion_1, ..., assertion_n) => class type_1 ... type_m where ...
```

An instance declaration has two parts.

- *context*: the left side of =>
- *head*: the right side of =>

When GHCi resolves a constraint, each instance declaration tries to be matched with the constraint through initialization of the head of instance declaration. Let's say you have the following statements:

```
instance ctx1 => C Int a    where ...
instance ctx2 => C a   Bool where ...
```

Implicitly, GHCi knows that exactly one instance should fit the constraint on which it tries to resolve.

Rules for the Head

There are rules for the head of an instance.

- *First rule*. -XTypeSynonymInstances, which defines an instance of a type class for the type synonyms

- *Second rule*. -XFlexibleInstances, which permits to define an instance of a type class with arbitrary encapsulated types from the head of the instance

The rules become less restrictive when used.

With -XTypeSynonymInstances, the heads of the instance could use type synonyms. The following code is correct.

```
Type Pt x = (x, x)
Instance C (Pt x) where ...
```

With -XFlexibleInstances, the head could mention arbitrary imbricated types. This flag implies the previous flag.

Rules for the Context

The -XFlexibleContexts moderates a rule according to the context of an instance declaration, which should have the C a format (a is a type variable that occurs in the head). More specifically, this flag permits constraints over a class that has the format (C t1 … tn) in the context of an instance declaration, but it does not interfere with the restrictions over equality.

The declaration of an instance should respect the rules for instance termination.

Rules for Instance Termination

-XUndecidableInstances defines instances that could result in type-checker non-termination. These are the rules.

- For every class restriction from the context

  a. A type variable should not have more appearances in the restriction than in the head.

  b. The constructors and the variable for the restrictions are fewer.

  c. The constraints do not mention type functions.

- For any functional dependency of the class, each type variable from the right should appear in the left of the substitution mapping.

These conditions assure that the termination of the resolution occurs. In every level of reduction, the problem shrinks with at least one constructor.

Other Lists

In the previous section, you used only finite lists, but in Haskell, lists can be infinite because of the lazy evaluation property. The following list represents an infinite list of integer numbers, which starts with 10.

```
[10..]
```

■ **Note** The evaluation could be interrupted with CTRL+C command.

If you want a list of the first 50 integers, you would not write all of them; you would do like this:

```
Prelude> [1..50]
```

This approach is called *ranges*, which enumerates the elements of a list (it has an enumeration rule!) in a compact manner.

```
Prelude> ['a'..'e']
"abcde"
Prelude> [5,10..50]
5,10,15,20,15,30,35,40,45,50
```

Still, the enumeration rule should be intuitive. You cannot write [1,3,9,27..50] to get all powers of 3 less than 50. In order for elements to be in decreasing order, it is not enough to write [50..1]; you should write [50,49..1].

Haskell allows ranges in floating-point numbers, but it is imprecise; often the results are not the expected ones.

In the next example, you write two ways to retrieve the first five multiples of 2.

```
Prelude> [2,4..5*2]
2,4,6,8,10
Prelude> take 5 [2,4..]
```

Three functions create infinite lists: cycle, repeat, and replicate.

```
Prelude> take 4 (cycle [1, 2])
[1,2,1,2]
Prelude> take 2 (cycle "Haskell")
"HaskellHaskell"
Prelude> take 5 (repeat 2)
2,2,2,2,2
Prelude> replicate 5 2
2,2,2,2,2
```

You know that in mathematics, the sets could be defined using predicates. A simple example is $A = \{3x \mid x \in N, x < 7\}$. For this set, 3x is called the output; x represents the variable; N represents the positive numbers set; and x < 7 represents the predicate. A simple way to get this set is to write take 7 [0,3..], but you could also proceed as follows.

```
Prelude> [3*x | x <- [0..6]]
0,3,6,9,12,15,18
```

This representation of lists is known as *list comprehension*.

Now, let's use more predicates. If you want numbers that are multiples of 5, in the range 100 to 150, you would proceed as follows.

```
Prelude> [x| x <- [100, 150], x `mod` 5 == 0]
100,105,110,115,120,125,130,135,140,145,150
```

Arrays

Haskell permits the use of an array, which has only one constructor, Array. As any data structure, they are immutable, so they cannot change the value. Still, it exists to "modify" an array, but this means that it created a new array with extra features, without altering the original array.

Immutable Arrays

The immutable arrays belong to the Data.Array.IArray module. The operations applied on them are the same as those applied on Array.

Mutable Arrays

Mutable arrays belong to the Data.Array.IO module. They permit operations through elements that are updated in-place. The create, update, and query functions for arrays that pertain to the IO monad.

```
import Data.Array.IO
main = do myArray <- newArray (1,5) 20 :: IO (IOArray Int Int)
          a <- readArray myArray 1
          writeArray myArray 1 25
          b <- readArray myArray 1
          print (a,b)
```

The preceding code builds an array with five elements, all of them having the value 20. Next, it reads the element from the first index and changes it, and then reads it again. In the last step, it prints the pair that contains the initial value and the new value.

Another mutable array belongs to the Data.Array.ST module, which permits the use of mutable array from the ST monad.

```
import Control.Monad.ST
import Data.Array.ST

oldNewValue = do myArray <- newArray (1,5) 20 :: ST s (STArray s Int Int)
                 a <- readArray myArray 1
                 writeArray myArray 1 25
                 b <- readArray myArray 1
                 return (a,b)

main = print $ runST oldNewValue
```

The preceding code essentially does the same thing as the previous example, but it uses a different approach.

In addition to these two types of arrays, there are other types that belong to the following modules: Data.Array.Diff, Data.Array.Unboxed, and Data.Array.Storable.

Finite Maps

Finite maps (or simple, maps) represent lookup tables for functional programming. In imperative programming, hash tables are equivalent to maps in Haskell. There are a couple of forms (key and value). When you work with maps, you need to import the Data.Map module.

```
import Data.Map
daysOfWeek = fromList
        [ ("M",  "Monday")
        , ("T",  "Tuesday")
        , ("W",  "Wednesday")
        , ("Th", "Thursday")
        , ("F",  "Friday")
        , ("S",  "Saturday")
        , ("Su", "Sunday") ]
```

A map could be converted to a list by using toList.

```
Prelude> toList daysOfWeek
    [("F","Friday"),("M","Monday"),("S","Saturday")
    ,("Su","Sunday"),("Th","Thursday"),("T","Tuesday")
    ,("Wed","Wednesday")]
```

As you can see, the order is not kept.

If you need only the keys, then use the keys command; if you need only the elements, then use the elems command.

```
Prelude> keys daysOfWeek
    ["F","M","S","Su","Th","T","W"]
*Main> elems daysOfWeek
    ["Friday","Monday","Saturday","Sunday","Thursday","Tuesday","Wednesday"]
```

You could also search a value in the map by using the lookup function, as follows.

```
Prelude> Data.Map.lookup "W" daysOfWeek
    "Wednesday"
```

You use the long version of the lookup function because there also exists a lookup function in Prelude, and you need to disambiguate so that GHCi knows what function to use.

Layout Principles and Rules

This section briefly talks about xmonad and wxHaskell.

xmonad

The following appears on the Haskell community's official site (http://xmonad.org/about.html):

> *xmonad is a tiling window manager for the X Window system, implemented, configured, and dynamically extensible in Haskell. This demonstration presents the case that software dominated by side effects can be developed with the precision and efficiency you expect from Haskell by utilizing purely functional data structures, an expressive type system, extended static checking and property-based testing. In addition, you describe the use of Haskell as an application configuration and extension language.*

As mentioned, xmonad is a dynamic window manager for Windows. Written in Haskell, it automatically presents windows and permits any number of workspaces and floating windows. Additionally, it supports many screens, each with its own workspace. Most elements can be customized.

xmonad can be installed in one of the following packages.

- xmonad: the standard package

- xmonda-contrib: uses different algorithms, settings, and so forth, from third parties

- xmonad-git or xmonad-contrib-git: the package for developers (includes additional dependencies)

xmonad is very powerful. It has an application in cloud computing, too, because it can act as a window manager for big data engineering.

wxHaskell

wxHaskell is a compact and native graphical user interface (GUI) for Haskell (written in C++), on which developers create a GUI with a functional language. There are many applications developed using wxHaskell, including Dazzle, hsReversi, GeBoP, Proxima, Functional Forms, HCPN, and HpView.

The following is samples code that creates a frame and a menu in the frame.

```
fr <- frame [text := "Main Window", clientSize := sz 600 600]
pnl <- panel f []

mainMenu <- menuPane [text := "File"]
openItem <- menuItem timerMenu [text :="Open..."]
saveItem <- menuQuit timerMenu [help := "Save"]
```

The Final Word on Lists

Pattern matching is a very important aspect of lists.

```
Prelude> let xs = [(-1, 0), (54,-23), (2,1), (15,-8), (5,12), (0,1)]
xs :: (Num t1, Num t) => [(t, t1)]
Prelude> [x+y | (x,y) <- xs]
[-1,31,3,7,17,1]
```

If pattern matching breaks down, then it moves to the next component.

The list itself could be utilized in pattern matching. Something could be matched with the empty list [ ], or whatever pattern that includes [ ]. The [1,2,3] is actually a representation for 1:2:3:[ ], because you first add 3 to the empty list, and then 2, and then 1, obtaining [1,2,3], so you have used the former pattern. This represents the pattern x:xs, which adds the x element as the head of the xs list. The x:xs pattern is widely utilized, especially in the recursive functions. Note that when you use the : symbob in patterns, it is applied to lists that have at least one element.

If you want to link, for example, the first two components to variables and the remaining elements to another variable, you can use x:y:ys. The matching will be applied only to lists with at least two components.

Let's implement our own function that retrieves the head of a list.

```
headFunction :: [x] -> x
headFunction [] = error "The list in empty."
headFunction (a:_) = aChecking if it works:
```

And some arguments.

```
Prelude> headFunction [1,2,3,4]
1
Prelude> headFunction ['a', 'b']
'a'
```

Let's look at our example. It uses the function error, which has a parameter and a string. When this error arises, the program crashes and the message is the string given as a parameter.

Now, let's display the first two elements of a list.

```
elements :: (Show a) => [a] -> String
elements [] = "The list has no elements."
elements (a:[]) = "The only element of the list is " ++ show a
elements (a:b:[]) = "The only two elements of the list are " ++ show a ++ " and " ++ show b
elements (a:b:_) = "The list has more than 2 elements, but the first are " ++ show a ++ "
and " ++ show b
```

The function covers all cases: an empty list and a list with one or more elements. Remember that a:[] is equivalent to [a], and a:b:[] is equivalent to [a,b], but you cannot write a:b:_ with squared braces.

Now let's write our length function, using patterns and recursion.

```
lengthFunction [] = 0
lengthFunction (_:xs) = 1 + lengthFunction xs
```

Let's test the function.

```
Prelude> lengthFunction []
0
Prelude> lengthFunction [1,2,3]
3
Prelude> lengthFunction "abc"
3
```

A special pattern is as pattern. It represents a way to split an element according to a pattern, and links it to names, but it is retained as a reference to the whole element. This is done using an @ in front of the pattern; for example, ys@(y:z:zs). This matches the same element that y:z:zs matches, but the entire list ys could be obtained.

Advanced Types

Until now, you have used many data types, such as Bool, Int, and Char, but Haskell allows us to define our data types. This is done by using the data keyword.

```
Prelude> data BoolValue = False | True
data BoolValue = False | True
```

Let's say that you want to represent a triangle by giving the values of the sides: (15, 5.3, 12.7), but this triple could represent anything. But what if you would have a square? This is defined by the length of the side. So, you need a more general type, such as Figure.

```
Data Figure = Triangle Float Float Float | Square Float
```

The value constructor of the Triangle has three elements of type Float. Also, a Figure could be Square, defined only by a variable whose type is Float.

```
Prelude> data Figure = Triangle Float Float Float | Square Float
data Figure = Triangle Float Float Float | Square Float
Prelude> :t Triangle
Triangle :: Float -> Float -> Float -> Figure
Prelude> :t Square
Square :: Float -> Figure
```

Next, let's compute the perimeters of the two figures.

```
perimeter :: Figure -> Float
perimeter (Triangle a b c) = a + b + c
perimeter (Square a) = 4 * a
```

Let's observe that the type of the perimeter is Figure. You have chosen Figure because it is a type; unlike Triangle or Square. Now, let's compute the perimeter for a triangle, and then for a square.

```
Prelude> perimeter $ Triangle 5 6 7
18.0
Prelude> perimeter $ Square 12.5
50.0
```

You tell Haskell which figure should have computed the perimeter by using the $ symbol. If you want that our data type to be derived from the Show type class, you proceed like this:

```
data Figure = Triangle Float Float Float | Square Float deriving (Show)
```

Now, you can write this in GHCi.

```
Prelude> Square 5
Square 5.0
```

You can use a previously defined data type to define a new data type. Let's say you have a data type called Data, which takes three Ints for the year, the day, and the month. Now, you want to define a new data type called User, which takes two elements: an Int for the id and Data for the birthdate.

```
Prelude> data Data = Int Int Int deriving (Show)
data Data = Int Int Int
Prelude> data Person = Int Data
data Person = Int Data
```

Our defined data types could be exported into modules, including the functions.

```
module Figures
( Figure(..)
, perimeter
) where
```

43

Through Figure(..), you have put the value constructors for Figure in the module, so when this module is imported, it could use anything with Triangle and Square.

Monads

It is a little difficult to define a *monad*. In a few words, a monad provides a manner through which operations are chained together. In principle, all you do is write execution levels, and then link them together using a bind function (called >>=). The calls could be written to the bind operator, or it could be used as a syntax such that the compiler is forced to call that function. The purpose of a bind function is to pass the result of the current step to the next step. This is called the *identity monad*. But the other monads must do something in addition to be considered good. In fact, every monad implements the bind function in its own manner, and you could write a function that does a particular thing between execution steps. The following are some examples of monads.

- *Failure monad.* If every step is marked as succeed/failed, you can bind to execute the following step just as if the last one succeed; thus, if the result of a step failed, the entire sequence is automatically cancelled without any additional test.

- *Error or exception monad.* Allow us to implement our own exceptions.

- *List monad.* Every step has multiple results, and the bind function is applied over them, passing every result to the next step. This writes loops in every place that has multiple results.

Other useful monads are the Maybe monad, the Failure monad, the Reader/Writer monad, and the State monad.

A monad has three important components:

- The type constructor m

- The function return

- The bind operator >=

The following shows how to use the Maybe monad.

```
return :: x -> Maybe x
    return a  = Just a

    (>>=)  :: Maybe x -> (x -> Maybe y) -> Maybe y
    m >>= g = case m of
                Nothing -> Nothing
                Just a  -> g a
```

Maybe represents the monad. The value is brought by the return through Just. If a value exists for m, then it applies g on it, and then the value is returned to the Maybe monad.

The monads fit very well with cloud computing.

Other Advanced Techniques

This section discusses higher order functions. In Haskell, a function could have another function as a parameter, or it could have another function as a result. These kinds of functions are called *higher order functions*. They are powerful when it comes to solving problems or issues with programs.

Every function in Haskell takes one parameter. How come? Let's say that you want to obtain the minimum value between 2 and 3, by applying the min function. This function takes 2 as a parameter, and returns a value; then, the obtained value is compared (also applying min function) with 3. The following are the same.

```
Prelude> min 2 3
2
Prelude> (min 2) 3
2
```

If a function is called with too few parameters, then it becomes partially applied.

Now let's write a function that has another function as a parameter. You write a function that returns the minimum value between 10 and another value.

```
Prelude> minTen x = min 10 x
Prelude> minTen 5
5
```

The infix functions could be partly applied when using sectioning. You do that using parenthesis.

```
Prelude> multiplyTwo = (*2)
Prelude> multiplyTwo 3
6
```

If you call multiplyTwo, then it is the same as 3*2, or (*2) 3.

In the following statement, you present a way in which a function is taken as a parameter and applied twice.

```
fTwo f x = f (f x)
```

The preceding example uses parenthesis because they are essential. First, f is applied on x, and then f is again applied, but the result is f x.

The following calls the fTwo function.

```
Prelude> fTwo (*2) 3
12
```

In the previous example, you see that functions of higher order are very useful in complex applications. Next, let's write a function that adjoins to lists and then applies a function on all elements.

```
joinAndFunction _ [] _ = []
joinAndFunction _ _ [] = []
joinAndFunction f (a:as) (b:bs) = f a b : joinAndFunction f as bs
Prelude> joinAndFunction (*) [1,2,3] [1,2,3]
[1, 4, 9]
```

In this manner, a single higher order function is used in many ways, bringing many benefits.

map, filter, takeWhile

The map function has a function and a list as parameters. It applies the function over each element of the list.

```
map _ [] = []
map f (x:xs) = f x : map f xs
Prelude> map snd [('a', 'b'), ('c', 'd')]
"bd"
```

Another useful function is filter. It has functions as parameters, which return a Boolean value (i.e., a predicate), and a list. It returns the elements that are satisfying the conditions of the predicate.

```
filter _ [] = []
filter p (x:xs)
| p x        = x : filter p xs
| otherwise = filter p xs
```

The map and filter functions could be replaced by list comprehension.

The takeWhile function has a predicate and a list as parameters. It returns the elements while the predicate stays True. It stops at the first element where the predicate becomes False.

```
Prelude> sum (takeWhile (<5000) [n^3 | n <- [1..], even (n^3)])
```

The preceding code computes the sum of even cubes smaller than 5000.

Lambdas

In essence, lambdas are unnamed functions, created to be used once. In general, they are used in functions of higher order, and they stay between parentheses. Also, you can use pattern matching inside of them. The distinction is that one parameter cannot have more than one pattern.

The following is an example.

```
Prelude> addNo a b c = a + b + c
Prelude> addNo 3 4 5
12
```

Summary

This chapter covered the main foundations for the user and programmer to understand the remainder of the book. It included the following topics.

- A quick overview of the main advantages and disadvantages of object-oriented programming and functional programming

- The basic elements used in Haskell and functional programming

- Arithmetic operations

- An introduction to pairs, triples, lists, monads, and more

- Advanced techniques in higher order functions

CHAPTER 3

███

Parallelism and Concurrency with Haskell

Haskell offers important implementations that support developing concurrent and parallel programming. To move forward, you need to understand a little bit of the terminology.

- *Parallelism* consists of running a Haskell program on multiple processors. Its goal is to improve performance. The most normal way of doing this is to stay invisible without bringing any semantic changes.

- *Concurrency* consists implementing a Haskell program using multiple I/O threads. The primary goal of using concurrency is not based on improving performance, but in creating simple and reliable source code. Regarding the semantics of the program, this is absolutely and necessarily non-deterministic.

Concurrent Haskell does not require a new set of language constructs for the programmer to use. Everything is about concurrency; it appears as a simple library, `Control.Concurrent`. The following are the functions within this library.

- Forking threads
- Killing threads
- Sleeping
- Synchronized mutable variables, known as `MVars`
- Bound threads

GHC Haskell, with the help of software transactional memory (STM), coordinates the activities regarding Concurrent Haskell threads. The STM library must be used for concurrent functionalities. The following are the main functionalities supported by this library.

- Atomic blocks
- Transactional variables
- Operations for composing transactions: `retry` and `orElse`
- Data invariants

© Stefania Loredana Nita and Marius Mihailescu 2017
S. L. Nita and M. Mihailescu, *Practical Concurrent Haskell*, DOI 10.1007/978-1-4842-2781-7_3

GHC Haskell includes all the support necessary to run programs in parallel on a symmetric, shared-memory multiprocessor (SMP). In default mode, GHC Haskell runs the programs on one processor. For running the programs on multiple processors and in parallel, you have to link your program with the -threaded, and run it with the TS -N option. The run-time mode plans the running threads within Haskell among the available OS threads; it runs as many as possible in parallel as specified with the -N RTS option.

GHC Haskell supports parallelism on a multiprocessor that has the process of shared-memory as a destination. Glasgow Parallel Haskell (GPH) supports running Parallel Haskell programs using clusters of machines and single multiprocessors. GPH is developed independently and is distributed as an extension to GHC.

In this chapter we provide some examples (*Implement a chat server, Simple servers* and *Haskell for multi-core*) from Haskell documentation, at `https://wiki.haskell.org`.

Annotating the Code for Parallelism

From the beginning, you have to understand that ordinary single-threaded programs written in Haskell do not have the benefit of enabling SMP parallelism alone. The parallelisms have to be exposed to the compiler. This is done by using forking threads with Concurrent Haskell. There is a simple method for creating parallelism from pure code by using the par combinator, which is related to seq. Both of these are available and may be used from the parallel library in the following way.

```
infixr 0 `par`
infixr 1 `pseq`

par  :: variable_A -> variable_B -> variable_B
pseq :: variable_A -> variable_B -> variable_B
```

The expression (x 'par' y) sparks the evaluation of x (to weak head normal form) and returns y. Sparks are queues used to execute in FIFO order, but they are not executed immediately. If there is any idle state in the CPU detected at run-time, a spark is converted into a real thread. The new thread is run on the idle state of the CPU. Doing this allows the available parallelism to be spread among the real CPUs.

Let's consider the following example, which actually represents a parallel version of an old example of computing the Fibonacci numbers (to run the Fibonacci example, you need to install parallel package).

```
import Control.Parallel

countFibonnaciNumber :: Int -> Int
countFibonnaciNumber number | number <= 1 = 1
        | otherwise = par number1 (pseq number2 (number1 + number2 + 1))
                    where number1 = countFibonnaciNumber (number-1)
                          number2 = countFibonnaciNumber (number-2)
```

If value n is greater than 1, then par is used for forcing the thread to evaluate countFibonnaciNumber (number-1), pseq is used to force the parent thread to evaluate countFibonnaciNumber (number-2) before going on to add these two subexpressions. Using divide and conquer technique, just a new thread is sparked for one branch, while the parent thread evaluate the other branch. The pseq function is used because it assures that number2 is evaluated before number1 in the expression (number1 + number2 + 1). Reordering the expression as (number1 + number2 + 1) is not enough, because the compiler could generate a situation in which evaluation is not done from left to right.

As a remark, pseq is used often than seq. They are very similar, but the difference is at run-time. The arguments of seq function are evaluated in any order, but pseq function evaluates firstly its first argument, then the second one. This behavior helps to control the order of evaluation.

When par is used, the sparked computation is needed in a further time and it should not be small. If it is too small, then the program loses its efficiency.

There is the posibility to collect information from the run-time statistics about how well par is working.

More sophisticated combinators for expressing parallelism are available from the Control.Parallel. Strategies module in the parallel package. This module builds functionality around par, expressing elaborate patterns of parallel computation, such as a parallel map.

Parallelism for Dataflow

The Eval monad and Strategies, which are working in conjunction with sluggish assessment, are used to express parallelism. A Strategy expends a language identification of information structure and assesses parts of it in parallel. This model has a few advantages: it permits the decoupling of the computation from the parallelism, and it permits parallel assessment methodologies to be manufactured compositionally. As it is, Strategies and Eval are not generally the most helpful or viable approach to express parallelism. We might not have any desire to fabricate a language identification information structure, for instance.

In this section, we'll investigate another parallel programming model, the Par monad, with an alternate arrangement of trade-offs. The objective of the Par monad is to be more unequivocal about granularity and information conditions, and to maintain a strategic distance from the dependence on apathetic assessment. In this programming model, the developer needs to give more detail about how to acquire control. The Par monad has some other intriguing advantages; for instance, it is actualized as a Haskell library and the usage can be promptly changed to oblige elective booking techniques.

The interface is based on calling the Par monad.

```
newtype Par object_A
instance Applicative Par
instance Monad Par

runningPar :: Par object_A -> object_A
```

The Par computation is passed as an argument to fork the "child," which is executed in parallel with the invoker of fork (the "parent"). As you can see, nothing is returned by fork to the parent. In this situation, a question is rising: how is the result get back when a parallel computation begins with fork? It is known that Ivar type and its operations is used to pass values between par computations.

```
data IVar object_A

new :: Par (IVar object_A)
put :: NFData object_A => IVar object_A -> object_A -> Par ()
get :: IVar object_A -> Par object_A
```

Think of an IVar as beginning with void. The put operation stores a quality in this case, and get is the value. On the off chance that the get operation finds the void container, then it holds up until the case is filled by a put. So an IVar gives you the chance to impart values between parallel Par calculations, since you can put a worth in the container in one place and get it in another.

Once filled, the box stays full. As you can see from the preceding code, the get operation will not remove the value from the box. We will obtain an error if we have to call put more than once on the same IVar.

You have to see the IVar type as related to the MVar type, which you shall see later in the "Threads and MVars" section. The principal difference in IVar is that can be written only once. Consider that an IVar is like the future or a promise, some important concepts that you may find familiar and similar to other parallel or concurrent languages.

■ **Note**   Although there are not constraints which prevents to return an IVar from runPar and pass it to another runPar, you should not do this. This warning becomes from the fact that Par monad presumes that Ivar values are created and utilized in the same runPar. If this assumption is violated, then run-time errors, deadlock or something worse could occur. Still, this situation could be prevented by using qualified types similar with ST monad.

Figure 3-1 makes it clear that we are making a dataflow diagram: that is, a diagram in which the hubs (fib n, etc.) contain the calculation and information streams down the edges (i and j). To be concrete, every fork in the system makes a hub, each new hub makes an edge, and get and put interface the edges to the hubs.

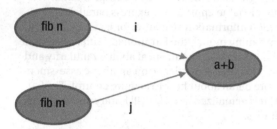

Figure 3-1. *Flow diagram for Fibonacci numbers*

Figure 3-1 shows that the two hubs containing fib n and fib m are autonomous of each other, and that is the reason that they can be processed in parallel, which is precisely what the monad-standard library will do. Notwithstanding, the dataflow chart doesn't exist in any unequivocal structure at run-time; the library works by monitoring every one of the calculations that can be played out (a work pool), and partitioning those among the accessible processors utilizing a proper planning procedure. The dataflow chart is only an approach to imagine and comprehend the structure of the parallelism. Lamentably, at this moment, there's no real way to produce a visual representation of the dataflow chart from some Par monad code; yet ideally, somebody will eventually compose an apparatus.

Utilizing dataflow to express parallelism is a significantly old thought; there were individuals exploring different avenues for custom equipment structures composed around dataflow back in the 1970s and 1980s. As opposed to those plans that were centered around misusing fine-grained parallelism naturally, here we are utilizing dataflow as an express parallel programming model. Yet, we are utilizing dataflow here for the same reasons that it was appealing in those days: rather than saying what could possibly be done parallel, we just depict the information conditions along these lines, uncovering all the verifiable parallelism to be misused.

The Par monad is very suited for communicating dataflow systems; it can likewise express other regular examples. For instance, we can produce something like the parMap combinator. To make it less demanding to characterize parMap, let's first form a basic deliberation for a parallel calculation that profits an outcome.

```
spawn :: NFData object_A => Par object_A -> Par (IVar object_A)
spawn varP = do
  varI <- new
  fork (do varX <- varP; put varI varX)
  return varI
```

The preceding is an example in which the spawn function forks the computation in parallel and returns an object of type IVar that can be used in to wait for the result. spawn is found within Control.Monad.Par.

A parallel map is formed on calling spawn to invoke and apply the function for all the elements of the queue, and then waiting for the response with all the results.

```
parMapM :: NFData object_B => (object_A -> Par object_B) -> [object_A] -> Par [object_B]
parMapM varF as = do
  varIBS <- mapM (spawn.varF) as
  mapM get varIBS
```

(parMapM is also provided by Control.Monad.Par, even if in a more generalized form than the version shown here.)

Note that the capacity connotation, f, gives back its outcome in the Par monad; this implies f itself can make further parallelism by utilizing fork and the other Par operations. At the point when the capacity contention of a guide is monadic, the tradition is to add the M postfix to the capacity name— consequently, parMapM.

It is very direct to set and define a variant of parMapM that will take a non-monadic function by inserting a return.

```
parMap :: NFData object_B => (object_A -> object_B) -> [object_A] -> Par [object_B]
parMap varF as = do
  varIBS <- mapM (spawn.return.varF) as
  mapM get varIBS
```

One other thing to consider is that unlike parMap, parMapM and parMap wait for the outputs before returning. Depending on the context, this may or may not be the most useful behavior. If you don't want to wait for the results, then you could always use mapM (spawn.f), which returns a list of IVars.

So far, what we have discussed represents all the necessary elements that need to be fulfilled and understood by a programmer in order to start creating software that is eligible to be ported in a cloud-computing environment.

Concurrent Servers for a Network

Concurrent network servers are implemented simultaneously with the String IO. Here on each acknowledge from the fundamental string, we make another Handle, and forkIO a lightweight Haskell string to compose a string back to the client. Depends on the run-time scheduler to awaken the primary string in an opportune manner (i.e., by means of the current "select" instrument).

```
import Network
import Control.Concurrent
import System.IO

main = withSocketsDo $ do
    socket <- listenOn $ PortNumber 5002
    loop socket

loop socket = do
    (something,_,_) <- accept socket
    forkIO $ body something
    loop socket
```

```
  where body something = do
      hPutStr something message
      hFlush something
      hClose something

message = "HTTP/localhost 200 OK\r\nContents-Dimension: 5\r\n\r\nsomething\r\n"
```

Next, by using a byte string, IO means that we allocate nothing in the body, and avoid a couple of copies to do the IO.

```
{-# LANGUAGE OverloadedStrings #-}
import Data.ByteString.Char8

import Network hiding (accept)
import Network.Socket
import Network.Socket.ByteString (sendAll)
import Control.Concurrent

main = withSocketsDo $ do
    socket <- listenOn $ PortNumber 5002
    loop socket

loop socket = do
  (connection, _) <- accept socket
  forkIO $ body connection
  loop socket
  where body x = do sendAll x message
                    Network.Socket.sClose x

message = "HTTP/localhost 200 OK\r\nContents-Dimension: 5\r\n\r\nsomething\r\n"
```

The next step is quite critical: instead of using the RTS select mechanism to wake up threads, we use a custom epoll handler. Based on epoll event handling and the IO byte string, in our case, the epoll replaces GHC's select model as quickly as possible. The designing method here shows that the concurrent primitives could be implemented in terms of epoll (please note the following code uses Unix—System.Event, System. Posix—and it could not be complied in Windows).

```
import Network hiding (accept)
import Network.Socket (fdSocket, accept)
import Network.Socket.ByteString
import Data.ByteString.Char8
import System.Event
import System.Posix
import System.Posix.IO

main = withSocketsDo $ do
    sock <- listenOn $ PortNumber 5002
    let fd = fromIntegral (fdSocket sock)
    mgr <- new
    registerFd mgr (client sock) fd evtRead
    loop mgr
```

```
client sock _ _ = do
    (c,_) <- accept sock
    sendAll c msg
    sClose c
```

This is significantly better. By the way, under the same conditions, this Python epoll version achieves 10K req/sec.

Moving forward, we can observe traditional invokes to accept and sendAll using Haskell's concurrent IO layer, which is having some redundant threading calls. Simon Marlow, the co-developer of GHC, provides additional explanations for threads (https://wiki.haskell.org/Simple_Servers):

> *The Haskell program as it stands won't scale up on a multicore because it only has a single accept loop, and the subtasks are too small. The cost of migrating a thread for load-balancing is too high compared to the cost of completing the request, so it's impossible to get a speedup this way. If you create one accept loop per CPU then in principle it ought to scale, but in practice it won't at the moment because there is only one IO manager thread calling select(). Hopefully this will be fixed as part of the ongoing epoll() work that was mentioned earlier.*

> *Regarding the slowdown you see with -threaded, this is most likely because you're running the accept loop in the main thread. The main thread is special - it is a "bound thread", which means it is effectively a fully-fledged OS thread rather than a lightweight thread, and hence communication with the main thread is very expensive. Fork a subthread for the accept loop, and you should see a speedup with -threaded.*

—Simon Marlow

Threads for Parallel Programming

Haskell development and invokers have an easy and flexible thread system that plans the logical threads on the free and available threads in operating systems. These light and cheap threads can be created with forkIO. (We won't discuss full OS threads that are created via forkOS, as they have significantly higher overhead and are only useful in a few situations).

```
forkIO :: IO () -> IO ThreadId
```

Let's consider the following simple example for a Haskell application. It creates a hash for two files and shows the result as an output in the console (to run the following code, you need to install the pureMD5 package first).

```
import Data.Digest.Pure.MD5 (md5)
import qualified Data.ByteString.Lazy as L
import System.Environment (getArgs)

main = do
    [fileA, fileB] <- getArgs
    hashAndPrint fileA
    hashAndPrint fileB

hashAndPrint f = L.readFile f >>= return . md5 >>= \h -> putStrLn (f ++ ": " ++ show h)
```

53

The preceding example represents a straight solution that creates a hash for the two files one at a time, showing the result as an output on the console. How do we proceed if we want to use more than one processor to create that hash for those files in parallel?

A simple solution is to turn on a new thread that creates the hash in parallel and displays the answers as they are computed.

```
import Control.Concurrent (forkIO)
import Data.Digest.Pure.MD5 (md5)
import qualified Data.ByteString.Lazy as L
import System.Environment (getArgs)

main = do
    [fileA,fileB] <- getArgs
    forkIO $ hashAndPrint fileA
    hashAndPrint fileB

hashAndPrint f = L.readFile f >>= return . md5 >>= \h -> putStrLn (f ++ ": " ++ show h)
```

Now, we have a rough program with great performance boost.

You will probably have some bugs. The first one represents the finishing process of the main thread, which has as a goal the finishing of the hashing process for the `fileB`, after the process is done. The program quits before the child thread finishes with `fileA`. The second bug is potentially garbled output due to two threads writing to `stdout`. Both of these problems can be solved using interthread communication (we'll pick up this example in the `MVar` section).

Working with mutable variables (`MVars`) that can be locked has a huge impact on communicating data, such as obtaining a string for a function to print, but it is also common for developers to lock their features as a signaling mechanism.

The mutable variables `MVars` are known and represented as a polymorphic mutable variable which might or not, to contain a value at any given time. The most usual functions include:

```
newMVar :: a -> IO (MVar a)
newEmptyMVar :: IO (MVar a)
takeMVar :: MVar a -> IO a
putMVar :: MVar a -> a -> IO ()
isEmptyMVar :: MVar a -> IO Bool
```

Although they are generally self-explanatory, note that `takeMVar` will block until the `MVar` is filled, and `putMVar` will obstruct until the current `MVar` is void. Taking a `MVar` will leave the `MVar` void while giving back the worth. In the `forkIO` illustration, we built up a system to hash two records in parallel and finished with two little bugs in light of the fact that the project ended rashly (the primary string would leave when done). A second issue is that strings can struggle with each other's utilization of `stdout`. Now let's sum up the case to work on any number of documents, piece until the hashing is finished, and print every one of the outcomes from only one string so that no `stdout` confusion happens.

```
{-# LANGUAGE BangPatterns #-}
import Data.Digest.Pure.MD5
import qualified Data.ByteString.Lazy as L
import System.Environment
import Control.Concurrent
import Control.Monad (replicateM_)
```

```
main = do
    files <- getArgs
    str <- newEmptyMVar
    mapM_ (forkIO . hashAndPrint str) files
    printNrResults (length files) str

printNrResults i var = replicateM_ i (takeMVar var >>= putStrLn)

hashAndPrint str f = do
    bs <- L.readFile f
    let !h = show $ md5 bs
    putMVar str (f ++ ": " ++ h)
```

We characterize another variable, str, as a vacant MVar. After the hashing, the outcome is accounted for with putMVar -. Recall that this capacity squares when the MVar is full, so no hashes are dropped by virtue of the variable memory. printNrResults utilizes the takeMVar capacity, which hinders until the MVar is full, or once the following document is done being hashed for this situation. Take note of how the worth is assessed before the putMVar call. In the event that the contention is an evaluated chunk, then printNrResults will need to assess the thunks before it prints the outcome—and our endeavors will have been useless. Knowing the str MVar is filled "length of the records" times, we can give the principle string a chance to exit subsequent to printing the given number of results; along these lines, ending the system.

```
$ ghc exMVar.hs -o exMVar-threaded --make -O2 -threaded
$ time ./exMVar-threaded +RTS -N2 -RTS 2GB 2GB 2GB 2GB
  2GB: b8f1f1faa6dda5426abffb3a7811c1fb
  2GB: b8f1f1faa6dda5426abffb3a7811c1fb
  2GB: b8f1f1faa6dda5426abffb3a7811c1fb
  2GB: b8f1f1faa6dda5426abffb3a7811c1fb

  real    0m40.524s

$ time ./exMVar-threaded +RTS -N1 -RTS 2GB 2GB 2GB 2GB
  2GB: b8f1f1faa6dda5426abffb3a7811c1fb
  2GB: b8f1f1faa6dda5426abffb3a7811c1fb
  2GB: b8f1f1faa6dda5426abffb3a7811c1fb
  2GB: b8f1f1faa6dda5426abffb3a7811c1fb

  real    1m8.170s
```

Threads and MVars

An MVar t represents a mutable location that has two types of values: empty and contains a value of type t. It is designed to have two main operations.

- putMVar fills the mutable variable if it does not have anything, and if it has a value it, will block it.

- takeMVar creates an empty mutable variable if it is full; if it has a value, it will block it.

The ways that they are used are different, as described in the following.

- Mutable variables can be synchronized.

- Within some channels, takeMVar is responsible for receiving and putMVar is responsible for sending.

- A mutable variable could be seen as a semaphore. takeMVar is responsible for waiting on the state of the signal and putMVar is in accordance with the signal.

Mutable variables were introduced in the paper "Concurrent Haskell" by Simon Peyton Jones, Andrew Gordon, and Sigbjorn Finne (https://www.microsoft.com/en-us/research/wp-content/uploads/1996/01/concurrent-haskell.pdf). Since then, some of the details regarding the implementation process have been changed, such as the put method of a mutable variable was used to indicate an error, but now this method is used to identify blocks.

Mutable variables (MVars) offer a lot of flexibility in cooperation with IORefs. Compared to STM, there is less flexibility. One of their primary goals is to be more appropriate for building synchronization primitives and realizing internal threads communication. When we discuss the race process between threads, we have to state that they are very susceptible to those conditions, with deadlocks or exceptions that cannot be caught. If there are complex atomic operations (e.g., reading within multiple variables), it is recommended to avoid them and to use STM.

The larger functions from this module are represented by the composition between takeMVar and putMVar, followed by exceptions management. This mechanism and composition guarantee the atomicity if all the rest of the threads perform takeMVar and putMVar. If this does not happen, we assist to a block process of the threads.

Let's take a skip channel as an example, presented as a data structure adapted from the original "Concurrent Haskell" article by Simon Peyton Jones et al. It is a very interesting example of concurrent data structure. This kind of channel can be used to write on without blocking, and the return process from the channel returns the most appropriate value, or it is blocked if there are no new values. The dupSkipChan operation supports different readers.

A pair of mutable variables form a skip channel. The first mutable variable contains the current value together with a queue of semaphores that are notified when there are changes. The second mutable variable is represented by a semaphore for a particular reader and it is occupied if there is a value within the channel, a value that the reader is unable to read, and without any value, in the second case.

```
data SkipChan a = SkipChan (MVar (a, [MVar ()])) (MVar ())

newSkipChannel :: IO (SkipChan a)
newSkipChannel = do
    semaphore <- newEmptyMVar
    main <- newMVar (undefined, [semaphore])
    return (SkipChan main semaphore)

putSkipChan :: SkipChan a-> a-> IO ()
putSkipChan (SkipChan main _) v = do
    (_, semaphores) <- takeMVar main
    putMVar main (v, [])
    mapM_ (semaphore -> putMVar semaphore ()) semaphores

getSkipChan :: SkipChan a -> IO a
getSkipChan (SkipChan main semaphore) = do
    takeMVar semaphore
```

```
    (v, semaphores) <- takeMVar main
    putMVar main (v, semaphore:semaphores)
    return v

dupSkipChan :: SkipChan a -> IO (SkipChan a)
dupSkipChan (SkipChan main _) = do
    semaphore <- newEmptyMVar
    (v, semaphores) <- takeMVar main
    putMVar main (v, semaphore:semaphores)
    return (SkipChan main semaphore)
```

Distributed Programming

In order to prove how the transmission works and what the most important concepts about distributed programming are, we will implement a server for chat in the following section.

We will show how to emerge an easy example of chat server that could be bounded to telnet for the primary operation for a chat application. It is expected that the server allows many users to be connected. When a message arrives to the server, it is transmitted to all users that have established a connection to the server at that time. In our model, we will utilize the Network.Socket library that permits low-level links to the C-socket API.

The cabal file should contain the following code.

```
executable chat-server-exe
    hs-source-dirs:       app
    main-is:              Main.hs
    ghc-options:          -threaded -rtsopts -with-rtsopts=-N
    build-depends:        base, network
    default-language:     Haskell2010
```

Socket Server

Let's begin with an easy-to-implement server. Observe that the server's code starts with a main function that generates a reutilizable socket. Next, a TCP connection is opened, using port 4242, which permits at most two queued connections.

```
-- in Main.hs
module Main where

import Network.Socket

main :: IO ()
main = do
    mySocket <- socket AF_INET Stream 0   -- A socket is creted
    setSocketOption mySocket ReuseAddr 1    -- The socket immediately reusable - eases debugging.
    bind mySocket (SockAddrInet 4242 iNADDR_ANY)    -- Listen on TCP port 4242.
    listen mySocket 2                               -- Set a max of 2 queued connections
    mainLoop mySocket -- Will be implemented
```

The `mainLoop` function builds a socket-server example equivalent to the classical "Hello World!" When there is a certain socket, do the following: accept the connection, receive and pass an easy "Hello World!", close the open connection, and reutilize the genuine socket.

```
-- in Main.hs

mainLoop :: Socket -> IO ()
mainLoop mySocket = do
    connection <- accept mySocket -- accept a connection and handle it
    runconnection connection -- run our server's logic
    mainLoop mySocket -- repeat

runconnection:: (Socket, SockAddr) -> IO ()
runconnection (mySocket, _) = do
    send mySocket "Hello!\n"
    close mySocket
```

When a socked is accepted, it returns the pair with the type (`Socket, SockAddr`), which represents a new socket object that could be utilized for sending and receiving information on an arbitrary connection. When the `runconnection` function ends, the socket object shuts down. In this simple example, SockAddr is the primary socket address for port 4242.

System.IO for Sockets

To avoid bugs, you should not use the send and recv functions, because `Network.Socket` does not correctly represent the binary data in these functions. When implementing with `Network.Socket`, utilizing the functions that are used in the `ByteString` module is recommended. To avoid complicating the example, use `System.IO` for incomes and outcomes. Note the fact that `System.IO` is not using `ByteString`, but is using a plain `String`. The following code shows how to import the new module and how to turn Socket into Handle.

```
-- in the imports our Main.hs add:
import System.IO

-- and we'll change our `runConn` function to look like:
runconnection:: (Socket, SockAddr) -> IO ()
runconnection (mySocket, _) = do
    myHandle <- socketToHandle mySocket ReadWriteMode
    hSetBuffering myHandle NoBuffering
    hPutStrLn myHandle "Hello!"
    hClose myHandle
```

Concurrency

Until now, the server permitted just one connection at a time. If it is limited to only read the flow of the messages, then that is sufficient; but in practice, it is more complicated because the server should manipulate the chat.

Prelude provides a library called `Control.Concurrency`, which creates threads and switches the context. The hackage page is very useful in this example, and we recommend accessing it.

forkIO manages every client of the chat, and creates threads for every connection. The following is the signature of forkIO.

```
forkIO :: IO () -> IO ThreadId
```

The output is ignored because we do not need the thread's identifier.

```
-- add to our imports:
import Control.Concurrent

-- and in our mainLoop function...
mainLoop mySocket = do
    connection <- accept mySocket
    forkIO (runconnection connection)    -- split off each connection into its own thread
    mainLoop mySocket
```

Communication Between Threads

We should make the connections to communicate with each other. At first look, this task is difficult to accomplish because we are required to administrate the event handlers/pub-sub implementations, which means we should learn about MVar, TVar, TMVar, and when to use each. We do not cover these topics, but we encourage you to read about them. Still, we need to accomplish the described task, but we will use Control.Concurrent.Chan, which assures boundless FIFO channels that permit one write operation and many read end operations. This module is quite simple, and the fact that Chan data type is abstract is an advantage. The Chan data type contains *->*. To make it complete, we should choose a message type that is serializable. Because we want a simple application, let's choose String and alias Msg, to make it more semantically understandable.

```
-- in Main.hs
type Message = String
```

In the first step, the required module is imported.

```
import Control.Concurrent.Chan   -- at the top of Main.hs with the others
```

Main assures the creation of socket connections and passes them to mainLoop, which shows that the socket connections are working in the same channel. The mainLoop function opens the channel to every thread in runConnection. The code is presented here.

```
main = do
    -- [...]
    channel <- newChan         -- notice that newChan :: IO (Chan a)
    mainLoop mySocket channel   -- pass it into the loop

-- later, in mainLoop:

mainLoop :: Socket -> Chan Message -> IO ()    -- See how Chan now uses Message.
mainLoop mySocket channel = do
    connection <- accept mySocket
    forkIO (runconnection connection channel) -- pass the channel to runconnection
    mainLoop mySocket channel
```

Now we need runconnection to make a duplicate of the channel communicating with it. To do this, some helpers are needed—liftM and fix. liftM permits the lifting of an arbitrary function on a particular data structure, and fix permits defining a monadic fixed point.

```
-- at the top of Main.hs
import Control.Monad (liftM)
import Control.Monad.Fix (fix)
```

Next, let's utilize some functions that belong to Control.Concurrent.Chan: writeChan, readChan, and dupChan. Their names are intuitive, so we will not insist over them. The dupChan function creates a novel channel by duplicating a Chan, so that more than one thread can read from it. This channel is empty at its creation and it does not have any written data. This permits broadcasting.

```
runconnection:: (Socket, SockAddr) -> Chan Msg -> IO ()
runconnection (mySocket, _) channel = do
    let broadcast message = writeChan channel message
    myHandle <- socketToHandle mySocket ReadWriteMode
    hSetBuffering myHandle NoBuffering
    commLine <- dupChan channel

    -- fork off a thread for reading from the duplicated channel
    forkIO $ fix $ \loop -> do
        line <- readChan commLine
        hPutStrLn myHandle line
        loop

    -- read lines from the socket and echo them back to the user
    fix $ \loop -> do
        line <- liftM init (hGetLine myHandle)
        broadcast line
        loop
```

Let's observe that runconnection runs on a different thread, and splits another worker thread to send messages to the user that has established a connection.

The Final Code

We are almost done. We need to resolve two problems in our code. The primary problem is that the genuine channel is never read, which represents a major leakage in our code. To resolve it, we just need to create an additional thread that assures access to it.

The last problem is that the connection is not closed properly. To do that, we need an exception handling for the case of extension, and the additional amendments.

- The messages should be resounded to the sender.

- Make an association between a connection and a name.

- Message should be changed to alias (Int, String).

To use exception handlers, we need to import Control.Exception. The whole code is shown here.

```
module Main where

import Network.Socket
import System.IO
import Control.Exception
import Control.Concurrent
import Control.Concurrent.Chan
import Control.Monad (liftM, when)
import Control.Monad.Fix (fix)

main :: IO ()
main = do
  mySocket <- socket AF_INET Stream 0
  setSocketOption mySocket ReuseAddr 1
  bind mySocket (SockAddrInet 4242 iNADDR_ANY)
  listen mySocket 2
  channel <- newChan
  forkIO $ fix $ \loop -> do
    (_, message) <- readChan channel
    loop
  mainLoop mySocket channel 0

-- Message is changed to alias (Int, String)
type Message = (Int, String)

mainLoop :: Socket -> Chan Message -> Int -> IO ()
mainLoop mySocket channel messageNum = do
  connection <- accept mySocket -- Association between a connection and a name
  forkIO (runconnection connection channel messageNum)
  mainLoop mySocket channel $! messageNum + 1

-- Messages are sent to the user.
runconnection :: (Socket, SockAddr) -> Chan Message -> Int -> IO ()
runconnection (mySocket, _) channel messageNum = do
  let broadcast message = writeChan channel (messageNum, message)
  myHandle <- socketToHandle mySocket ReadWriteMode
  hSetBuffering myHandle NoBuffering

  hPutStrLn myHandle "Welcome to the chat. Please choose a username: "
  userName <- liftM init (hGetLine myHandle)
  broadcast ("--> " ++ userName ++ " in now online.")
  hPutStrLn myHandle ("Hello, " ++ userName ++ "!")

  commLine <- dupChan channel

  -- Fork a thread which will read messages of the duplicated channel.
  readerFromDuplicateChan <- forkIO $ fix $ \loop -> do
      (nextNum, line) <- readChan commLine
      when (messageNum /= nextNum) $ hPutStrLn myHandle line
      loop
```

```
handle (\(SomeException _) -> return ()) $ fix $ \loop -> do
    line <- liftM init (hGetLine myHandle)
    case line of
        -- When an exception occurs, a message is sent and the loop is broken.
        "quit" -> hPutStrLn myHandle "Bye!"
        -- If there is no exception, then continue looping.
        _       -> broadcast (userName ++ ": " ++ line) >> loop

killThread readerFromDuplicateChan                       -- Kill after the loop ends
broadcast ("<-- " ++ userName ++ " is now offline.") -- Send a last broadcast hClose
myHandle
```

Running the Server

The preceding code provides a functioning server. After we build the executable and fire up the server, we can use our chat. Run the server and then establish a connection to it using telnet, as follows.

```
$ telnet localhost 4242

Trying 127.0.0.1...
Connected to localhost.
Escape character is '^]'.
Welcome to the chat. Please choose a username:
```

Eval Monad for Parallelism

Haskell is a lazy language. Due to laziness, expressions are evaluated just when they are required, and are not evaluated if they are not required. The way how laziness works, should not worry us, but there are situations in which we tell the compiler how a program should be run. These are situations in which parallelism is used. Before knowing how parallelism works, we should know firstly how lazy evaluation works. so this section explores the basic concepts, and use GHCi as a playground.

Let's start with something very simple.

```
Prelude> let x = 1 + 2 :: Int
```

The above line of code creates a binding between variable x and the expression 1 + 2. For simplicity, let's suppose the type is Int. We know that 1 + 2 = 3, so we could instead just write let x = 3 :: Int. But when we work with parallel code, there is a huge difference between this two approaches, because 1 + 2 represents an expression which was not evaluated yet, which could be computed in parallel with something else. Anyway, this is a didactical example, because in practice something as trivial as 1 + 2 is not computed in parallel.

Returning to example, at this moment x is not evaluated. Usually, in Haskell, we can't tell that x is *unevaluated*, but GHCi provides commands that allow us to inspect the structures of expression, without influencing the expression in any way. For example, :sprint command is used to display the value of an expression without being evaluated.

```
Prelude> :sprint x
x = _
```

The special symbol _ indicates *unevaluated*. Another term for an unevaluted expression is *thunk*, which is the object in memory representing the unevaluated computation 1 + 2. In this case, the thunk looks something like what's shown in Figure 3-2.

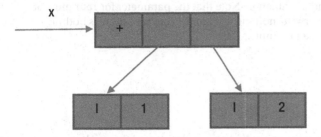

Figure 3-2. *Representation of 1+2*

Here, x is a pointer to an object in memory representing the function + applied to the integers 1 and 2.

The thunk representing x is evaluated whenever its value is required. A simple situation which determine evaluation is printing the value. So, just type x into Prelude.

```
Prelude> x
3
```

Now if we use :sprint to check the value of x, we get 3, which means x was evaluated.

```
Prelude> :sprint x
x = 3
```

In terms of the objects in memory, the thunk representing 1 + 2 is actually overwritten by the (boxed) integer 3. So any future demand for the value of x gets the answer immediately; this is how lazy evaluation works.

That was a simple example. Below it is a more complex example.

```
Prelude> let x = 1 + 2 :: Int
Prelude> let y = x + 1
Prelude> :sprint x
x = _
Prelude> :sprint y
y = _
```

Again, x is bound to 1 + 2, but now we have also bound y to x + 1, and :sprint shows that both are unevaluated as expected.

To create parallelism in Haskell, the Control.Parallel.Strategies module is used. The general form of the used elements is

```
data Eval a
instance Monad Eval

runEval :: Eval a -> a

rpar :: a -> Eval a
rseq :: a -> Eval a
```

The main element is the Eval monad, which has the following two functions: rpar and rseq. Eval represents the identity monad, where rpar and rseq are equivalent to par and pseq, respectively, and it produces successions of parallel calculations used to evaluate lazy data structures in parallel. The result is extracted using the runEval function, which is totally pure. The rpar function is used to create parallelism, whereas the rseq function is used to force sequential evaluation. Note that the parameter for rpar must be an unevaluated calculation—namely, a thunk; otherwise, nothing will happen because there is nothing to evaluate or to produce the parallelism. Let's look at an example.

```
runEval $ do
  p <- rpar (fct a)
  q <- rpar (fct b)
  return (p,q)
```

In the preceding example, the arbitrary fct function is applied on a and on b, and the results are computed in parallel. Let's say that fct a takes longer than fct b. After using rpar, we return the results as a pair. From an execution point of view, fct a and fct b begin at the same time, in parallel; whereas the return occurs straightaway, not waiting for the two appliances of the function to terminate. The remaining program continues the execution, whereas the two calls are evaluated in parallel.

The following is another example, this time using both rpar and rseq.

```
runEval $ do
    p <- rpar (fct a)
    q <- rseq (fct b)
    return (p,q)
```

In the preceding example, fct a and fct b are evaluated in parallel also, but return does not wait until fct b is finished, thanks to the rseq function, which holds on until its argument is evaluated. If we add rseq to waiting fct a, then the program waits for fct a and fct b to complete.

```
runEval $ do
  p <- rpar (fct a)
  q <- rseq (fct b)
  rseq p
  return (p,q)
```

The preceding examples represent patterns for parallel computing in Haskell. We use them as follows.

- rpar - rseq are not very useful, because usually we do not know which of the two calls of the arbitrary function is waiting longer.

- It depends on the particular case in which we need to use rpar - rpar or rpar - rseq - rseq. If we want more parallelism and we are not focused on the results, we should use rpar - rpar because the result is obtained straightaway. If we cannot "add" more parallelism, or if one of the results is needed in order to continue, then we should use rpar - rseq - rseq.

The following is another pattern.

```
runEval $ do
  p <- rpar (fct a)
  q <- rpar (fct b)
  rseq p
  rseq q
  return (p,q)
```

This works similarly to `rpar - rseq - rseq`. It is the most complicated example, but it could be the most used because of its symmetry.

Summary

This chapter discussed the most important characteristics and elements of parallelism and concurrence in Haskell. It covered the most important issues and their advantages and disadvantages, making a workflow for those who want to learn how to develop applications in Haskell in a distributed environment, such as the cloud.

As a quick overview, the following topics were covered.

- The parallelism and dataflow in Haskell with examples

- Concurrent servers working within a network

- Implementing threads within a parallel programming concept

- The difference between threads and `MVars`, and the advantages and disadvantages

- Creating a server in Haskell as an example of distributed programming, pointing out the necessary steps for developing an application that needs a distributed environment

- Creating a discussion for the `Eval` monad, which can be used for parallelism with examples and case studies

CHAPTER 4

Strategies Used in the Evaluation Process

In programming languages, evaluation strategies represent a collection of rules that are used when expressions are evaluated or computed. The way in which arguments are passed to functions represents a particular case for evaluation strategies.

There are two main approaches in evaluation strategies:

- *Strict* strategies, in which the arguments are calculated before they are applied

- *Non-strict* strategies, in which the arguments are calculated only when they are needed, or on demand.

The second category is also known as *lazy evaluation*, which is mainly used in functional programming, and in particular, by the Haskell programming language.

The first section of the chapter presents a simple example of how lazy evaluation uses redexes. The next section discusses the Strategies library used in deterministic parallelism in Haskell, and which introduces scan family functions and skeletons.

Redexes and Lazy Evaluation

One of the most important techniques used to execute Haskell program code is lazy evaluation. It has many benefits, but it could present a problem with memory terms, if it is not used properly.

In Haskell, a program is performed through *expression evaluation*. A technique called *graph reduction* is used in evaluation. It prevents duplicate steps in the process of expression evaluation. Let's look at an example.

```
upSquare c = c*c
```

The preceding function could be called with an argument such as 2+3.

```
upSquare (2+3)
```

The evaluation works as follows: from the definition of function, c becomes c = 2+3:

```
upSquare (2+3)
=> (2+3)*(2+3)
```

© Stefania Loredana Nita and Marius Mihailescu 2017
S. L. Nita and M. Mihailescu, *Practical Concurrent Haskell*, DOI 10.1007/978-1-4842-2781-7_4

Then, the + and * operators are evaluated.

```
(2+3)*(2+3)
=>5*(2+3)
=>5*5
=>25
```

In the preceding example, the same steps are performed many times; namely, 2+3 is evaluated twice, even if it is the same. To avoid these useless evaluations, so you apply a technique called *graph reduction*. This means that the expressions could be represented as graphs, as shown in Figure 4-1.

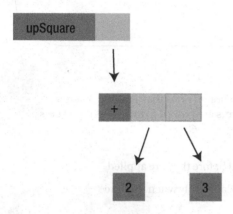

Figure 4-1. *Expression as graph*

In Figure 4-1, the blue section (on the left) represents the function, and the green section (on the right) represents the arguments for that function. In a similar way, the expressions are represented in the memory, with the help of pointers. All defined functions are linked to a reduction rule. For our example, the rule is shown in Figure 4-2.

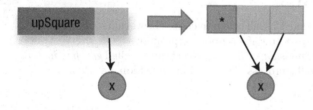

Figure 4-2. *Rule for reduction*

The circle with label x is replacing a subgraph. For the * operator function, there is a single subgraph, because the arguments have the same value. If you commonly use this kind of subgraph, you can prevent useless operations.

A *reducible expression* (*redex*) represents a subgraph that fits with a rule. A redex can be reduced; namely, the focused pair is updated in accordance with the rule. The redexes shown in Figure 4-3 are in the upSquare example: upSquare could be reduced or the + operator function could be reduced.

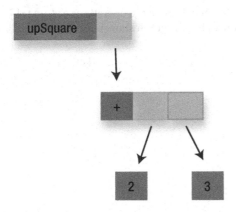

Figure 4-3. *Redexes for upSquare*

In the first step, let's apply the reduction for the upSquare function, and then, we evaluate the redex for +, obtaining the sequence shown in Figure 4-4.

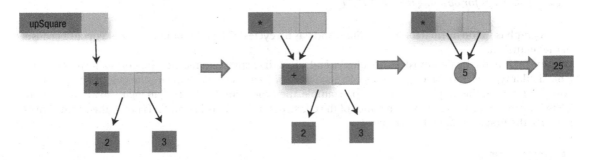

Figure 4-4. *Reduction process for upSquare*

It updated the colored redex at each stage. In the second-to-last graph, we introduced a novel redex, corresponding to the multiplication rule. The result is 25.

If there is no expression in the graph that can be reduced, then the process of reduction is finished and we obtain the result. The last form of expression is called *normal form*, which represents the result of an evaluation process. In our example, Figure 4-5 shows the result.

Figure 4-5. *The result of upSquare(2+3)*

For every expression, there is a graph. For example, the list obtained through the operations 9:10:11:[ ] (which is in the normal form, because there is nothing else to reduce) has the graph shown in Figure 4-6 associated with it.

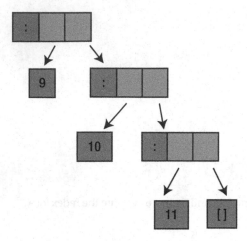

Figure 4-6. *Steps for obtainig the list [9,10,11]*

A graph is in the normal form if it is finite and has no cycles. The cycles or infinity could occur because of the recursion.

In Haskell, the evaluation does not always end when the expression reaches the normal form. There is a particular type of normal form called *weak head normal form (WHNF)*. If the topmost node of a graph is a constructor, then the graph is in WHNF. For example, the expression (2+3) : [] in Figure 4-7 is stated in the WHNF form because its root is an instance of the constructor (:) of the list, and it is not in the normal form because the first parameter has a redex.

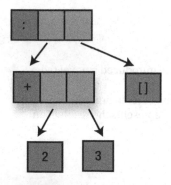

Figure 4-7. *Example of WHNF form*

A graph that is not in the WHNF is called an *unevaluated expression*, or *thunk*. Even if an expression is in WHNF, the parameters for the constructor could be unevaluated expressions. A good example is the following piece of code.

```
Prelude> onesList = 1 : onesList
```

The onesList is a list obtained by adding the digit 1 to itself (so, it becomes infinite). Even the associated graph has a topmost constructor, its argument is an unevaluated expression.

Usually, expressions contain more redexes. From this fact rises a natural question: In what order are they reduced?

Many programming languages are based on *eager evaluation*, which means the arguments of a function are first reduced to normal form, and then the function itself is reduced. This technique is not adopted by Haskell, however. In Haskell, the evaluation technique is lazy evaluation, which means that the topmost function is evaluated first. If necessary, it evaluates some arguments of the function. Let's consider the logicalAnd function, which implements logicalAnd.

```
logicalAnd :: Bool -> Bool -> Bool
logicalAnd True x = x
logicalAnd False x = False
```

This function works with two reduction rules: one for True as the first argument, and one for False as the first argument, as shown in Figure 4-8.

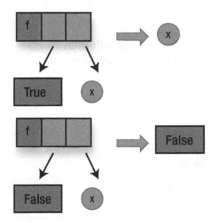

Figure 4-8. *Reduction rules for* logicalAnd *function*

The logicalAnd ('x' == 'y') ('a' == 'b') expression is represented in Figure 4-9.

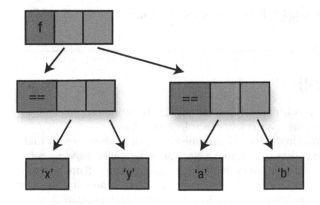

Figure 4-9. *Evaluation of* logicalAnd ('x' == 'y') ('a' == 'b')

The parameters of the function are redexes. The first parameter of the function verifies if the first argument fits the True constructor. So, the next step in lazy evaluation is to reduce the first parameter, as shown in Figure 4-10.

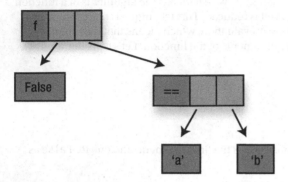

Figure 4-10. *Lazy evaluation and reducing rules*

The last argument is no longer verified, because we already achieved a redex. Lazy evaluation always tries to reduce the topmost node; so, using the definition of logicalAnd, we obtain False, as shown in Figure 4-11.

Figure 4-11. *The final result for logicalAnd ('x' == 'y') ('a' == 'b')*

This is in normal form, so the reduction process stops, and the result is obtained.

■ **Note**   The result obtained by applying lazy evaluation is never different from the result obtained by applying eager evaluation, if the expression is terminating; otherwise, eager evaluation may diverge, but lazy evaluation could still return some partial information.

In Haskell, the process of evaluation does not draw graphs "behind the scenes," but uses a model called STG (spineless, tagless, G-machine) to reduce graphs.

Parallel Strategies in Haskell

In Haskell, there are many techniques for deterministic parallelism. The Strategies library supplies methods for controlling granularity through chunking, assessment control, and sparking.

The *spark* represents the smallest unity of work in the Haskell runtime system. It binds to a thunk that can be evaluated. The runtime system procedure choses sparks from a circular buffer, called a *spark pool*, when runnable threads do not exist. Even if the sparks are not evaluated, the computation will not become stuck. The normal schedule flow does not wait for a spark that remained unevaluated, because its evaluation is ongoing. Because Haskell uses lazy evaluation, operations on lists do not require that to evaluate the whole list. The Strategies library allows you to indicate the level of evaluation expected for the input.

It is not necessary to compile programs with the -threaded flag. The GHC runtime system could provide data about logging details of inner events. This could be combined with a good profiling tool, such as ThreadedScope. Let's compile a program using these options:

```
ghc --make -threaded -eventlog -rtsopts -O2 myprogram.hs
```

eventlog is used for profiling events and rtsopts sets runtime options.

Let's take the Fibonacci example and write it in three different ways.

```
nfibo :: Integer -> Integer
nfibo n | n < 2 = 1
nfibo n = nfibo (n-1) + nfibo (n-2)

-- The version using Eval monad
efibo :: Integer -> Integer
efibo n | n < 2 = 1
efibo n = runEval $ do
        nf1 <- rpar (efibo(n-1))
        nf2 <- rpar (efibo(n-2))
        return (nf1 + nf2)

-- The version using Strategy
sfibo :: Integer -> Integer
sfibo n | n < 2 = 1
sfibo n = withStrategy strat nf1 + nf2
        where nf1 = nfibo(n-1)
                  nf2 = nfibo(n-2)
                  strat v = do rpar nf1; rse1 nf2; return v
```

The Eval monad and Strategies are very close. Strategies performs a more powerful abstraction for easing the issues that come from regulating granularity. It forces the evaluation to be made by the user.

```
type Strategy a = a -> Eval a

using :: a -> Strategy a -> a
x `using` s = runEval (s x)
withStrategy :: Strategy a -> a -> a ->a
withStrategy s x = runEval (s x)
```

In the preceding code, using and withStrategies are logically the same. They provide syntactic sugar. The Strategies library could be considered an extension of the Eval monad, which has syntactic sugar and control over evaluation orderliness.

In the preceding Fibonacci function implementation, it is difficult to determine how sfib will be executed, because the rpar strategy does not provide any guarantee for the evaluation process; it is used to alert the runtime system to first deal with the thunks if runnable threads that need to be scheduled do not exist.

Scan Family

An important family of functions, called scan, allows itself to be parallelized. Let's look at an implementation that uses Strategies, from *A tutorial on Parallel Strategies in Haskell* by Oscar Andersson and Yanling Jin.

```
scanP :: (Num a, NFData a) => Int -> (a -> a -> a) -> [a] -> [a]
scanP d f list = concat reducedList
        where
                scanList = map (scan1 f) (chunk d list) `using` parList rdeepseq
                reducedList = reduce f scanList
                strat v = do rpar reducedList; return v

reduce :: (a-> a -> a) -> [[a]] -> [[a]]
reduce f [ ] = [ ]
reduce f x:[ ] = [x]
reduce f x:y:xs= x : reduce f (map (f $ last x) y : xs)

chunk :: Int -> [a] -> [[a]]
chunk _ [ ] = [ ]
chunk n xs = as : chunk n bs where (as, bs) = splitAt n xs
```

The following is the foremost building block of Strategies, in which the `using` function evaluates an expression utilizing a strategy.

```
x `using` s = runEval ( s x)
parList :: Strategy a -> Strategy [a]
```

The parList is one of the simplest strategies of the library, because every item on the list is evaluated by parList in parallelism, being sparks, as stated by a particular strategy. In our example, the control is retained in the reduce stage, so the granularity constructed into Strategies is not utilized. Let's continue by using chunking built-in to Strategies.

```
scanList = map (scan1 f) (chunk d list) `using` parListChunk 4 rdeepseq
```

Another important strategy is rdeepseq. First, let's take a look at a special type class called NFData. It adds a restriction such that every argument of type a should be assessed to normal form, so it cannot be applied to other reductions on the expression. Broadly, thunks that are not evaluated do not remain, because the expression is assessed when it is in normal form.

The rdeepseq is a function that forces the evaluation to a normal form, making Haskell a stricter programming language. As you have seen, rpar strategy leaves the evaluation for the spark tool, while rseq evaluates only the expressions that are in WHNF.

The rdeepseq function could also be used in sequential approach.

```
evalList :: Strategy a -> Strategy [a]
```

evalList represents the analogs of parList in the sequential approach.

These techniques can provide powerful algorithms if they are used properly.

Skeletons

Another use of strategies is in defining skeletons, because they supply a high level of abstraction in distributed computation patterns. The following is a standard example of *divide and conquer* from original article *Architecture aware parallel programming in Glasgow Parallel Haskell* by Mustafa Kh Aswad, where the strategies are used to separate algorithms from parallelism.

```
divConq :: (a -> b)
        -> a
        -> (a -> Bool)
        -> (b -> b -> b)
        -> (a -> Maybe (a,a))
        -> b
divConq f arg threshold combine divide = go arg
        where
                go arg =
                        case (divide arg) of
                            Nothing -> f arg
                            Just (lo, ro) -> combine l1 r1 `using` strat
                                where l1 = go lo
                                        r1 = go ro
                                strat x = do r l1; r r1; return x
                                r | threshold arg = rseq
                                          | otherwise = rpar
```

The DivConq function splits the main problem (which is not trivial) into subproblems of the same type, and then it applies the f schema to every subproblem. Next, the results of the subproblems are combined to obtain the final result. The sparks of sub-parts l1 and r1 are encoded by strat, and threshold manages the degree of parallelism. The degree of parallelism is returned based on the argument. It returns False if no further division is done.

Next, mergesort shows how the divide-and-conquer skeleton works. The sort function merges two lists and then does the sorting, utilizing the classical Haskell function.

```
sort :: Ord a => [a] -> [a] -> [a]
sort [ ] yl = yl
sort xl [ ] = xl
sort xl@(x:xs) yl@(y:ys)
        | x <= y = x : sort xs yl
        | x > y = y : sort xl ys

mergeSort :: Ord a => [a] -> [a]
mergeSort [ ] = [ ]
mergeSort [x] = [x]
mergeSort xs = sort (mergeSort xs1) (mergeSort xs2)
        where (xs1, xs2) = splitAt (length xs `div` 2) xs
```

The next code represents the implementation of mergesort in parallel, using the preceding skeleton.

```
mergeSort_dc :: Ord a => Int -> [a] -> [a]
mergeSort_dc thres xs = divConq f xs threshold combine divide
        where
                f :: Ord a => [a] -> [a]
```

```
f x = x
threshold :: [a] -> Bool
threshold x = length x < thres
combine x1 x2 = sort x1 x2
divide :: [a] -> Maybe ([a], [a])
divide x = case (splitAt (length x `div` 2) x) of
            ([ ], x2) -> Nothing
            (x1, [ ]) -> Nothing
            res -> Just res
```

Summary

This chapter covered the main strategies used in the evaluation process, including the following topics:

- Redexes and lazy evaluation

- The smaller units at work during the Haskell runtime system

- Scan functions

- Skeletons for the high level of abstraction in distributed computation patterns

■ ■ ■

CHAPTER 5

Exceptions

In any programming language, error handling is an important task. In general, when we talk about an unexpected behavior in our program, we refer to two terms: errors and exceptions. We need to distinguish between them to make the appropriate decision for our program.

The term exception is newer to programming than the error. An exception represents an anticipated, but improper case at runtime; whereas an error represents an inaccuracy, which can only be solved by changing the program.

The following are types of errors:

- *Syntax error.* Occurs because there is a "spelling" mistake in the programming language

- *Semantic error.* Occurs because the statements are used incorrectly

- *Logical error.* Occurs because some specifications are not respected

The following are time errors:

- *Compile-time errors.* Syntax errors and static semantic errors that are identified by the compiler

- *Runtime errors.* Dynamic semantic errors and logical errors that are not identified by the compiler

Errors

The following are the error and exception functions in Haskell programming:

- *Errors.* `error, assert, Control.Exception. catch, Debug.Trace.trace`

- *Exceptions.* `Prelude.catch, Control.Exception.catch, Control.Exception.try, IOError, Control.Monad.Error`

Observe that the keyword `catch` belongs in both categories. But take a deeper look: they are different because `Prelude.catch` manages only exceptions; whereas `Control.Exception.catch` is used to catch types of unspecified values (such as undefined, error, and many other things).

© Stefania Loredana Nita and Marius Mihailescu 2017

S. L. Nita and M. Mihailescu, *Practical Concurrent Haskell*, DOI 10.1007/978-1-4842-2781-7_5

Using the error Function

The error function, which belongs to `Prelude`, stops the execution of a program and returns an error message with custom text. `undefined` is a particular type of error with standard text. In Haskell, there is no difference between an undefined value and an infinite loop, in practice. Broadly, `error` and `undefined` are the same.

```
let a = a + 2 in a :: Int
```

The simplest ways to throw, generate, or indicate an error condition is with the `error` function. The following is a function that computes the *n*th number of the Fibonacci series.

```
fibo 0 = 1
fibo 1 = 1
fibo n = fibo(n-1) + fibo(n-2)

Prelude> fibo 3
3
```

What happens if the input is less than zero?

```
Prelude> fibo (-1)

*** Exception: <interactive>: Non-exhaustive patterns in function fibo
```

To avoid this case, we could complete our function as follows.

```
 fibo n | n < 0 = error "The argument should be positive!"
 fibo 0 = 1
 fibo 1 = 1
 fibo n = fibo(n-1) + fibo(n-2)
```

In practice, the error function is not used in error handling; instead, `Maybe` or `Either` are used, as presented in the next two sections.

Maybe

Let's start with a simple example. We have a list of integers and we want to divide each by a number.

```
Prelude> divide x = map (x `div`)
divide :: Integral b => b -> [b] -> [b]
Prelude> divide 100 [2, 10, 20, 50]
[50,10,5,2]
```

The preceding function worked as we wanted. We can test it on an infinite list; the result is as follows.

```
Prelude> take 10 (divide 100 [1..])
[100,50,33,25,20,16,14,12,11,10]
```

But the division has a special case: division with a zero. Let's see what happens.

```
Prelude> take 10 (divide 100 [0..])
[*** Exception: divide by zero
Prelude> divide 100 [2, 10, 0, 20, 50]
[50,10,Prelude> *** Exception: divide by zero
```

In the first example, we get the divide by zero error because our list begins with a zero. In the second example, you can see how lazy initialization is applied: the allowed divisions are computed, and when 0 becomes the nominator, we get the divide by zero error, and the program stops.

How do we avoid situations like the preceding?

Let's use Maybe, Nothing, or Just.

```
divide :: Integral x => x -> [x] -> Maybe [x]
divide _ [] = Just []
divide _ (0:_) = Nothing
divide a (b:ys) =
    case divide a ys of
      Nothing -> Nothing
      Just res -> Just ((a `div` b) : res)
```

The use of Maybe is the most common method to show that an error occurred. Another way is to return Nothing, if the zero element belongs to the list. There is also Just if 0 is not an element of the list.

```
Prelude> divide 100 [2, 10, 0, 20, 50]
Nothing
Prelude> divide 100 [2, 10, 20, 50]
Just [50,10,5,2]
Prelude> divide 100 [1..]
*** Exception: stack overflow
```

The first two examples work perfectly, but we get an error if the list is infinite. This is due to the use of Maybe. Because the result is Maybe [x], the whole list is traversed to determine if it contains the 0 element. Also, before compute the current outcome, in every stage of divide, the former outcomes need to be known. Therefore, an infinite list is not accepted as input in the error-handling version of the divide function.

In most programs, we know the special cases in which it would crash. Let's think about two simple functions in lists: head and tail. If the input list is empty list, then we will get errors in both cases.

```
Prelude> head []
*** Exception: Prelude.head: empty list
Prelude> tail []
*** Exception: Prelude.tail: empty list
```

Let's write our own head and tail functions, in which we handle the empty list case. Let's begin with the function for tail.

```
tailEmptyHandling :: [x] -> Maybe [x]
tailEmptyHandling [] = Nothing
tailEmptyHandling (_:ys) = Just ys
```

When we use our function, we get the following.

```
Prelude> tailEmptyHandling []
Nothing
Prelude> tailEmptyHandling [1,2,3]
Just [2,3]
```

If we want the tail of an infinite list, we could proceed as follows, where we actually get only the first 10 elements of an infinite list.

```
Prelude> case tailEmptyHandling [1..] of {Nothing -> Nothing; Just a -> Just (take 10 a)}
Just [2,3,4,5,6,7,8,9,10,11]
```

Next, let's see what the function for head looks like.

```
headEmptyHandling :: [x] -> Maybe x
headEmptyHandling [] = Nothing
headEmptyHandling (y:_) = Just y
```

These are the results.

```
Prelude> headEmptyHandling []
Nothing
Prelude> headEmptyHandling [1,2,3]
Just 1
```

So, you have seen how to handle an empty list or an infinite list for a head and tail function. Now, let's return to our previous example and remember that, if the list contains a 0 value, no matter the index, the result will always be Nothing. But we want Nothing to be returned only for the 0 values, and the result of the division to be returned for the rest of the elements. We could proceed as follows.

```
divide :: Integral x => x -> [x] -> [Maybe x]
divide divident divisor =
    map ok divisor
    where ok 0 = Nothing
          ok x = Just (divident `div` x)
```

The following are the results.

```
Prelude> divide 100 [2, 10, 20, 50]
[Just 50,Just 10,Just 5,Just 2]
Prelude> divide 100 [2, 10, 20, 0, 50]
[Just 50,Just 10,Just 5,Nothing,Just 2]
```

The fact that we used divide :: Integral x => x -> [x] -> [Maybe x], instead of divide :: Integral x => x -> [x] -> Maybe [x] helps to maintain the laziness. An important benefit is that you can see exactly where the special case of division occurred.

A useful library is safe, that could be found at this web page. It is useful because it works on Data.List and throws exceptions in different situations. For every unsafe function, there are more versions of it. For example, tail has the following versions.

- tail :: [a] -> [a]: The error occur on tail []
- tailMay :: [a] -> Maybe [a]: Transforms errors in Nothing
- tailDef :: [a] -> [a] -> [a]: Default to return on errors
- tailNote :: String -> [a] -> [a]: Could be used for a particular error message
- tailSafe :: [a] -> [a]: Returns a sensible default if possible; [] in the case of tail

Either

The use of Either is similar to the use of Maybe, but there is an important difference: Either can bind connected information for both a failure and a success. A function that returns Either has two sides: the right/correct value is returned with Right, and the wrong/incorrect value is returned with Left. The association between Right/Left and success/failure is not restricted. You can reversely bind them, but the convention is that the Right side is linked to success and the Left side is linked to failure.

The following shows the divide function written using Either.

```
divide :: Integral x => x -> [x] -> Either String [x]
divide _ [] = Right []
divide _ (0:_) = Left "divide: found 0"
divide divident (divisor:ys) =
    case divide divident ys of
      Left y -> Left y
      Right outputs -> Right ((divident `div` divisor) : outputs)
```

These are the results.

```
Prelude> divide 100 [2, 10, 20, 50]
Right [50,10,5,2]
Prelude> divide 100 [2, 10, 0, 20, 50]
Left "divide: found 0"
```

The implementation of Either is similar to the implementation of Maybe. Here, Right is corresponding to Just, and Left is corresponding to Nothing. An important feature of Either is that you can write your own failure message. The following example is modified so that there are restrictions on dividing by 2.

```
data DivisionError x = DivisionZero
                | IllegalDivisor x
                  deriving (Eq, Read, Show)

divide :: Integral x => x -> [x] -> Either (DivisionError x) [x]
divide _ [] = Right []
divide _ (0:_) = Left DivisionZero
divide _ (2:_) = Left (IllegalDivisor 2)
divide divident (divisor:ys) =
    case divide divident ys of
      Left y -> Left y
      Right outcomes -> Right ((divident `div` divisor) : outcomes)
```

The following shows the results of calling our function.

```
Prelude> divide 100 [2, 10, 0, 20, 50]
Left (IllegalDivisor 2)
Prelude> divide 100 [12, 10, 0, 20, 50]
Left DivisionZero
Prelude> divide 100 [12, 10, 20, 50]
Right [8,10,5,2]
```

Exceptions

As in many programming languages, Haskell allows you to handle exceptions. Only in the IO monad does Haskell catch exceptions, because the order of the evaluation is not specified. A special syntax is not necessary because the techniques through which exceptions are caught are mostly functions.

Control.Exception is an important module that works with exceptions. In this module, different functions exist. Many types are defined to handle exceptions. Every exception that occurs has the Exception type, because it is the main type.

try is a common function that handles exceptions. It has two sides: Left – returns an exception, and Right – returns the output, if the program was run successfully. Let's look at the following example.

```
Prelude> :m Control.Exception
Prelude > let a = 2 `div` 2
Prelude > let b = 2 `div` 0
Prelude > print a
1
Prelude > print b
*** Exception: divide by zero
Prelude > try (print a) :: IO (Either SomeException ())
1
Right ()
Prelude > try (print b)
Left divide by zero
```

First, we just call the print function without handling a possible exception, but then we use the try function to catch possible exceptions that occur in calling print. The exception was thrown when we called the print function, not when we defined b. When an expected situation occurs—namely, printing a valid result, two lines are displayed: the first is caused by print, which provides result 1, and the second is caused by GHCI, which says that the function was called successfully, without exceptions.

Lazy Evaluation and Exceptions

Let's run the following program.

```
Prelude> let c = undefined
Prelude > try (print c)
Left Prelude.undefined
Prelude > outcome <- try (return c)
Right *** Exception: Prelude.undefined
```

As, you can see it is not a problem to assign the undefined value to c, but an exception occurs if you try to print it. But, why is there Right *** Exception: Prelude.undefined, if there is an exception? This is because Right comes from assignation, which works fine, but when it tries to print undefined, it gets an exception.

To avoid this kind of situations, use evaluate.

```
Prelude > let c = undefined
Prelude > outcome <- try (evaluate c)
Left Prelude.undefined
Prelude > outcome <- try (evaluate b)
Left divide by zero
```

evaluate is similar to return, but the system is forced to analyze the input.

The handle Function

Most times, we want our program to work in the case of success. But other times, we want it to work in case of failure; for example, we want to display a message. For that, we use the handle function, which has two sides: the second side is the function we want to call, and the first side is called in case of failure.

```
Prelude> :m Control.Exception
Prelude > let a = 2 `div` 2
Prelude > let b = 2 `div` 0
Prelude > handle (\_ -> putStrLn " Divide by zero ") (print a)
1
Prelude > handle (\_ -> putStrLn "Divide by zero") (print b)
Divide by zero
```

In the preceding example, we used a kind of brute force, because for any exception that arises, the message will be the same. Instead, you could use handleJust, which permits you to use particular types of exceptions, when the elements are described by a single type exception. For other types of exceptions, like arithmetic exceptions, I/O exceptions, custom exception, and so forth, a more powerful mechanism, such as Catch, is needed.

```
import Control.Exception

exeptionCatch:: Exception -> Maybe ()
exeptionCatch (ArithException IllegalDivision) = Just ()
exeptionCatch _ = Nothing

handle :: () -> IO ()
handle _ = putStrLn "We have an illegal operation: 0 as divisor."

myPrint :: Integer -> IO ()
myPrint a = handleJust exceptionCatch handle (print a)
```

exceptionCatch represents a function that is establish if the targeted exception occurs, returning Just(), which goes to the handle function, or otherwise, Nothing.

```
Prelude> let a = 2 `div` 2
Prelude > let b = 2 `div` 0
Prelude > myPrint a
1
Prelude > myPrint b
We have an illegal operation: 0 as divisor.
```

Input/Output Exceptions

In most cases, exceptions occur because of the input/output. For that, Haskell has a special module called System.IO.Error, which defines the main functions try and catch. If the exceptions that occur do not have an IOError type, then they will not be captured.

■ **Note** System.IO.Error and Control.Exception have the same functions, but they act differently. You need to import these modules carefully. If both of them are imported, then there is an error when you use their functions, because the callings are ambiguous. So, you need to import them qualified, or conceal the symbols of one from the other. Another important aspect to remember is that the default catch used by Prelude is the System.IO.Error version.

The throw Function

Another aspect of exception handling is throw. In the earlier examples in this chapter, the exceptions were thrown by the system, but we can throw them on our own. The most used functions for this purpose are throw, throwIO, and ioError:

- throw belongs to Control.Exception and it could generate any Exception

- throwIO belongs to Control.Exception, but it generates exceptions (of type Exception) just for IO monad

- ioError belongs to Control.Exception and System.Error.IO, and it is used to engender exceptions associated with I/O

Dynamic Exceptions

Data.Dynamic and Data.Typeable modules are used for dynamic exceptions. They are very useful, especially when working with databases, because they return the errors from SQL queries. Usually, SQL exceptions have three elements: a number representing the error code, a state, and a message. In this section, we will implement a function that simulates SQL errors.

```
{-# LANGUAGE DeriveDataTypeable #-}
import Data.Dynamic
import Control.Exception
```

```
data SqlException = SqlException {state :: String,
                                 exceptionCode :: Int,
                                 exceptionMessage :: String}
                deriving (Eq, Show, Read, Typeable)
```

In the last line of code, the data type becomes accessible for dynamic type, derived from Typeable. The first line is used to engender an object of type Typeable.

The following defines functions that implement catch and handle SQL errors. Observe that Haskell's catch and handle are not able to figure out the error, because it does not fall under the Exception type class.

```
{- | It is executed the specified IO command.
When the SqlException occurs, it is executed the given
handler which returns its result. When our exception does
not occur, operate normally.-}
catchSqlEception :: IO x -> (SqlException -> IO x) -> IO x
catchSqlEception =  catchDyn

{- | This is the same as catchSql, but the arguments are reverted. -}
handleSqlException :: (SqlError -> IO x) -> IO x -> IO x
handleSqlException = flip catchSql
```

catchDyn is restricted to catch only SqlException.

If the program throws an exception, but it is not caught by any function, it will display a common error message; but when it comes to dynamic exceptions, which are unknown to the system, the message will not be clear. Instead, we could add a feature to our program so that all exceptions can be caught.

```
{- | There are caught SqlException and, then they are re-raised
Like IO errors and with failure. -}
featureHandleSqlException :: IO x -> IO x
featureHandleSqlException activity =
    catchSql activity myHandler
    where myHandler ex = fail ("Sql exception occured " ++ show ex)
```

The following throws a SqlException exception.

```
throwSqlException :: String -> Int -> String -> a
throwSqlException state exceptionCode exceptionMessage =
    throwDyn(SqlException state exceptionCode exceptionMessage)

throwSqlExceptionIO :: String -> Int -> String -> IO x
throwSqlExceptionIO state exceptionCode exceptionMessage =
    evaluate (throwSqlException state exceptionCode exceptionMessage)
```

Let's see how it worked.

```
ghci> throwSqlExceptionIO "state" -100 "exception message"
*** Exception: (unknown)
ghci> featureHandleSqlException $ throwSqlException "state" -100 "exception message"
*** Exception: user error (SQL error: SqlError {state = "state", exceptionCode = -100,
    exceptionMessage = "exception message"})
ghci> featureHandleSqlException $ fail "non-Sql exception"
*** Exception: user error (non-Sql exception)
```

Summary

In this chapter, you learned

- how errors can be used in Haskell.
- the differences in using `Maybe` and `Either`.
- `Exceptions` in Haskell.
- the way lazy evaluation handles exceptions.
- the exceptions for input and output.
- the way the `handle` and the `throw` functions work.
- about dynamic exceptions.

CHAPTER 6

■ ■ ■

Cancellation

When working with interactive applications, a thread may need to break another thread execution in a particular situation. The following are some general examples.

- In web applications, the client presses an Abort button. In this case, some activities need to be aborted; for example, a thread downloads something, or a thread runs script, or a thread renders a page.

- An application with a thread that runs an interface, and another thread that does intense computations, needs to abort the computation thread if the client is changing the parameter from the user interface.

- Usually, in server-based applications, the client has time to emit a demand before closing the connection. This approach prevents any remaining hanging connections that use many resources.

It is very important to decide if the targeted thread has the property to accept the cancellation, or if it is instantly closes when a particular situation occurs. This represents a compromise.

- When a thread can choose, it raises a risk because the thread may not respond for a short time, or even worse, it could become permanently unresponsive. When threads are not responding, it could lead to hangings or deadlock, which is very bad from the client's point of view.

- When the cancellation is asynchronous, pieces of the program that change state must be kept safe from cancellation; otherwise, an update could be interrupted at an inappropriate time and could leave pieces of information in an improper state.

In reality, we have to choose between only implementing the first option and implementing both options. If the second option is preselected, protection of a crucial part leads to changing the choosing behavior during the crucial part.

In almost all imperative languages, the second option is not set as the default behavior because there are many parts where states are changed in a program. One major benefit of Haskell is that most code is functional, thus a condition could abort or safely suspend a thread, and then reload the thread without effect. In addition, specific to Haskell in a purely functional program, threads cannot ask for the cancellation conditions (due to the definition of a functional program itself), thus it cancels implicitly.

Hence, fully asynchronous cancellation represents the sensible implicit choice in Haskell. The only projection problem is to decide the way that cancellation is controlled by the program in the IO monad.

In this chapter, we talk mainly about asynchronous cancellation for threads, which is a sensible subject because it could occur at crucial moments in a program's execution. The way that asynchronous cancellation is used in a program should be determined in the code in the IO monad.

© Stefania Loredana Nita and Marius Mihailescu 2017

S. L. Nita and M. Mihailescu, *Practical Concurrent Haskell*, DOI 10.1007/978-1-4842-2781-7_6

Asynchronous Exceptions

A very useful function in exception handling is bracket from Control.Exception.

```
bracket :: IO a -> (a -> IO b) -> (a -> IO c) -> IO c
```

This function allows the programmer setting up exception handling to deallocate some resources or to apply tidy-up operations. If we call bracket a b c, then a represents the operation that assigns the resource, b represents the operation that frees the resource, and c represents the actual operation that works. The following is the definition of bracket.

```
bracket :: IO a -> (a -> IO b) -> (a -> IO c) -> IO c
bracket ahead after current = do
  a <- ahead
  c <- current a `onException` after a
  after a
  return c
```

You already know that exceptions are a useful part of the IO monad, and the best practice in writing code with the IO monad is to make use of bracket, and then to gain and issue resources in a proper way. An important fact is that bracket should continue its job even if a thread is aborted. Thus, in this case, the cancellation should act as an exception. There is a huge distinction between exceptions and cancellation. For example, one is a situation in which an exception occurs when the user tries to open a file that does not exist anymore and an exception occurs when the user clicks an Abort button. In a second example, it is an asynchronous exception, because interruption was unexpected. The exceptions that occur when throw and throwIO are used are called *synchronous exceptions*.

If we want to use asynchronous exceptions, Haskell delivers a powerful primitive called throwTo that is throws exceptions from one thread to another thread.

```
throwTo :: Exception e => ThreadId -> e -> IO ()
```

Identical to synchronized exceptions, the argument for throwTo must be of type Exception. ThreadId is the output of a prior running of forkIO. It could represent a thread that is running, is blocked, or has ended. To show how to utilize throwTo, we will create a little program in which we will use the new Async type (defined next) to handle errors. In this program, the user is downloading web pages concurrently, and can quit the downloading pressing the Q key. The following is the code with explanations.

```
data Async a = Async (MVar (Either SomeException a)) -- 1

async :: IO a -> IO (Async a)
async something = do
  variable <- newEmptyMVar
  forkIO (do r <- try something; putMVar variable r) -- 2
  return (Async variable)

waitCatch :: Async a -> IO (Either SomeException a)  -- 3
waitCatch (Async var) = readMVar variable

wait :: Async a -> IO a                              -- 4
wait a = do
  x <- waitCatch a
```

```
case x of
  Left b  -> throwIO b
  Right a -> return a
```

- When MVar has Right a, the computation has successfully completed and returns the value a; when it has Left e, the computation throws exception e.

- The action is included in try that outputs Either SomeException a —the necessary type for MVar.

- There are two ways in which the result of Async could be waiting. First, waitCatch is returning Either SomeException a, which means the handling could be done right up. The second approach is to use wait, whose type is below. When wait is finding that in Async occurs an exception, it will throw again that exception.

```
wait :: Async a -> IO a
```

The preceding example is extended to permit cancellation. The following cancel operation is added.

```
cancel :: Async a -> IO ()
```

This function aborts an existing Async. If the operation is yet ended, then the function cancel has not any impact.

The implementation of cancel requires the ThreadId from the thread that runs the Async; thus, it needs to register it into Async type, together with MVar, which keeps the output. So, the Async type has the following definition.

```
data Async a = Async ThreadId (MVar (Either SomeException a))
```

Implement cancel as follows.

```
cancel :: Async a -> IO ()
cancel (Async t var) = throwTo t ThreadKilled
```

ThreadKilled belongs to Control.Exception. It is an exception that is thrown by cancel when a thread is called, even if it is already cancelled.

We now need to implement an async operation that will keep the output of the forkIO function from the Async constructor; namely, ThreadID.

```
async :: IO a -> IO (Async a)
async something = do
    mVar <- newEmptyMVar
    tVar <- forkIO (do r <- try something; putMVar mVar r)
    return (Async tVar mVar)
```

The following is an example (from Simon Marlow's talk *Parallel and Concurrent Haskell*, also available here https://github.com/simonmar/parconcexamples/blob/master/geturlscancel.hs) in which web pages are downloaded, but we want to also have the option to cancel the download.

```
sites = ["http://www.google.com",
         "http://www.bing.com",
         "http://www.yahoo.com",
```

```
                "http://www.wikipedia.com/wiki/Spade",
                "http://www.wikipedia.com/wiki/Shovel"]

main = do
  as <- mapM (async . timeDownload) sites                    -- 1

  forkIO $ do                                                -- 2
    hSetBuffering stdin NoBuffering
    forever $ do
      c <- getChar
      when (c == 'q') $ mapM_ cancel as

  rs <- mapM waitCatch as                                    -- 3
  printf "%d/%d succeeded\n" (length (rights rs)) (length rs) -- 4
```

Let's take a look at the code.

1. Begin the download like in the initial example.

2. Branch a thread that reads characters through standard input until it meets the Q character, in which case the cancel function is called for Asyncs.

3. Expect the state of the output (completed or aborted).

4. Display a report that mentions the number of successful operations. If the program is started and you press Q very quickly, the output should look like the following.

    downloaded: http://www.google.com (14538 bytes, 0.17s)
    downloaded: http://www.bing.com (24740 bytes, 0.22s)
    q2/5 finished

The program uses a long and complex HTTP library that does not supply assistance for cancellation and asynchronous I/O; Haskell provides modular cancellation assistance. A significant piece of code is not necessary for supporting it, even if some specifications should be taken into consideration when working with states.

Using Asynchronous Exceptions with mask

At the beginning of the previous section, we mentioned that a damaging cancellation could occur in the middle of an important action. For example, when an update process is suddenly interrupted, the data is left in an uncertain state, maybe forever. This is why you should supervise the way the asynchronous exceptions occur while running crucial sections. A solution could be the ability to postpone the asynchronous exception until the execution of crucial sections has finished; but this approach is not what we actually need.

Let's imagine the following scenario: the takeMVar is called by a thread, which uses the value of MVar to make a computation, and then the output is stored by MVar. The implementation should allow asynchronous exceptions, but at the same time, it should be secure. For example, if an asynchronous exception occurs in the middle of a computation, then the value of MVar would be left empty. But this is not what should happen; instead, the initial value should be put back into MVar.

The following is a piece of code that illustrates that scenario. The function situation has two arguments: an m variable whose type is MVar, and an f function that makes a computation over the value of m in the IO monad.

```
situation :: MVar a -> (a -> IO a) -> IO ()
situation m f = do
  a <- takeMVar mVar                                   -- 1
  rVar <- f a `catch` \e -> do putMVar mVar a; throw e -- 2
  putMVar mVar rVar                                    -- 3
```

There are two places where MVar will be left without a value: from 1 to 2, and from 2 to 3. Actually, we could not intervene directly to be sure that the MVar value is not empty. But Haskell contains a great combinator called mask.

```
mask :: ((IO a -> IO a) -> IO b) -> IO b
```

The benefit of mask is that it delays the asynchronous exception so that its parameter has enough time to execute successfully. It is a little difficult, but the following is an example that shows how the combinator operates.

```
situation :: MVar a -> (a -> IO a) -> IO ()
situation mVar f = mask $ \restore -> do
  a <- takeMVar mVar
  rVar <- restore (f a) `catch` \e -> do putMVar mVar a; throw e
  putMVar mVar rVar
```

The argument of mask is a function, which has the restore function as a parameter that brings an asynchronous exception to its actual state while the argument of mask is executing.

This described approach is useful because it brings a solution to our problem: exceptions can be raised only while (f a) is running, and there is a handler to catch every exception that occurs.

But we have not solved all of our problems, because the following is exposed: takeMVar is blocked for too much time and it is an inner mask combinator, thus the thread will not respond. Moreover, there is no relevant cause to hide exceptions while takeMVar is executing, rather the exception could occur almost until the stage in which takeMVar is returning.

On the other hand, in Haskell, by definition, the takeMVar should behave as described. Only a few operations would be interrupted while executing, including takeMVar, because takeMVar could block for an unknown time, and every operation that could block for an unknown time is designated as interruptible. These special types of operations could be interrupted by asynchronous exceptions, even if they are within a mask combinator.

Within mask, asynchronous exceptions are no longer asynchronous, but they could be activated by computations. Thus, asynchronous exceptions become synchronous exceptions inner mask combinator. The operations that could be interrupted are operations that could block for an undefined time. This is the expected behavior in almost all cases, as in our example.

Let's return to the situation function. putMVar could be blocked for an undefined time, so it becomes interruptible, which leads us to the conclusion that problem is not safe yet, since an asynchronous exception could occur by blocking putMVar.

The property to be interrupted is very rigorously defined, so the situation function is OK. This is because an operation could be interrupted only if it really blocks; but this is not the case for putMVar because when it is called, the value of MVar is absolutely empty, so it will not be interrupted.

Are we sure that the MVar is really empty? Actually, we are not precisely sure, because another thread could call the putMvar function, applied on the same MVar after takeMVar from the problem function is performed. Still, we know that MVar is performed in a consistent manner, such that every call of takeMVar is succeeded by a putMvar. This represents a usual approach for a large number of MVar operations—a certain usage of MVar brings a protocol, in which operations should succeed or else there is the risk of deadlock.

Ultimately, there is a solution that permits a function to not be interrupted, and an asynchronous exception not to occur. The solution is uninterruptibleMask.

```
uninterruptibleMask :: ((IO a -> IO a) -> IO b) -> IO b
```

This is the same as mask, but it does not allow asynchronous exceptions to interrupt the interruptible functions. You need to pay attention to uninterruptibleMask, because the wrong use of it could produce significant damage, such that the application would no longer respond.

For debugging purposes, in the Control.Exception library there is a great function that allows us to verify if a current thread stands in the mask state or not.

```
getMaskingState :: IO MaskingState

data MaskingState
  = Unmasked
  | MaskedInterruptible
  | MaskedUninterruptible
```

As you can see, there are three constructors that could be returned by getMaskingState, one at a time, which are quite intuitive.

- Unmasked. The targeted thread is not an inner mask or uninterruptibleMask.

- MaskedInterruptible. The targeted thread is an inner mask.

- MaskedUninterruptible. The targeted thread is an inner uninterruptibleMask.

There are higher-level combinators that exempt programmers from the necessity to use the mask combinator. As an example, the problem function from earlier is provided by the Control.Concurrent.MVar library, and its name is modifyMVar, because it is applicable when operating with MVars.

```
modifyMVar_ :: MVar a -> (a -> IO a) -> IO ()
```

Another variation of modifyMVar permits a different outcome among the novel content of the MVar.

```
modifyMVar :: MVar a -> (a -> IO (a, b)) -> IO b
```

The following is a simple example that implements the well-known compare-and-switch (CAS) operation.

```
compareAndSwitchMVar :: Eq a => MVar a -> a -> a -> IO Bool
compareAndSwitchMVar m oldValue newValue =
  modifyMVar m $ \cur ->
  if cur == oldValue
      then return (newValue,True)
      else return (cur,False)
```

The parameters for compareAndSwitchMVar function are an MVar, a check valuable, and a new valuable. It works as follows: if the value of MVar is the same as the check value, then it changes with the new value and also returns True; else, the value of MVar is not changed and returns False.

If we want to work with more MVars, we should fit more calls of modifyMVar. The following modified the values of the two MVars in a safe way.

```
modifyTwoValues :: MVar a -> MVar b -> (a -> b -> IO (a,b)) -> IO ()
modifyTwoValues maValue mbValue f =
  modifyMVar_ mbValue $ \b ->
    modifyMVar maValue $ \a -> f a b
```

When it is blocked inside modifyMVar, and an exception occurs, the content of MVar is restored to the initial value, with the help of an outside modifyMVar_.

Be careful with the order in which two or more values are taken. It should be the same order everywhere; otherwise, the program will have deadlock.

Extending the bracket Function

Let's write a bracket function using mask, such that the function is safe if asynchronous exceptions occur.

```
bracket :: IO a -> (a -> IO b) -> (a -> IO c) -> IO c
bracket ahead after something =
  mask $ \restore -> do
    a <- ahead
    rVar <- restore (something a) `onException` after a
    _ <- after a
    return rVar
```

The IO actions are executed inside of mask, such as ahead and after. The bracket function assures that when ahead is returning, after is executed at a later time. The fact that ahead has a blocking process is legal. For example, if an exception occurs when ahead blocks, there is no damage. However, ahead could execute just a single blocking process. If a second blocking process raises an exception, it will not result in after being executed. If more blocking operations are necessary, then you should fit calls to bracket, as in the modifyMVar example.

Another thing to pay attention to is the use of blocking operations in after. If this is really necessary, be sure that the blocking operation can be interrupted and accept an asynchronous exception.

Writing Safe Channels Using Asynchronous Exceptions

Channels represent models for communications between processes, and synchronization between them through *message passing* (a method that invokes comportment on a computer, in which the programs are not called by names as in the classical method, but use object models to differentiate the general function from the particular implementations). Channels are useful because they facilitate the access of threads to the messages. Threads or processes can access a message that is sent through a channel if it has a reference to that channel.

In Haskell, channels belong to Control.Concurrent.Chan. The first step is to declare a channel, then to send data between threads using pipes, and then to extract data for different readers.

The following is a simple example in which file names are hashed and then printed using channels (see https://wiki.haskell.org/Haskell_for_multicores#Message_passing_channels).

```
{-# LANGUAGE BangPatterns #-}
import Data.Digest.Pure.MD5
import qualified Data.ByteString.Lazy as L
import System.Environment
```

```
import Control.Concurrent
import Control.Concurrent.Chan
import Control.Monad (forever, forM_, replicateM_)

nrWorkers = 2

main = do
    files <- getArgs
    str <- newChan
    fileChan <- newChan
    forM_ [1..nrWorkers] (\_ -> forkIO $ worker str fileChan)
    forM_ files (writeChan fileChan)
    printNrResults (length files) str

printNrResults i var = replicateM_ i (readChan var >>= putStrLn)

worker :: Chan String -> Chan String -> IO ()
worker str fileChan = forever (readChan fileChan >>= hashAndPrint str)

hashAndPrint str f = do
        bs <- L.readFile f
        let !h = show $ md5 bs
        writeChan str (f ++ ": " ++ h)
```

In the remaing c ontent of section, there are examples that belong to Simon Marlow, from his talk "Parallel & Concurrent Haskell 3: Concurrent Haskell", available at http://community.haskell.org/~simonmar/slides/cadarache2012/3%20-%20concurrent%20haskell.pdf. When working with MVars, we can make the code safer against asynchronous exception if we replace the use of takeMVar and putMVar with modifyMVar_. For example, the following function reads from a buffered channel, which is not safe when it deals with asynchronous exceptions.

```
readChan :: Chan a -> IO a
readChan (Chan readVar _) = do
  stream <- takeMVar readVar
  Item val new <- readMVar stream
  putMVar readVar new
  return val
```

When the execution of the primal takeMVar raises an asynchronous exception, the readMVar remains free, which leads to deadlock because of further read operations over Chan. modifyMVar helps achieve safer code.

```
readChan :: Chan a -> IO a
readChan (Chan readVar _) = do
  modifyMVar readVar $ \stream -> do
    Item val tail <- readMVar stream
    return (tail, val)
```

The preceding modification is not sufficient. Do not forget that readMVar has the following definition.

```
readMVar :: MVar a -> IO a
readMVar m = do
  a <- takeMVar m
```

94

```
  putMVar m a
  return a
```

Looking at the readMVar definition, notice that when an exception occurs after the execution of takeMVar, but before the execution of readMVar, the content of the MVar is empty; therefore, it is necessary to assure the safety here, also. To do that, more options exist. One option is to utilize modifyMVar to reinstate the initial value. Another option is to utilize an extent of modifyMVar.

```
withMVar :: MVar a -> (a -> IO b) -> IO b
```

withMVar is similar with modifyMVar, but it does not modify the value of the MVar; thus, it is better for the goal of readMVar.

The easiest option is to only keep readMVar safe by using a mask. This approach is also adopted by the Control.Concurrent.MVar library.

```
readMVar :: MVar a -> IO a
readMVar m =
  mask_ $ do
    a <- takeMVar m
    putMVar m a
    return a
```

In the preceding implementation, mask_ is similar to mask; still, it does not have a restore function as a parameter. This implementation is enough because takeMVar and putMVar do not exist in any operation; thus, it is not needed in the exception handler.

The writeChan is a little more difficult. The initial definition is

```
writeChan :: Chan a -> a -> IO ()
writeChan (Chan _ writeVar) val = do
  newHole <- newEmptyMVar
  oldHole <- takeMVar writeVar
  putMVar oldHole (Item val newHole)
  putMVar writeVar newHole
```

To protect our code against exception, one idea is the following implementation.

```
wrongWriteChan :: Chan a -> a -> IO ()
wrongWriteChan (Chan _ writeVar) val = do
  newHole <- newEmptyMVar
  modifyMVar_ writeVar $ \oldHole -> do
    putMVar oldHole (Item val newHole)    -- 1
    return newHole                        -- 2
```

Still, it is not safe, because in lines 1 and 2, an asynchronous exception could occur, which will let old_hole full and writeVarbounding to old_hole, which breaks the invariants of the data structure.

To resolve this last issue, all we need to do is apply mask_ over the entire sequence.

```
writeChan :: Chan a -> a -> IO ()
writeChan (Chan _ writeVar) val = do
  newHole <- newEmptyMVar
  mask_ $ do
```

```
oldHole <- takeMVar writeVar
putMVar oldHole (Item val newHole)
putMVar writeVar newHole
```

Observe that both putMVars are ensured against blocking; thus, they cannot be interrupted.

timeout Variants

A function that limits the amount of time for an action to work is a popular approach in concurrent programming when using asynchronous exceptions. For this purpose in Haskell, there is timeout from the System.Timeout module wrapper. Its type is

```
timeout :: Int -> IO a -> IO (Maybe a)
```

timeout t m acts as follows.

- Similar to fmap Just m, m returns an outcome or leads to an exception (inclusive to the asynchronous one) in t microseconds.

- In other cases, it raises an exception in the format Timeout u. Timeout represents a novel data type, and u represents a single valuable whose type is Unique, so this specific instance of timeout is distinguished from any others. In this case, calling timeout gets Nothing.

In reality, the necessary t microsecond is approximated by timeout. In the first case, it is necessary that the execution of m be done under the conditions of the current thread, as m could need myThredId. It is also expected that m be interrupted by a thread that throws an exception to the current one, using throwTo. Having this anticipated behavior, nesting timeouts would help.

The following implementation for timeout is from the System.Timeout library (with some minor changes). It is a little complicated, but we will explain it. The main point is to branch a thread, which is waiting for t microseconds, until it calls throwTo for throwing the Timeout exception; thus, it is necessary that timeout terminate the thread until it returns.

```
timeout t m
  | t < 0     = fmap Just m                          -- 1
  | t == 0    = return Nothing                       -- 2
  | otherwise = do
      pid <- myThreadId                              -- 3
      u <- newUnique                                 -- 4
      let ex = Timeout u                             -- 5
      handleJust                                     -- 6
        (\e -> if e == ex then Just () else Nothing) -- 7
        (\_ -> return Nothing)                       -- 8
        (bracket (forkIO $ do threadDelay t          -- 9
                              throwTo pid ex)
                 (\tid -> throwTo tid ThreadKilled)  -- 10
                 (\_ -> fmap Just m))                -- 11
```

Here are a few explanations.

- Lines 1 and 2: Treat the simple cases of timeout being less or equal to zero.

- Line 3: Get the ThreadId that belongs to the current thread.

- Lines 4 and 5: newUnique generates a novel value, which creates a novel Timeout exception.

- Line 6: handleJust handles exceptions and has the type

```
handleJust :: Exception e
           => (e -> Maybe b) -> (b -> IO a) -> IO a
           -> IO a
```

- Line 7: The first parameter of handleJust says which exceptions are caught. For this example, we need to catch an exception of Timeout type that contains the unique valuable generated.

- Line 8: The secondary parameter of handleJust handles the exceptions. In our case, it is returning Nothing because timeout takes place.

- Line 9: This operation is running in handleJust. In this part, the novel thread is forked, making use of bracket, which assures that the novel thread is always terminated until the timeout function outputs. In the novel thread, threadDelay has a delay of t microseconds, and throwTo throws an exception whose type is Timeout to the initial thread.

- Line 10: Terminates the youngest thread every time.

- Line 11: The computation m (the secondary parameter of bracket) is running inside bracket, which will lead to the outcome Just.

We could check the correctness of the program in three cases.

- m finishes and outputs a value.

- The second thread (the new one) throws an exception; whereas m is still doing its tasks.

- Both threads call throwTo at the same time.

The first two cases could be easily verified by running the program with specific arguments. The third case in the list is a little difficult. What happens in this case? It is actually conditioned by the implementation of throwTo. When bracket is called, it should not be allowed to output; whereas a Timeout exception could yet arise; this is necessary for timeout to work correctly. Therefore, when throwTo terminates the second thread, its call should be synchronous. In the event that it outputs, the second thread will not be able to throw an exception. This behavior is assured by the implementation of throwTo, which returns immediately after the exception occurs in the desired thread. As a consequence, throwTo could still be blocking when the second thread runs mask with asynchronous exceptions, which could be interrupted and get asynchronous exceptions.

For the third case, throwTo is called from both threads, which represents the expected and correct behavior.

Catching Asynchronous Exceptions

The behavior of an asynchronous exception is the same as a synchronous exception. It can be caught with catch or another function that catches exceptions from Control.Exception. Let's say it was caught an asynchronous exception. We need to make some computations, but other asynchronous exception have occurred in the actual thread, which interrupts the initial function that handles exceptions. This behavior is not what we expect, because it could cause damage; the exception handlers could be interrupted by asynchronous exceptions.

The preceding behaviors can be avoided using mask and restore, as follows.

```
mask $ \restore ->
  restore action `catch` handler
```

We have already used this approach in some examples. The expected behavior is that asynchronous exceptions from mask stand inside the exception handler. Haskell brings a great benefit by doing this automatically, so there is no need to use mask explicitly. When returned from the handling exception, they are outside of mask again.

You need to pay attention and not remain in the default mask. The following is an example that shows this situation. The program inputs are file names by command line, and the output is represented by the number of lines for each file. If the file with a given name does not exist, then it is ignored.

```
main = do
  fs <- getArgs
  let
    loop !n [] = return n
    loop !n (f:fs)
      = handle (\e -> if isDoesNotExistError e
                      then loop n fs
                      else throwIO e) $
          do
            getMaskingState >>= print
            h <- openFile f ReadMode
            s <- hGetContents h
            loop (n + length (lines s)) fs

  n <- loop 0 fs
  print n
```

The names of the files are read in the recursive loop function, where it tries opening and reading the content of each file, and saves the number of lines in the n variable. For every file, handle is called to assure exception handling. If isDoesNotExistError from System.IO.Error occurs, showing that the specified file does not exist, the exception handling is calling the recursive loop function to do the same operations over the remaining file names.

At first look, the program is working, but a problem could occur when getMaskingState is called. Next, the program runs with more file names that could not be found.

```
$ ./catch-mask xxx yyy
Unmasked
MaskedInterruptible
0
```

In the first iteration of the loop function, the state is Unmasked, which is good; but in the next iteration, it is reported that the current state is MaskedInterruptible, which is bad, because the synchronous exception should not be masked starting at the secondary iteration.

This situation has occurred because the loop function was called recursively by the exception handler, which means that the calling is done in the default mask from handle.

The following is the improved program.

```
main = do
  fs <- getArgs
  let
    loop !n [] = return n
    loop !n (f:fs) = do
      getMaskingState >>= print
      r <- Control.Exception.try (openFile f ReadMode)
      case r of
        Left e | isDoesNotExistError e -> loop n fs
               | otherwise              -> throwIO e
        Right h -> do
          s <- hGetContents h
          loop (n + length (lines s)) fs

  n <- loop 0 fs
  print n
```

The loop function is not called any more recursively inside a mask. In addition, we have limited the purpose of the exception handler to only openFile, which is better than in the previous version.

You need to pay attention to this approach. In situations where handling asynchronous exceptions is needed, it is best that the exception handling is done within mask, so that current work is not interrupted by other asynchronous exception until it ends the first exception. This is why catch or handle are more suitable.

mask and forkIO Operations

Now, let's return to the async function from the previous sections.

```
async :: IO a -> IO (Async a)
async action = do
  m <- newEmptyMVar
  t <- forkIO (do r <- try action; putMVar m r)
  return (Async t m)
```

This implementation is actually a mistake. When the Async is aborted, an exception is raised immediately after try; at putMVar, the thread terminates, but the content of MVar remains empty. The program experiences deadlock if it is waiting for the outcome of Async.

The code could be put inside a mask, but this will not help because, if an exception occurs before try, then the behavior will be similar. It follows a natural question: Which is the way in that asynchronous exceptions are put inside mask, in the place between creation of the thread and execution of try? Calling mask function within forkIO is not sufficient, because throw could be applied on an exception before calling mask.

This is why forkIO creates a thread that receives the state of mask as it is in the parent thread. So, it could create a thread that occurs in the masked state by encapsulating the forkIO call within the mask.

```
async :: IO a -> IO (Async a)
async action = do
  m <- newEmptyMVar
  t <- mask $ \restore ->
         forkIO (do r <- try (restore action); putMVar m r)
  return (Async t m)
```

Another variation of forkIO is shown next. It allows you to take some action after a thread is completed.

```
forkFinally :: IO a -> (Either SomeException a -> IO ()) -> IO ThreadId
forkFinally action fun =
  mask $ \restore ->
    forkIO (do r <- try (restore action); fun r)
```

Here is the improved version if the async function.

```
async :: IO a -> IO (Async a)
async action = do
  m <- newEmptyMVar
  t <- forkFinally action (putMVar m)
  return (Async t m)
```

Finally, the program is safe now.

Summary

In this chapter, you saw how asynchronous cancellation works for threads, and how to proceed when a thread can accept the cancellation, or is instantly aborted if a certain situation occurs. You also used useful operations such as bracket, timeout, mask, and forkIo. You were introduced to channels and you learned how to make them safe using asynchronous exceptions.

CHAPTER 7

■ ■ ■

Transactional Memory Case Studies

Safety and ease in programming are two advantages of transactional memory. If the transactions are used correctly, then it is almost impossible for problems to occur in parallel code (for example, deadlocks). The programmer mostly needs to assign transactions (and maybe some transaction variables). It is not necessary to identify the locks or their correct order to prevent deadlocks or other problems. How do you use transactions correctly? All shared data is passed through transaction variables to threads. Transactional data is accessed only through transactions; and in transactions, there are no operations that can be rolled back.

This chapter explains what transactional memory is and how it works in Haskell.

Transactions

A transaction consists of grouped activities that are not individually visible by an external observer. The results of the combined activities are seen by the external observer. A database transaction has several properties: atomicity, consistency, isolation, and durability—known as *ACID properties*.

- *Atomicity* means that all actions that compound a transaction must terminate successfully; but if an action fails, then the transaction has not finished successfully. When a transaction is successful, then it commits; otherwise, it aborts.

- *Consistency* depends on the application, but generally, it represents a selection of states for data. This means a new state of data is created by a transaction; but if a failure occurs, then the data is returned to its state prior to the transaction.

- *Isolation* means that transactions run separately. They do not interact with each other, even if they are executed in parallel.

- *Durability* means that once a transaction successfully completes and commits, the result is irreversible and available for further transactions.

Introducing Transactional Memory

Transactions seem to be a good technique for programming languages. It assures consistency in the information used by other processes.

The basic concept is easy to understand. In a system based on concurrency or parallelism, the read and write operations are coordinated properly, applying abstraction provided by the characteristics of the transactions. Nowadays, programmers coordinate read and write operations using basic techniques, such as locks or mutexes, to avoid interaction between concurrent threads.

© Stefania Loredana Nita and Marius Mihailescu 2017   101
S. L. Nita and M. Mihailescu, *Practical Concurrent Haskell*, DOI 10.1007/978-1-4842-2781-7_7

Because of their properties, transactions can be used in concurrency such that a program encapsulates a task in a transaction. The successful execution is assured by atomicity; then, the outcome is committed, or the task is aborted if there is a failure. Isolation assures that the result is always the same, whether the transaction is executed alone or there are concurrent transactions.

For transaction memory, atomicity becomes failure atomicity, assuring consistency. For example, if a transaction is not completed successfully, then some pieces of information could remain in an uncertain state and affect other transactions. To control concurrency, it is necessary to have a technique for implementing failure atomicity, so that the data can be reverted to a previous state in the event of failure.

Software Transactional Memory

Read logs and *write logs* supply *software transactional memory* (STM) systems the information needed for conflict detection and solution. Read logs have a version number that provides useful information to a thread (because when an object update occurs, its version number is increased). The thread checks if a concurrent thread has changed an object that it uses for reading. If a conflict occurs, then the thread will use *undo logs* to cancel a transaction.

There are many characteristics that differentiate STM systems. This is usually based on the purpose of the system. The following are a few examples.

- *Low sequential overhead*. In these systems, the transaction instructions run as quickly as allowed.

- *Good scalability*. A parallel amount of work utilizing transactions can enhance execution as processors are included. This is very useful in cloud computing systems.

- *Strong progress guarantees*. For example, blocking is avoided. Another criteria is the programming semantics provided by the STM systems.

The evaluation of the transactional memory systems is influenced by the way that systems with multiple processors work. From a computational point of view, choosing a more expensive method leads to lower synchronization or cache movement. Hardware dissimilarities could sway the capabilities of STM systems; for cxample, the STM system model for memory vs. classical memory accessions.

Software Transactional Memory in Haskell

STM supplies compounding atomic transactions, which allow you to combine read and write operations, or other types of memory operations, into one atomic operation. As you have seen, the transactions could abort or retry.

The STM transactions are found in the STM monad.

```
data STM a
instance Monad STM
```

Transactions are executed using a special function called atomically, which is covered in a later in this chapter.

```
atomically :: STM a -> IO a
```

A very important and useful primitive is represented by retry, a function that cancels the actual transaction and reloads it in case any dependencies are modified during transactions in different threads.

```
retry :: STM a
```

The STM package supplies the essential transactional variables, but there are other complicated structures that are delivered by other packages. The following are a few structures from stm:Control.Concurrent.STM.

- TVar: A localization of memory that is imparted; a correspondent of IORef, but its type is transactional.

- TMVar: A changeable variant correspondent to IORef.

- TChan: Channels corresponding to Chan from the base.

- TQueue: A channel with high speed, but does not support channel replication.

- TBQueue: Limited and non-replicable channels.

- TArray: The corresponding transactional arrays from the array package.

The stm-containers and stm-chans packages also supply transactional structures.

As technology becomes more complex, processors contain more cores, and software products become more elaborated, there is an increasing need for transactional memory. Mainly, the software transactional memory represents the act of synchronizing common memory and avoiding deadlock.

GHC is one of the best compilers. It supplies very good assistance to STM systems. To work with STM, Haskell makes use of monads.

The following are simple examples that implement typical concurrent programming models.

```
module STM where
import Random
import Control.Monad
import Control.Concurrent
import Control.Concurrent.STM
```

The first example implements the semaphores, or locks, as they are also named. In the snipped code, we use traditional obtain and release to achieve and issue the semaphore.

```
type Semaphore = TVar Bool
newSem :: Bool -> IO Semaphore
newSem available = newTVarIO available
 obtain :: Semaphore -> STM ()
 obtain sem = do b <- readTVar sem
            if b
                then writeTVar sem False
                else retry
 release :: Semaphore -> STM ()
 release sem = writeTVar sem True
```

One of the powerful characteristic of STM's implementation in GHC is the retry combinator, because it manipulates conditional synchronization. When a state is not accomplished, it is called retry. At the right moment, the process is awoken by the runtime system.

Next is an example of an unlimited buffer, in which processes can add or retrieve information. In the following piece of code, we do not concentrate on efficiency, but on clarity of implementation.

```
type Buffer a = TVar [a]
newBuffer :: IO (Buffer a)
newBuffer = newTVarIO []
put :: Buffer a -> a -> STM ()
```

```
put buffer item = do ls <- readTVar buffer
                        writeTVar buffer (ls ++ [item])
get :: Buffer a -> STM a
get buffer = do ls <- readTVar buffer
                case ls of
                  [] -> retry
                  (item:rest) -> do writeTVar buffer rest
                                    return item
```

In the preceding example, the main operation is writing. When there is only one process that writes on the buffer, it can be read an arbitrary number of times. If there are many processes, just one of them could access the buffer at a certain time, because the semaphore implementation gives a reciprocal exclusion. The first process that made a request is first served.

An easy but important pattern is resource allocation. In the following, we use a relaxed variant of resource allocation, in which a counter is used to keep the quantity of disposable resources. When a process requests a certain quantity of resources, and it is not disposable, then it blocks.

```
type Resource = TVar Int
acquire :: Resource -> Int -> STM ()
acquire res nr = do n <- readTVar res
                    if n < nr
                       then retry
                       else writeTVar res (n - nr)

release :: Resource -> Int -> STM ()
release res nr = do n <- readTVar res
                    writeTVar res (n + nr)
```

The next example is the dining philosophers, a representative problem for concurrent programming, and a good example of STM use. To check if the simulation works right, we need to display what the philosophers are doing. To do that, we need to pay attention to how we print output in standard out, because the classical I/O primitives in Haskell are thread unsafe. We have a buffer where the processes write, and a thread that reads from the buffer and prints the output. This is useful because only one process gives the output, so it will not be an unexpected output. The forks are implemented as binary semaphores, as before.

```
simulation n = do forks <- replicateM n (newSem True)
                  outputBuffer <- newBuffer
                  for [0..n-1] $ \i ->
                    forkIO (philosopher i outputBuffer
                           (forks!!i)
                           (forks!!((i+1)`mod`n)))
                  output outputBuffer
 output buffer =
    do str <- atomically $ get buffer
       putStrLn str
       output buffer
for = flip mapM_
```

In the first line of code, the system is prepared for simulation, such that `simulation` is a function with just one argument; namely, the number of philosophers. The next step is to create the number of forks and the buffer, and then generate the philosopher processes that receive their corresponding forks. In the last step, the principal thread enters a loop that reads the output from the buffer and then displays the read messages.

```
philosopher :: Int -> Buffer String -> Semaphore -> Semaphore -> IO ()
philosopher n out fork1 fork2 =
    do atomically $ put out ("Philosopher " ++ show n ++ " is thinking.")
        randomDelay
        atomically $ do
          p fork1
          p fork2
        atomically $ put out ("Philosopher " ++ show n ++ " is eating.")
        randomDelay
        atomically $ do
          v fork1
          v fork2
        philosopher n out fork1 fork2
randomDelay = do r <- randomRIO (100000,500000)
                 threadDelay r
```

As you can see, the preceding code is quite simple, but its strength is that it is able to sequentially create transactions and then atomically execute them. Let's observe that the philosopher processes run in the IO monad and access the transactional memory when they synchronize. This is a classic example of transactional memory use.

When a philosopher starves, `randomDelay` occurs, which calls `threadDelay` at a certain time.

A Bank Account Example

The following is a function that transfers an amount of money.

```
sendAmount :: Account -> Account -> Int -> IO ()
-- Send 'amount' from account 'from' to account 'to'
sendAmount fromAccount toAccount moneyAmount
  = atomically (do deposit toAccount moneyAmount
                   withdrawAmount fromAccount moneyAmount)
```

The inside do block is quite simple: `deposit` is called to put an amount in a repository, and `withdrawAmount` is called to retrieve an amount. We will implement these functions later in this chapter. First, let's observe the `atomically` function. The parameter is an action that is executed atomically. So, there are two important characteristics of a transaction to observe:

- *Atomicity*. The repercussions of atomic transactions are obvious to other threads at the same time. In our example, this means that an estate in which the amount was stored, but not withdrawn, could not be identified by another threads.

- *Isolation*. When atomic transactions are performed, the action is not affected by other threads.

Let's imagine a basic running model for atomicity: it is only one global lock. The atomically act gets the lock, runs the action, and discharges the lock. This usage guarantees that two atomic pieces will not be executed at the same time, and so the atomicity is guaranteed.

This model sounds very simple, but it still has disadvantages. First, isolation is not ensured because there is no condition that stops a thread to write the same IORef outright (namely, outside atomically, without keeping the general lock); whereas a certain thread is approaching an IORef inside an atomic piece (which holds the general lock). Another disadvantage is low performance, because each atomic sequence will be serialized, although interference is impossible. This problem is discussed later. For the moment, let's review the atomically function.

```
atomically :: STM a -> IO a
```

As you can see, the parameter of the atomically function is an action that has STM a. An STM action is similar to an IO action in regards to side effects, but those of the STM actions are much lower. The most important operations done in an STM action are reading and writing transactional variables, which have TVar a type; like IORefs, it could be read or written in an IO action.

```
readTVar  :: TVar a -> STM a
writeTVar :: TVar a -> a -> STM ()
```

Like IO actions, the STM actions can be formed with the same do notation, because it has an implementation for every type. The following code presents the withdraw function.

```
type Account = TVar Int

withdrawAmount :: Account -> Int -> STM ()
withdrawAmount account amount = do
    bal <- readTVar account
    writeTVar account (bal - amount)
```

The Account type is has one variable, whose type is Int to represent the repository balance. The withdrawAmount function subtracts the desired amount from the total amount of the account, an operation that is implemented as an STM action.

The following is the entire sendAmount function.

```
depositAccount :: Account -> Int -> STM ()
depositAcoount account amount = withdraw account (- amount)

import System.IO
import Control.Concurrent.STM

type Account = TVar Int

withdrawAmount :: Account -> Int -> STM ()
withdrawAmount account amount = do
    bal <- readTVar account
    writeTVar account (bal - amount)

depositAccount :: Account -> Int -> STM ()
depositAccount account amount = withdrawAmount account (- amount)
```

```haskell
sendAmount :: Account -> Account -> Int -> IO ()
-- Transfer 'amount' from account 'from' to account 'to'
sendAmount fromAccount toAccount moneyAmount
    = atomically (do depositAccount toAccount moneyAmount
                     withdrawAmount fromAccount moneyAmount)

displayAccount :: Account -> IO Int
displayAccount account = atomically (readTVar account)

main = do
    fromAccount <- atomically (newTVar 200)
    toAccount <- atomically (newTVar 100)
    sendAmount fromAccount toAccount 50
    v1 <- displayAccount fromAccount
    v2 <- displayAccount toAccount
    putStrLn $ (show v1) ++ ", " ++ (show v2)
```

newTVar represents two accounts: the sender and the beneficiary.

Observe that the sendAmount function realizes four read and write actions: reading and writing to the sender account, and reading and writing to the beneficiary account. The readings and writings run atomically, and satisfy the requirements described in the beginning of this chapter.

Read and write operations outside a TVar transaction are prevented by the type system. Let's do the following.

```haskell
wrong :: Account -> IO ()
wrong account = do
    hPutStr stdout "Withdrawing..."
    withdrawAmount account 10
```

This program won't compile:

```haskell
import System.IO
import Control.Concurrent.STM

type Account = TVar Int

withdrawAmount :: Account -> Int -> STM ()
withdrawAmount account moneyAmount = do
    bal <- readTVar acc
    writeTVar account (bal - moneyAmount)

wrong :: Account -> IO ()
wrong account = do
    hPutStr stdout "Withdrawing..."
    withdrawAmount account 10

main = do
    account <- atomically (newTVar 200)
    wrong account
    hPutStr stdout "\nDone!\n"
```

The program will be cancelled because the hPutStr and withdraw actions have different types, IO and STM, respectively, so they cannot be put in the same single block.

The following is the error message.

```
Couldn't match type 'STM' with 'IO'
        Expected type: IO ()
          Actual type: STM ()
```

If we make the withdrawAmount action an argument for an atomically function, then it will work fine.

```
right :: Account -> IO ()
right account = do
    hPutStr stdout "Withdrawing..."
    atomically (withdrawAmount account 10)
```

The program is compiled and could be executed as follows.

```
import System.IO
import Control.Concurrent.STM

type Account = TVar Int

withdrawAmount :: Account -> Int -> STM ()
withdrawAmount account moneyAmount = do
    bal <- readTVar account
    writeTVar account (bal - moneyAmount)

right :: Account -> IO ()
right account = do
    hPutStr stdout "Withdrawing..."
    {-hi-}atomically{-/hi-} (withdrawAmount account 10)

main = do
    account <- atomically (newTVar 200)
    right account
    hPutStr stdout "\nDone!\n"
```

Transactional Memory Version

Isolation and atomicity should be enough for STM use. But it is also important to keep a clean implementation of a model to understand every step. One advantage of STMs is that it has a clean and easy-to-use interface that can be implemented in different ways.

An example of implementation called *optimistic execution* is in the database area. An empty thread is assigned for many local transactions whenever an *atomically* act occurs; after that, the locks are not taken during an act action. Every time an act is running, there is a log in which writeTVar it is writing the address of TVar in that log, but not the value of TVar. The writeTVar writes every time it is called. Similarly, when readTVar is called, the address corresponding to TVar is searched into the log (only if writeTVar was previously called). If there is no TVar address value in the log, then it reads the TVar value, which is saved in the log. Of course, at the same time, there could be more threads that read and write values and TVar addresses.

When the act is performed, the log is verified, and if the result is success, then the log is committed. To validate a log, every record of TVar in the log is verified such that the value in the log must match the actual TVar value. If there is a match, the verification has succeeded, and then in the commit, every record from write in the log is written in the real TVars.

The presented steps are dependent one of each other, such that, the implementation does not allow the interrupts, utilizes locks or instructions for example, make a comparison and then exchange. All these are needed for ensuring that the verification and commit are not seen by another threads. These steps are part of the implementation; the programmer is unaware of them.

Earlier, we presented a successful case. When it fails, however, the transaction's view of memory is wrong. Thus, the transaction is aborted, the log is reinitialized, and the act is executed again, this procedure is named *re-execution*. This is possible, because the writes have not been registered into the memory. It is very important that act contains only read and write operations so as not to influence other threads. Let's examine the following piece of code.

```
atomically (do x <- readTVar xv
               y <- readTVar yv
               if x>y then launchRockets
                     else return () )
```

launchRockets :: IO () has secondary effects over other threads. Locks are not taken when the atomic pieces are executed, so when a concurrent thread changes the values of xv and yv, an inconsistent view of memory will occur. If this happens, then the run of launchMissiles is at fault; it will be discovered later that the verification has failed, and the transaction should run again. But in Haskell, we have type system, which impedes executing IO actions inside STM actions, thus, the previous piece of code will be cancelled by the type checker. This is another benefit of differentiation between IO and STM actions.

```
import System.IO
import Control.Concurrent.STM

launchRockets :: IO ()
launchRockets = hPutStr stdout "Zzzing!"

main = do
    xv <- atomically (newTVar 2)
    yv <- atomically (newTVar 1)
    atomically (do x <- readTVar xv
                   y <- readTVar yv
                   if x > y then launchRockets
                         else return () )
```

Blocking and Choice

Atomic blocks (or pieces) are inappropriate for coordination of concurrent programs. They dismiss two important characteristics: blocking and choice. In this section, you will see how to elaborate a base STM interface, so that blocking and choice are included in a modular approach.

Let's consider the situation when a user tries to withdraw an amount greater than what is available; in this case, a thread should prevent this action. These situations occur often in concurrent programming. Other examples are when a thread tries to read from an empty buffer, or it is waiting for an occurrence; in these cases, the thread should block. To make this happen in STM, all we need to do is add the retry function, whose type is

```
retry :: STM a
```

The following is an improved `withdraw` function that aborts if the desired amount is greater than the available amount.

```
limitWithdrawAmount :: Account -> Int -> STM ()
limitWithdrawAmount account moneyAmount = do
    bal <- readTVar account
    if moneyAmount > 0 && moneyAmount > bal
    then retry
    else writeTVar account (bal - moneyAmount)
import System.IO
import Control.Concurrent.STM
import Control.Concurrent

type Account = TVar Int

limitWithdrawAmount :: Account -> Int -> STM ()
limitWithdrawAmount account moneyAmount = do
    bal <- readTVar account
    if moneyAmount > 0 && moneyAmount > bal
    then retry
    else writeTVar account (bal - moneyAmount)

delayDepo account moneyAmount = do
    hPutStr stdout "Waiting for deposit \n"
    threadDelay 3000000
    hPutStr stdout "OK! Depositing now!\n"
    atomically ( do bal <- readTVar account
                    writeTVar account (bal + moneyAmount) )

main = do
    account <- atomically (newTVar 100)
    forkIO (delayDepo account 1)
    hPutStr stdout "Withdrawing...\n"
    atomically (limitedWithdrawAmount account 101)
    hPutStr stdout "Success!\n"
```

The preceding code is branched a thread that calls `delayDeposit`; this function waits 3 seconds to deposit the sum. Meantime, the `limitedWithdrawAmount` function aborts because the available sum is too low; `limitedWithdrawAmount` is successful after a thread successfully completes the deposit.

The `retry` function is very easy: when a `retry` action occurs, the actual transaction is abandoned and reloaded at a future time. The theoretical correct procedure is that transaction to be retried instantly, but this is also not efficient, because the available amount is probably the same, in which case the transaction is retried. An efficient way is to stop the thread until another thread writes to the account. This approach raises a question: Is the implementation able to await the account? Yes, it is, because the account is read by the transaction as a retry function; this deed is registered in the transaction log.

The `limitedWithdrawAmount` condition has a communal model: it verifies that a Boolean statement is pleased. If it is not, the `retry` occurs. We have globalized all that we have explained in the following check function.

```
checkAcc :: Bool -> STM ()
checkAcc True = return ()
checkAcc False = retry
```

The following is another version of `limitedWithdrawAmount`.

```
limitedWithdrawAmount :: Account -> Int -> STM ()
limitedWithdrawAmount account moneyAmount = do
    bal <- readTVar account
    checkAcc (moneyAmount <= 0 || moneyAmount <= bal)
    writeTVar account (bal - moneyAmount)
```

Here is the code in which we added the check function.

```
import System.IO
import Control.Concurrent.STM
import Control.Concurrent

type Account = TVar Int

limitedWithdrawAmount :: Account -> Int -> STM ()
limitedWithdrawAmount account moneyAmount = do
    bal <- readTVar account
    checkAcc (moneyAmount <= 0 || moneyAmount <= bal)
    writeTVar account (bal - moneyAmount)

delayDepo account moneyAmount = do
    threadDelay 3000000
    hPutStr stdout "Depositing...\n"
    atomically ( do bal <- readTVar account
                    writeTVar account (bal + moneyAmount) )

main = do
    account <- atomically (newTVar 100)
    forkIO (delayDepo account 1)
    hPutStr stdout "Withdrawing...\n"
    atomically (limitedWithdrawAmount account 101)
    hPutStr stdout "Oh, phew!\n"
```

Now, let the user to make a choice: if the initial account does not have enough funds, then the user could choose to withdraw the amount from another account.

For that, we need the ability to choose an alternative action if the first one retries. To support choice, STM Haskell has a primitive action called orElse, whose type is

```
orElse :: STM a -> STM a -> STM a
```

Like atomically, orElse takes actions as its arguments, and glues them together to make a bigger action. Here are its semantics: The action (orElse a1 a2) first performs a1; if a1 retries (i.e., calls retry), it tries a2 instead; if a2 also retries, the whole action retries. It may be easier to see how orElse is used.

```
limitedWithdrawAmount2 :: Account -> Account -> Int -> STM ()
-- (limitedWithdrawAmount2 acc1 acc2 amt) withdraws amt from acc1,
-- if acc1 has enough money, otherwise from acc2.
-- If neither has enough, it retries.
limitedWithdrawAmount2 account1 account2 amount
```

```
  = orElse (limitedWithdrawAmount account1 amount) (limitedWithdrawAmount account2 amount)
import System.IO
import Control.Concurrent.STM
import Control.Concurrent

type Account = TVar Int

limitedWithdrawAmount :: Account -> Int -> STM ()
limitedWithdrawAmount account moneyAmount = do
    bal <- readTVar account
    checkAcc (moneyAmount <= 0 || moneyAmount <= bal)
    writeTVar account (bal - moneyAmount)

displayAccount name account = do
    bal <- atomically (readTVar account)
    hPutStr stdout (name ++ ": $")
    hPutStr stdout (show bal ++ "\n")

limitedWithdrawAmount2 :: Account -> Account -> Int -> STM ()
-- (limitedWithdrawAmount2 acc1 acc2 amt) withdraws amt from acc1,
-- if acc1 has enough money, otherwise from acc2.
-- If neither has enough, it retries.
limitedWithdrawAccount2 account1 account2 amount
  = orElse (limitedWithdrawAcount account1 amount) (limitedWithdrawAccount account2 amount)

delayDepo name account moneyAmount = do
    threadDelay 3000000
    hPutStr stdout ("Depositing $" ++ show moneyAmount++ " into " ++ name ++ "\n")
    atomically ( do bal <- readTVar account
                    writeTVar account (bal + moneyAmount) )

main = do
    account1 <- atomically (newTVar 100)
    account2 <- atomically (newTVar 100)
    displayAccount "Left pocket" account1
    displayAccount "Right pocket" account2
    forkIO (delayDepo "Right pocket" account2 1)
    hPutStr stdout "Withdrawing $101 from either pocket...\n"
    atomically (limitedWithdrawAmount2 account1 account2 101)
    hPutStr stdout "Successful!\n"
    displayAccount "Left pocket" account1
    displayAccount "Right pocket" account2
```

We use a showAcc helper function to display the content of an account before and after the withdrawal. We have two accounts, account1 and account2, both with insufficient funds for the limitedWithdrawAmount2 to succeed immediately. However, when the background thread deposits $1 into account2, the call succeeds.

Since the result of orElse is an STM action, you can feed it to another call to orElse and so choose among an arbitrary number of alternatives.

Summary

This chapter discussed how software transactional memory (STM) works in Haskell, and covered the most important operations that can be applied.

CHAPTER 8

■ ■ ■

Debugging Techniques Used in Big Data

In this chapter, you learn what big data means and how Haskell can be integrated with big data. You also see some debugging techniques.

Data Science

There is critical and developing interest in data science by the data-savvy experts at organizations, open offices, and charities. The supply of experts who can work successfully with information at scale is limited, however, which is reflected by the quickly rising salaries of information engineers, information researchers, analysts, and information investigators.

In a recent review by the McKinsey Global Institute, an expert remarked: "A shortage of the analytical and managerial talent necessary to make the most of big data is a significant and pressing challenge (for the United States)."

The report states that by 2018 there will be 4 to 5 million jobs in the United States that require data analysis aptitude. An extensive number of positions may be filled through preparing or retraining. There will be a need for 1.5 million managers and examiners with investigative and specialized abilities "who can ask the right questions and consume the results of analysis of big data effectively."

Information becomes inexpensive and omnipresent. We are currently digitizing easy content that was made over hundreds of years, and gathering new sorts of information from web logs, cell phones, sensors, instruments, and exchanges. The measure of computerized information that exists is developing at a tremendous rate—doubling every two years, and changing the way we live. International Business Machines (IBM) estimates that 2.5 billion gigabytes (GB) of information was produced each day in 2012, which represents 90% of all available data from all of history. An article in *Forbes* states that data is coming more quickly than at any other time, and by the year 2020, around 1.7 megabytes of new data will be made each second—for each person on the planet.

Meanwhile, new technologies are developed in order to understand and to use this avalanche of unstructured data gathered from many fields of activity. These provides a way to recognize patterns in all available information, which contains data of different types, helping to propel grant, enhance the human condition, and make business and social to grow. The ascent of big data can develop our comprehension of aspects ranging from physical and natural frameworks to human social and monetary behavior.

Essentially, each area of the economy now has access to a larger amount of information than would have been possible even 10 years ago. Organizations today are amassing new information at a rate that surpasses their ability to get value from it. The question confronting each organization is how to adequately utilize the information—not only their own information, but also the greater part of all of the information that is accessible and important.

© Stefania Loredana Nita and Marius Mihailescu 2017
S. L. Nita and M. Mihailescu, *Practical Concurrent Haskell*, DOI 10.1007/978-1-4842-2781-7_8

Our capacity to infer social and financial value from this recently accessible information is constrained by the absence of expertise. Working with this information requires particular new aptitudes and instruments. The information is often excessively voluminous, making it impossible to fit on one PC, to be controlled with conventional databases, or to use with standard design programming. The information is likewise more heterogeneous than the curated information of the past. Digitized, audio, visual, sensor, and blog content are often muddled, deficient, and unstructured. These types of information typically have unverifiable provenance and quality, and much of the time, they must be joined with other information to be helpful. Working with client-created information additionally raises protection, security, and moral issues.

Data science is rising with the convergence of the fields of sociology and software engineering. It is dealing with unorganized and organized information, and represents a field that involves everything that identifies with data cleansing, readiness, and investigation. Data science is the unification of mathematics, statistics, programming, and critical thinking. It requires the capacity to find and observe information in clever new ways, and to purge, prepare, and adjust this information. Basically, it is the umbrella of the systems utilized when attempting to understand information from data.

Data science has applications in a lot of fields, including Internet search, digital advertising, health care, travel, gaming, and energy management, among many others.

Big Data

Big data is a term for data sets that are so extensive or complex that conventional information handling applications are lacking to manage them. Its origin dates back to 1990. To understand this technology, this section offers a comprehensive description of big data.

Characteristics

Until now, there was no standard definition for big data. There are three commonly agreed upon characteristics of big data within the scientific community.

- *Volume.* In 2012, about 2.5 exabytes (2.5 billion gigabytes) of information were created every day. It continues at a rate that doubles approximately every 2 years. Today, a greater amount of information crosses the Web each second than was placed on the entire Web 20 years ago. This gives organizations a chance to work with numerous petabytes of information in just one data set—and not only from the web. For example, it is estimated that Walmart gathers more than 2.5 petabytes of information from its client exchanges. A petabyte is one quadrillion bytes, or around 20 million file organizers of content. An exabyte is 1,000 times that sum, or 1 billion gigabytes.

- *Velocity.* For some applications, the speed of data creation is considerably more imperative than the volume. Real-time or almost real-time data makes it workable for an organization to be significantly more coordinated than its rivals. Retrieving fast and useful information is a big advantage for a company.

- *Variety.* Big data is collected from messages, updates, and pictures appearing on social media; data sent from sensors; data collected from GPS; and many other sources. A number of the most critical origins of enormous information are moderately new. The immense measures of data from social media, for instance, are just as old as the systems themselves. For example, Facebook was inaugurated in 2004; Twitter in 2006. Cell phones are similar; they now have gigantic amounts of information attached to individuals, activities, and places. Accordingly, the organized databases of corporate data are currently ill suited for handling massive amounts of information. In the meantime, the declining costs of the stocking, memory, handling, transmission capacity, and so forth, imply that the existing costly information gathering methodologies are rapidly becoming distinctly conservative.

The preceding characteristics are known as the *3Vs,* defined by analyst Doug Laney of the META Group (now Gartner) in 2001. Even if these 3Vs are widely accepted by the community, in some reports, big data is seen as 5Vs. The other 2Vs come from the following.

- *Veracity.* This alludes to the untidiness of or the trust we have in the information. With many types of big data, quality and precision are less controllable (consider Twitter posts with hash tags, grammatical mistakes, and casual discourse, and also questionable dependability and accuracy); however, big data and examination innovations now permit us to work with this sort of information. The volume of this information regularly compensates for the absence of value or accuracy.

- *Value.* It is fine to have access to enormous amounts of information; however, unless we can transform it into something of value, it is useless. So, this last V can be seen as the most critical V in big data. It is imperative that organizations put forth a business defense for any endeavor to gather and influence massive amounts of information. It is so natural to fall into the buzz trap and gather enormous information activities without a reasonable comprehension of the expenses and the advantages.

Figure 8-1 illustrates a synthesizing of big data characteristics.

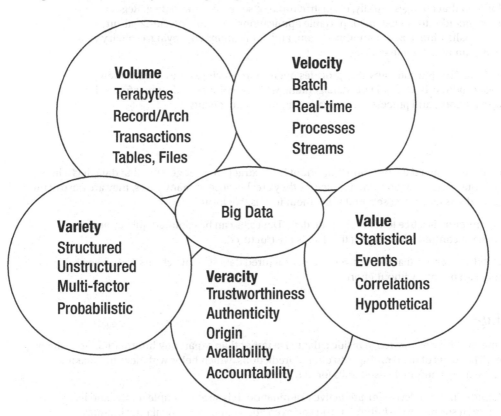

Figure 8-1. *Big data represented as 5Vs*

Tools

When we are working with data, there are more stages through which data passes until useful information is extracted. Let's look at the stages involved in the process of extracting information from big data, as well as some of the tools used in every category.

Storage and Management

Classical database systems cannot handle large amounts of data, so new systems for storage and management have been developed.

- *Hadoop.* Hadoop has become synonymous with big data. It's an open source programming structure for distributed systems of huge data sets on computer clusters. This means that data can be scaled up and down without hardware damage. Hadoop provides gigantic measures of capacity for any sort of data, tremendous preparing power, and the space to handle tasks or jobs without limit.

- *Cloudera.* Basically, it is a Hadoop brand name for with additional administration. It helps businesses construct an information center point that permits employees better access to information. Since it contains an open source component, Cloudera helps organizations manage their Hadoop system. They likewise convey a specific measure of information security, which is very important with sensitive or personal information.

- *MongoDB.* Consider it a replacement option for relational databases. It is very good for data that changes rapidly, or unstructured or semi-structured data. Regular uses include stocking data for portable applications, item inventories, real-time personalization, content administration, and applications conveying a solitary view over numerous frameworks.

- *Talend.* This is a company that provides open source technologies. One of their best products is Master Data Management, which combines real-time information, applications, and process incorporation assuring data quality.

Cleaning

It is a powerful thing to own data, but more important is to extract knowledge from that data. It is a little complicated to obtain information from data sets as they are, because in many cases, they are unstructured. The following products clean data sets and bring them to a usable form.

- OpenRefine is a free tool for cleaning data. Data sets can be explored quickly and without complication, even if the data is unstructured.

- DataCleaner is a that tool converts semistructured data sets into cleansed data sets that can be read without effort.

Data Mining

Data mining means finding knowledge inside a database rather than separating information from site pages into databases. The focus of data mining is to obtain predictions, which helps with decision making. The following are most commonly used tools for data mining.

- RapidMiner is a device for predictive examination. It is strong, simple to use, and has an open source group behind it. You can even add your own particular techniques into RapidMiner by using its dedicated APIs.

- IBM SPSS Modeler contains an entire suite of techniques used in data mining. It incorporates text examination, element analytics, and decision administration and improvement.

Other data-mining products include Oracle Data Mining (ODM), TeraData, FrameData, and Kagle.

Languages

Some languages provide great support for big data. The following are the most popular.

- R is a language for statistical and graphical usage.

- Python has become one of the most commonly used programming languages. It is flexible, free, and contains many libraries for data management and analysis. It is also used in web applications that need great scalability.

Haskell for Big Data

Of course, one of the most important languages used in big data is Haskell. The following are some of the tools that Haskell provides for working with large data set.

- hspark

- Hadron

- Cloud Haskell

- ZeroMQ

- Krapsh library

Next, we briefly describe these Haskell tools.

hspark

A new library inspired by Apache Spark, it is useful in distributed, in-memory computations. It performs simple Map-Reduce jobs over nodes from networks.

hspark implements an easy and extendible Digital Subscriber Line (DSL) for specifying a job. A configuration of a cluster is taken as input and the jobs are translated into a set of distributed jobs, making use of the distributed-process Cloud Haskell library.

The following are components of hspark.

- *Context*. Provides information about the cluster.

- *Resilient Distributed Dataset (RDD) DSL*. Expresses hspark jobs.

- *Execution*. Executes RDD and its dependencies.

Let's look at Alp Mestanogullari's and Mathieu Boespflug's "Hello World!" example using hspark (http://www.tweag.io/posts/2016-02-25-hello-sparkle.html). It is on an Amazon cluster.

```
# Build it
$ stack build hello
# Package it
$ mvn package -f sparkle -Dsparkle.app=sparkle-example-hello
# Run it
$ spark-submit --master 'spark://IP:PORT' sparkle/target/sparkle-0.1.jar
```

The following code counts the number of lines from the input file that contains at least one "a" character.

```
{-# LANGUAGE OverloadedStrings #-}
{-# LANGUAGE StaticPointers #-}

import Control.Distributed.Spark as RDD
import Data.Text (isInfixOf)

main :: IO ()
main = do
    conf <- newSparkConf "Hello sparkle!"
    sc <- newSparkContext conf
    rdd <- textFile sc "s3://some-bucket/some-file.txt"
    as <- RDD.filter (static (\line -> "a" `isInfixOf` line)) rdd
    numAs <- RDD.count as
    putStrLn $ show numAs ++ " lines with the letter 'a'."
```

Hadron

The purpose of the Hadron library is to use type-safety in the complex and sensitive world of Hadoop Streaming MapReduce. It will be presented in more detail in Chapter 13.

The following are its main characteristics.

- Binds into Hadoop using the Streaming interface.

- Operates Hadoop jobs in many steps, so programmers do not need to call Hadoop manually.

- Allows the user to interact with input/output data from the Hadoop Distributed File System (HDSF), Amazon S3, or other systems that Hadoop supports.

- Makes a set of long and complicated jobs easier to design and maintain.

- Provides built-in support for map-side joins.

- Provides many combinators from the Controller module, which covers simple tasks.

It provides three modules.

- Hadron.Basic: Constructs one MapReduce step, but it is not recommended for direct usage.

- Hadron.Controller: Automates instrumentation of map-reduce jobs with multiple stages.

- Hadron.Protocol: Describes data encode/decode strategies according to Protocol type.

Cloud Haskell

Cloud Haskell is a library used in distributed concurrency. It is covered in Chapter 9. The aim of this library is to provide support in writing programs for clusters. The supplied model is message-passing communication, which is very similar to Erlang.

It is available as a distributed process. The following are some of its characteristics.

- Builds concurrent programs making use of asynchronous message passing.

- Builds distributed computing programs.

- Builds fault tolerance systems.

- Runs on different network transport implementations.

- Supports static values (necessary for remote communication).

An important purpose of Cloud Haskell is the separation between transport and process layers, so that the transport back-end does not depend on anything. Novel connections can be created using `Control.Distributed.Process`.

ZeroMQ

The ZeroMQ library is an extension of a classical socket interface, adding characteristics that are usually supplied by specific messaging middleware products. Its sockets deliver an abstractization of asynchronous message queues, manifold messaging models, messages filtration, and so forth.

The `zeromq4-haskell` package is used to bind to the ZeroMQ library. The following is an example of ZeroMQ usage in displaying the input for a socket (https://gitlab.com/twittner/zeromq-haskell).

```
{-# LANGUAGE OverloadedStrings #-}
import Control.Monad
import System.Exit
import System.IO
import System.Environment
import System.ZMQ4.Monadic
import qualified Data.ByteString.Char8 as CS

main :: IO ()
main = do
    args <- getArgs
    when (length args < 1) $ do
        hPutStrLn stderr "usage: display <address> [<address>, ...]"
        exitFailure
    runZMQ $ do
        sub <- socket Sub
        subscribe sub ""
        mapM_ (connect sub) args
        forever $ do
            receive sub >>= liftIO . CS.putStrLn
            liftIO $ hFlush stdout
```

The preceding code defines a socket and then prints the data it receives.

The Krapsh Library

This project explores an alternative API to run complex workflows on top of Apache Spark. It is available at https://github.com/krapsh/kraps-haskell.

119

The Developer's Perspective

Through this API, complex transforms can be applied on top of Spark, making use of different programming languages. The advantage is that there is no need to communicate with Java objects. Every programming language only needs to implement an interface that does not rely on features specific to Java virtual machines, and that can be implemented using standard REST technologies.

A set of bindings is being developed in the Haskell programming language. It is used as the reference implementation. Despite its limited usage in data science, it is a useful tool to design strongly principled APIs that work across various programming languages.

The User's Perspective

Citing Readme file from github page of Krapsh library, the following are some features of the Krapsh library.

- *Lazy computations*. No call to Spark is issued until a result is required. Unlike standard Spark interfaces, even aggregation operations such as `collect()` or `sum()` are lazy. This allows Krapsh to perform whole-program analyses of the computation and to make optimizations that are currently beyond the reach of Spark.

- *Strong checks*. Thanks to lazy evaluation, a complete data science pipeline can be checked for correctness before it is evaluated. This is useful when composing multiple notebooks or commands. For example, a lot of interesting operations in Spark, such as machine learning algorithms, involve an aggregation step. In Spark, such a step would break the analysis of the program and prevent the Spark analyzer from checking further transforms. Krapsh does not suffer from such limitations and checks the entire pipeline at once.

- *Automatic resource management*. Because Krapsh has a global view of the pipeline, it can check when data needs to be cached or uncached. It is able to schedule caching and uncaching operations automatically, and it refuses to run a program that may be incorrect with respect to caching (for example, when uncaching happens before the data is accessed again).

- *Complex nested pipelines*. Computations can be arbitrarily nested and composed. It allows the conceptual condensing of complex sequences in operations into a single high-level operation. This is useful for debugging and understanding a pipeline at a high level without being distracted by the implementation details in each step. This follows the same approach as TensorFlow.

- *Stable format and language agnostic*. A complex pipeline may be stored as a JSON file in one programming language and read/restored in a different programming language. If this program is run on the same session, that other language can access the cached data.

Haskell vs. Data Science

As a programming language, Haskell offers a few engaging components. Specifically, it's one of only a few current languages that are not strict, which means expressions can have a value regardless of the possibility that their subexpressions do not; this keeps it from requiring everything to be assessed. The code can be cleaner because capacities do not need everything fixed to work.

It is especially valuable when working with functions that may be required later: rather than assessing everything now, only use them if and when important (recursions are particularly great).

While the non-strictness identifies *what* Haskell computes, the *how* is also significant—lazy evaluation. This influences the reduction order by attempting to reduce the highest function in the program, which means the parameters of the function are evaluated only if it is necessary. While this implies the lazy evaluation has a tendency to get the same or better complexity like eager evaluation, it could make the code to lead to space leaks. So, as a conclusion, lazy evaluation has better time performance, but may lead to space leaks.

Therefore, thanks to Haskell's non-strictness and lazy evaluation, it could be used functions like "bind" (>>=) which are useful when a value could not be obtained yet, and the bind chooses when to call the function. Basically, the control is taken by the bind function. Moreover, you can label values that outcome from impure calculation, and control the assessment order.

Haskell is used in many areas, including financial services and bioinformatics. Bank of America Merrill Lynch, BAE Systems, Capital IQ, Ericsson AB, Facebook, Google, Glyde, Intel, IVU Traffic Technologies AG, Microsoft, and NVIDIA are on the impressive list of companies that use Haskell.

Haskell has a solid base of financial code that is normally inaccessible to the public, yet it is the subject of a considerable number of blog articles and analysis on how you can construct exceptionally proficient, capable spilling frameworks that interact with Excel.

Haskell has a tendency to be a memory hog. Memory leaks can occur without careful attention to avoid them. This weakens its use for extensive data sets, but it is easy to prevent these issues. This means, it needs to know anytime where new laziness is created and deciding whether that is right or not. The data types that are strict and belong to UNPACK pragma remove space utilization and leakage.

For strict data types, there are two pragmas: `Strict` and `StrictData` (a subset of `Strict`). Using `Strict`, the fields of the constructor and the bindings (like `let`, `where`, `case` function arguments) are made strict. `StrictData` is almost the same, but it is applied only on constructor fields by using strict annotation (i.e., `!`).

```
data T = T !Int !Int
```

In the preceding definition, none of the constructor fields lead to space leak because they are fully evaluated to Ints when the constructor is called. (For more about `Strict` and `StrictData` pragmas, visit `https://wiki.haskell.org/Performance/Data_types` or `http://blog.johantibell.com/2015/11/the-design-of-strict-haskell-pragma.html`).

The UNPACK pragma tells the compiler that the content of a field from a constructor needs to be unpacked into the constructor itself; thus, it removes a level of indirection. The following example is from the official documentation (`https://downloads.haskell.org/~ghc/8.0.2/docs/html/users_guide/glasgow_exts.html#unpack-pragma`). It generates a constructor, T, that has two unboxed floats.

```
data T = T {-# UNPACK #-} !Float
           {-# UNPACK #-} !Float
```

Note that this approach could not be an optimization if it used incorrectly for example, when the T constructor is examined and the floats are sent to a function that is non-strict, it needs to be boxed again (automatically)—a process that needs additional computations. To have an effect, the UNPACK pragma should be used with the -o option (through which unboxing is avoided).

Haskell provides a very useful library called `vector`, which is used very often in data science. Other useful libraries include `ad`, `linear`, `vector-space`, `statistics`, `compensated`, and `log-domain`. They are not the same. We will let you further explore these libraries.

Haskell's best dense `matrix` library, `hmatrix`, is good and falls under General Public License (GPL). A disadvantage of these libraries is that they do not work as smoothly as the `vector` library. The Repa library is another good one; it is optimized for images and parallel matrix operations, such as as Discrete Fourier Transform (DFT).

If it is necessary that a graphics processing unit (GPU) be spared, then this is very easy when using the algorithms provided by the Accelerate library.

The following are the main reasons why Haskell is very good with data science.

- Type system doubles as a design language, crystallizes thoughts

- Catches errors early, refactors aggressively (in comparision to Ruby or Python)

- Purity of functions in Haskell is a huge win for long-term solutions/applications

- Stays at a very high level, yet still gets solid performance

- QuickCheck is very good, testing is better

- Simple multicore concurrency

- Promising future for parallel algorithms

Debugging Tehniques

The dubugging techniques for big data are the same as classical debugging techniques from Haskell. For example, Microsoft Azure provides support for Haskell. Additional information about the Microsoft Azure Cloud platfomr is at https://docs.microsoft.com/en-us/azure.

In this section, we present a simple example of how to use Azure and Haskell. It is from Phil Freeman's short blog tutorial "Haskell on Azure" (http://blog.functorial.com/posts/2012-04-29-Haskell-On-Azure.html). It uses the azure-servicebus package.

Microsoft Azure supplies storage services (table, queue, and blob storage services) revealing REST APIs. In the following, there is a union between the Happstack web server and blaze-html for building a simple web application that takes notes. It is easy to change in with a specific web server.

```
module Main where

import Data.Maybe
import Control.Monad
import Control.Monad.Trans
import System.Time
import System.Directory
import Happstack.Server
import qualified Text.Blaze.Html4.Strict as H
import qualified Text.Blaze.Html4.Strict.Attributes as A
import Network.TableStorage
import Text.Blaze ((!), toValue)
```

The next stept defines the account that will be used. it contains a service endpoint, a user name, and the secret key.

This example uses the development account, which means the Windows Azure storage emulator should exist and run on the computer on which the example is implemented.

```
account :: Account
account = developmentAccount
```

When deploying an account to staging or production, the developmentAccount could be replaced with a call to defaultAccount, having the account information extracted from the Azure management portal.

The application is very simple. It has three parts: many notebooks will exist, it will be possible to view the latest note in a notebook, and it will be possible to add a new note in a specific notebook. The notes can be fragmented, if necessary, according to the notebook's capacities. In the table storage model, this means that the notebook being used is determined by the note entities' partition key.

We should allow the generation of a new key. We will sort the note ids after the date of insertion so that the more recent notes are displayed first. We will generate a key based on the current time, subtracting the seconds component of time from the large value to reverse the order of the generated keys.

```
newId :: IO String
newId = do
  (TOD seconds picos) <- getClockTime
  return $ show (9999999999 - seconds) ++ show picos
```

With the preceding piece of code, now we can implement the method through which a new note is added. This will be a POST method that receives the arguments as form-encoded data in the request body.

After the generation of the key, it is uses the insertEntity IO action for adding the just-produced note object to the table notes. The elements of the note are the author and text properties, which are string columns.

If the adding procedure is successfully completed, then the redirect and get actions are performed to display the newly added note; otherwise, an error message is displayed—namely, 500 - Internal Server Error.

```
postNote :: ServerPartT IO Response
postNote = do
  methodM POST
  tmp <- liftIO getTemporaryDirectory
  decodeBody $ defaultBodyPolicy tmp 0 1000 1000
  text <- look "text"
  author <- look "author"
  partition <- look "partition"
  result <- liftIO $ do
    id <- newId
    let entity = Entity { entityKey = EntityKey { ekPartitionKey = partition,
                                                  ekRowKey = id },
                entityColumns = [ ("text", EdmString $ Just text),
                                  ("author", EdmString $ Just author)] }
    insertEntity account "notes" entity
  case result of
    Left err -> internalServerError $ toResponse err
    Right _ -> seeOther ("?partition=" ++ partition) $ toResponse ()
```

When a notebook is chosen, the last 10 notes are displayed. This is done using the queryEntity function, which retrieves the notes from the table, and filters them after the partition key.

```
getNotes :: ServerPartT IO Response
getNotes = do
  methodM GET
  partition <- look "partition" `mplus` return "default"
  let query = defaultEntityQuery { eqPageSize = Just 10,
                                   eqFilter = Just $ CompareString "PartitionKey"
                                   Equal partition }
```

```
  result <- liftIO $ queryEntities account "notes" query
  case result of
    Left err -> internalServerError $ toResponse err
    Right notes -> ok $ setHeader "Content-Type" "text/html" $ toResponse $ root partition
notes
```

The preceding implementation uses a very simple query, but there is a package called `tablestorage` that allows difficult queries, including many filters at once.

If the call of the function completes successfully, then it returns an HTML page, created using `blaze-html`; otherwise, a 500 error code is displayed. The root function performs these actions.

```
root :: String -> [Entity] -> H.Html
root partition notes = H.html $ do
  H.head $
    H.title $ H.toHtml "Notes"
  H.body $ do
    H.h1 $ H.toHtml "Add Note"
    H.form ! A.method (toValue "POST") $ do
      H.input ! A.type_ (toValue "hidden") ! A.name (toValue "partition") ! A.value
      (toValue partition)
      H.div $ do
        H.label ! A.for (toValue "text") $ H.toHtml "Text: "
        H.input ! A.type_ (toValue "text") ! A.name (toValue "text")
      H.div $ do
        H.label ! A.for (toValue "author") $ H.toHtml "Author: "
        H.input ! A.type_ (toValue "text") ! A.name (toValue "author")
      H.div $
        H.input ! A.type_ (toValue "submit") ! A.value (toValue "Add Note")
    H.h1 $ H.toHtml "Recent Notes"
    H.ul $ void $ mapM displayNote notes
```

The page has a form, where the user could submit a new note, with text areas for the text and the author arguments. The partition key is given as an unseen field, but the user can modify it by changing the query string.

Next is a form that lists the latest notes from the current notebook (partition key). These recent notes are displayed with the help of the `displayNote` function.

```
displayNote :: Entity -> H.Html
displayNote note = fromMaybe (return ()) $ do
  text <- edmString "text" note
  author <- edmString "author" note
  return $ H.li $ do
    H.toHtml "'"
    H.toHtml text
    H.toHtml "'"
    H.i $ do
      H.toHtml " says "
      H.toHtml author
```

The `edmString` helper function is used for extracting a column whose type is string from the available columns retrieved through the query.

The Maybe-valued function returns Just as a string when the column's name has string values, and Nothing is returned if there is no column or the type of column in not string. Functions for different column types could be found in the tablestorage package.

We use two routes—getNotes and postNotes—for creating the web application.

```
routes :: [ServerPartT IO Response]
routes = [ getNotes, postNote ]
```

The main function defines the constraints to create the notes table, if it does not exist. Using the createTableIfNecessary function checks this.

```
main :: IO ()
main = do
  result <- createTableIfNecessary account "notes"
  case result of
    Left err -> putStrLn err
    Right _ -> simpleHTTP nullConf $ msum routes
```

In order to deploy the application, cspack and csrun command-line utilities are used.

Some basic configuration files are needed. The web server will run as a worker, fact that needs to be set up in the ServiceDefinition.csdef file. We need to add a worker role definition, like in the following.

```
-- <ServiceDefinition name="Notes" xmlns="http://schemas.microsoft.com/
ServiceHosting/2008/10/ServiceDefinition">
--   <WorkerRole name="WebServer" vmsize="Small">
--     <Runtime>
--       <EntryPoint>
--         <ProgramEntryPoint commandLine="Main.exe" setReadyOnProcessStart="true" />
--       </EntryPoint>
--     </Runtime>
--     <Endpoints>
--       <InputEndpoint name="happstackEndpoint" protocol="tcp" port="80" />
--     </Endpoints>
--   </WorkerRole>
-- </ServiceDefinition>
```

The ServiceConfiguration.*.cfg files should contain a role section with the same worker role name.

```
-- <Role name="WebServer">
--   <ConfigurationSettings />
--   <Instances count="1" />
-- </Role>
```

After building the application, an executable Main.exe is obtained, which needs to be put under WebServer role subdirectory. The command used build for deployment is:

```
-- cspack /copyOnly ServiceDefinition.csdef
```

The package can then be deployed locally using

```
-- csrun Notes.csx ServiceConfiguration.Local.cscfg
```

At this step the operations which are available are: add a note, display the content of a note and move into another notebook by simply editing the query string.

To deploy the application in Azure, a cspkg file needs to be built, using the following command (note that credentials for development account needs to be replaced in code by credentials for management portal):

```
-- cspack ServiceDefinition.csdef
```

Next, we present some debugging methods that can be applied to big data.

Stack Trace

Late forms of GHC permit a dump of a stack follow (of cost focuses) when an error is raised. Keeping in mind the end goal to empower this, compile with -prof and run with +RTS - xc. (Since just the cost focus stack will be printed, you might need to include - fprof-auto - fprof-cafs to the aggregation venture to incorporate all definitions in the following.) Since GHC version 7.8, the errorWithStackTrace function can be used to automatically dump the stack follow.

The following is a simple example.

```
crash = sum [1,2,3,undefined,5,6,7,8]
main  = print crash

> ghc-7.6.3 test.hs -prof -fprof-auto -fprof-cafs && ./test +RTS -xc
*** Exception (reporting due to +RTS -xc): (THUNK_2_0), stack trace:
  GHC.Err.CAF
  --> evaluated by: Main.crash,
  called from Main.CAF:crash_reH
test: Prelude.undefined
```

A CAF (*constant applicative form*) is a super combinatory that isn't a lambda abstraction. Constant expressions and partial functions are included. A CAF does not contain free variables because it is super combinatory; but actually, it does not contain any variables because they are not lambda abstractions. Still, it could have identifiers that refer to another CAF.

```
x 3 where x = (*) 2
```

A CAF can be placed on the top level of a program. It can be compiled in a piece of graph shared with all users, or from shared code that overwrites itself when it is first inspected with a graph. The following CAF could go to the top of a program without bounds, but it could also be accessed within the code from one or more functions. Garbage collectors can reclaim these kinds of structures if each function has an associated list of CAFs to which it is making a reference. When a function is targeted by a garbage collector, then its associated CAFs are collected.

```
ints = from 1 where from n = n : from (n+1)
```

The following is an example of errorWithStackTrace.

```
import GHC.Stack

main = putStrLn $! (show $! fact  7)

fact :: Int -> Int
fact 0 = 1
fact 1 =1
```

```
fact 3 = errorWithStackTrace "error"
fact n | n > 0 = n * fact (n-1)
  | otherwise = errorWithStackTrace "wrong"

~/D/r/testTraceing $ ghc -prof -fprof-auto main.hs
[1 of 1] Compiling Main              ( main.hs, main.o )
Linking main ...
~/D/r/testTraceing $ ./main
main: error
Stack trace:
  Main.fact (main.hs:(6,1)-(10,74))
  Main.main (main.hs:3:1-36)
  Main.CAF (<entire-module>)
```

Printf and Friends

Printf debugging is a technique through which the flow of an execution is traced, and targeted values are printed. The easiest method to print a message on screen is to make use of Debug.Trace.trace.

```
trace :: String -> a -> a
```

According to its library, when called, trace outputs the string in its first argument, before returning the second argument as its result.

The following is the usual context in which trace is used.

```
myfun a b | trace ("myfun " ++ show a ++ " " ++ show b) False = undefined
myfun a b = ...
```

A benefit is that the enable and disable actions of trace are in a single line of comment.

You should remember that because of lazy evaluation, traces print if the value that they wrap is ever requested.

The trace function is situated in the base package. The htrace package characterizes a trace function like the one in the base; however, it has a space for better visual impact. Different tools can be found in the debug class on the Hackage page.

A more capable option for this method is Hood, which works well with the current ghc conveyance. Hugs has it effectively incorporated. Include an import Observe and begin embedding observations in the code. Note that because Hugs is no longer under development, it is only for readers who want to experiment or to explore the system; for example:

```
import Hugs.Observe
f'  = observe "Informative name for f" f
f x = if odd x then x*2 else 0
And then in hugs:
Main> map f' [1..5]
[2,0,6,0,10]

>>>>>>> Observations <<<<<<
```

```
Informative name for f
  { \ 5  -> 10
  , \ 4  -> 0
  , \ 3  -> 6
  , \ 2  -> 0
  , \ 1  -> 2
  }
```

The preceding code results a report of all calls of f and the result for every call. The GHood library appends a graphical support for Hood.

The Safe Library

The safe library of functions belongs to Prelude, which can crash. In the event that you get an error message (for example, pattern match failure, head []), you can then utilize headNote ("extra infomation") to get a more detailed error message for that specific call to head. The safe library likewise has functions that contains default values and wrap their calculations in Maybe as needed.

Offline Analysis of Traces

The most evaluated troubleshooting methods are situated in offline investigation of traces. The following tools are used in academic research. It is possible to work with older versions of Haskell.

Haskell Tracer HAT

Hat is perhaps the most evaluated source-level tracer. It is a large suite of tools.

The impediment of conventional Haskell tracers is that they could change the entire program or require a particular run-time framework. They are not generally best suited with the most recent libraries, but you can put them to use every now and again.

Hoed: The Lightweight Haskell Tracer and Debugger

Hoed is a tracer and/or debugger that brings many techniques from HAT. It can be used in untransformed libraries. It is used for debugging more programs than the traditional tracer.

To localize a fail, you need to do an annotation of the suspected function, and then follow the compilation as usual. When the program runs, it retrieves data about the targeted function. The last stept is connecting to a debugging session on a web browser.

Dynamic Breakpoints in GHCi

Active breakpoints and intermediary valuables observation are enabled by the GHCi debugger.

The breakpoints can be established directly in the code from the GHCi command prompt, as shown in the following example.

```
*main:Main> :break Main 2
Breakpoint set at (2,15)
*main:Main> qsort [10,9..1]
```

Local bindings in scope.

```
x :: a, xs :: [a], left :: [a], right :: [a]
```

```
qsort2.hs:2:15-46> :sprint x
x = _
qsort2.hs:2:15-46> x
```

The preceding is a computation without type and without being evaluated. seq is used for forcing the evaluation. :print is used for recovering its type.

```
qsort2.hs:2:15-46> seq x ()
()
qsort2.hs:2:15-46> :p x
x - 10
```

When a breakpoint is reached, the bindings are explored in the scope, and the evaluation of an expression is enabled, like in the GHCi prompt. The laziness could be explored in the :print instruction. A comprehensive description of how to use breakpoints in Haskell is at https://downloads.haskell. org/~ghc/7.4.1/docs/html/users_guide/ghci-debugger.html.

Source-Located Errors

The LocH library gives wrappers over assert to generate exceptions for source-located errors. The following exemple located fromJust.

```
import Debug.Trace.Location
import qualified Data.Map as M
import Data.Maybe

main = do print f

f = let m = M.fromList
              [(1,"1")
              ,(2,"2")
              ,(3,"3")]
        s = M.lookup 4 m
    in fromJustSafe assert s

fromJustSafe a s = check a (fromJust s)
This will result in:
$ ./a.out
a.out: A.hs:12:20-25: Maybe.fromJust: Nothing
```

This could be done automatically, making use of the LocH preprocessor. For example, a program that fails, as follows…

```
$ ghc A.hs --make -no-recomp
[1 of 1] Compiling Main            ( A.hs, A.o )
Linking A ...
$ ./A
A: Maybe.fromJust: Nothing
```

This could be converted into src-located through addition of the following line.

```
import Debug.Trace.Location
```

The last step is to recompile.

```
$ ghc A.hs --make -pgmF loch -F -no-recomp
[1 of 1] Compiling Main              ( A.hs, A.o )
Linking A ...
$ ./A
A: A.hs:14:14-19: Maybe.fromJust: Nothing
```

Other Tricks

When GHC is utilized, a program will show a stack trace in the console if there is an error condition.

Locating a Failure in a Library Function

The easiest way to locate a mismatch run-time error in the program, error that raises from libraries that provide the functions head, tail, fromJust or another similar, is to avoid using these functions; as a alternative, use explicit matching.

The following is an example.

```
g x = h $ fromJust $ f x,
```

The references to the g, f, and h functions are lost. An error occurs when f returns Nothing. Instead, consider the following.

```
g x = let Just y = f x in h y,
```

GHC displays

```
Main: M1.hs:9:11-22:
Irrefutable pattern failed for pattern Data.Maybe.Just y
```

It has indicated the source of the error.

Mysterious Parse Errors

GHC supplies -ferror-spans to indicate the beginning and the end of a wrong expression (for example, \x:xs->x instead of \(x:xs)->x).

Infinite Loops

To avoid infinite loops, let's consider the loop function called with one parameter.

1. Activate the -fbreak-on-error (:set -fbreak-on-error in GHCi).

2. Call the statement with :trace (:trace loop 'a').

3. Press Ctrl+C when the program is blocked in the loop, such that the debugger breaks that loop.

4. Utilize the `:history` and `:back` commands for localization of the loop.

Summary

In this chapter, you saw

- what big data means and the phases through which it passes to obtain relevant information.

- how Haskell can be integrated with big data and the tools that do this.

- techniques for debugging.

Haskell for Big Data and Cloud Computing

■ ■ ■

CHAPTER 9

Haskell in the Cloud

This chapter talks about programming in Cloud Haskell, a domain-specific language to develop programs in a distributed computing environment in Haskell. The chapter focuses on presenting the processes, messages between processes, how to use channels and ports, and closures.

The following are the main characteristics of the Cloud Haskell programming model.

- Explicit concurrency

- Lightweight processes

- Processes do not share the states

- Message passing is realized asynchronously, which is also known as an *actor model* and is also used by other languages, like Erlang

The packages that belong to Cloud Haskell are

- `distributed-process`: the core of CH package

- `distributed-process-simplelocalnet`: an easy back end for local networks

- `network-transport`: the Transport implementation

- `network-transport-tcp`: an instance of `Network.Transport`

- `distributed-process-azure`: Azure back end

All examples in this chapter belong to Cloud Haskell's creators at `http://haskell-distributed.github.io/`.

Processes and Messages

In parallel programming, processes and messages have crucial roles. In this section, you see how processes and messages are used in Cloud Haskell.

Before beginning, let's look at some introductory information about Cloud Haskell. It has a generic `network-transport` API (`http://hackage.haskell.org/package/network-transport`) and uses primitives from the `distributed-process` package (`https://github.com/haskell-distributed/distributed-process`) that provides primitives such as nodes and processes.

`Network.Transport` provides the following concepts.

- `EndPoints` in a network are actually nodes that represent a meaningful element.

- Every `EndPoint` is characterized by `EndPointAddress`.

- `EndPointAddress` creates a connection between `EndPoint`.

© Stefania Loredana Nita and Marius Mihailescu 2017
S. L. Nita and M. Mihailescu, *Practical Concurrent Haskell*, DOI 10.1007/978-1-4842-2781-7_9

- EndPointAddress can be serialized, but an EndPoints connection cannot be serialized.

- A connection between two EndPoints is unidirectional and trivial.

- The Connection object sends outgoing messages. It is the sending end of the connection.

- Incoming messages are gathered from all incoming connections of an EndPoint into a special queue for receiving messages that it shares between all incoming connections.

- EndPoint receives notifications about other events that could occur, such as a new connection or a lost connection.

Processes

In addition to Haskell, this chapter requires that stack is installed (https://github.com/commercialhaskell/stack/wiki/Downloads). It also uses the distributed-process and network-transport-tcp libraries. All you need to do to create a new project in stack is type the following line into a new directory.

```
$ stack new
```

A folder will be created for some files. Also, you need to add distributed-process and network-transport-tcp to the build-depends section.

Create the First Node

You have seen that Cloud Haskell contains lightweight processes that are contained by a node. The initial state of the node should contain a network transport implementation and also a remote table, which is needed to store the components of the system such that physically unrelated nodes know from what node(s) they receive messages. For the moment, let's just create a table. In the app/Main.hs file, let's add the imports.

```
import Network.Transport.TCP (createTransport, defaultTCPParameters)
import Control.Distributed.Process
import Control.Distributed.Process.Node
```

Also, a socket is needed for the TCP network transport, so let's use the IP and the port as follows.

```
main :: IO ()
main = do
  Right t <- createTransport "127.0.0.1" "10501" defaultTCPParameters
  node <- newLocalNode t initRemoteTable
  ....
```

With this piece of code, we have created a running node.

Topologies

The topology is chosen by the user from the Cloud Haskell back end. The simplelocalnet back end is the main topology that comes with Cloud Haskell. It contains a grid of fully connected nodes with an optionally configured master-slave topology. The nodes discover each other through a User Datagram Protocol (UDP) multicast.

Other back ends may have various types of nodes or discover nodes in a different way.

The simplelocalnet Topology

The following presents a program that uses simplelocalnet, which looks for a list of pair nodes and transmits messages to a recorded (named) process, which is a process registered with the local registry.

```
import System.Environment (getArgs)
import Control.Distributed.Process
import Control.Distributed.Process.Node (initRemoteTable, runProcess)
import Control.Distributed.Process.Backend.SimpleLocalnet
import Control.Monad (forever, forM_)

main = do
  [host, port] <- getArgs

  backend <- initializeBackend host port initRemoteTable
  node    <- newLocalNode backend
  peers   <- findPeers backend 1000000
  runProcess node $ forM_ peers $ \peer -> nsendRemote peer "echo-server" "hello!"
```

The preceding program is not very practical, but we want to underline two important functions.

- initializeBackend connects to an existing communication infrastructure.

- findPeers can be evaluated every time we need to get a list of existing nodes that marked their presence through a broadcast.

Master-Slave Configuration

Let's improve the preceding example by adding a non-operational slave process and a master process that lists its slaves and displays a message for each slave. The first one that needs to be started is a master.

```
main :: IO ()
main = do
  args <- getArgs

  case args of
    ["master", host, port] -> do
      backend <- initializeBackend host port initRemoteTable
      startMaster backend (master backend)
    ["slave", host, port] -> do
      backend <- initializeBackend host port initRemoteTable
      startSlave backend
```

The following is the code for a master node.

```
master :: Backend -> [NodeId] -> Process ()
master backend slaves = do
  -- Do something interesting with the slaves
  liftIO . putStrLn $ "Slaves: " ++ show slaves
  -- Terminate the slaves when the master terminates (this is optional)
  terminateAllSlaves backend
```

137

Obtaining Information About Processes

If we want to obtain information about a certain Cloud Haskell process that is running, we can use the getProcessInfo function, whose ProcessInfo type has the id of the local process and a comprehensive list of the recorded names, monitors, and bindings to process. If the process we want is not running, then the result will be Nothing.

Messages to Processes

Next, we use runProcess, whose arguments are a node and a Process action, and the result will be a Process monad. We need to remark that each process has its own identifier that is utilized for sending messages to processes that are already running. Another important component is the *mailbox*, where the messages from other processes are stored and organized as a queue in order of arrival.

```
-- in main
  _ <- runProcess node $ do
    -- get our own process id
    self <- getSelfPid
    send self "hello"
    hello <- expect :: Process String
    liftIO $ putStrLn hello
  return ()
```

Deadlock will not occur in the preceding example when the thread sends and receives messages, because the messages are sent asynchronously. Moreover, if the receiver's mailbox does not exist, it will not raise an error and the evaluation of send will not obstruct the sender, even if it sends messages to itself. The expect function or the receive* functions could be used by a process to send a message from its mailbox. When a process expects a certain type of message (in this case, it is "selected" via the type annotation "Process String"; in other cases, the type of message might be inferred) and it is not in the mailbox, the process is blocked until it receives the expected message.

Next, we create two processes that are in the same node and make them communicate reciprocally.

```
import Control.Concurrent (threadDelay)
import Control.Monad (forever)
import Control.Distributed.Process
import Control.Distributed.Process.Node
import Network.Transport.TCP (createTransport, defaultTCPParameters)

replyBack :: (ProcessId, String) -> Process ()
replyBack (sender, msg) = send sender msg

logMessage :: String -> Process ()
logMessage msg = say $ "handling " ++ msg

main :: IO ()
main = do
  Right t <- createTransport "127.0.0.1" "10501" defaultTCPParameters
  node <- newLocalNode t initRemoteTable
  runProcess node $ do
```

```
-- Spawn another worker on the local node
echoPid <- spawnLocal $ forever $ do
  -- Test our matches in order against each message in the queue
  receiveWait [match logMessage, match replyBack]

-- The `say` function sends a message to a process registered as "logger".
-- By default, this process simply loops through its mailbox and sends
-- any received log message strings it finds to stderr.

say "send some messages!"
send echoPid "hello"
self <- getSelfPid
send echoPid (self, "hello")

-- `expectTimeout` waits for a message or times out after "delay"
m <- expectTimeout 1000000
case m of
  -- Die immediately - throws a ProcessExitException with the given reason.
  Nothing  -> die "nothing came back!"
  Just s -> say $ "got " ++ s ++ " back!"

-- Without the following delay, the process sometimes exits before the messages are
exchanged.
liftIO $ threadDelay 2000000
```

The example uses receiveWait to obtain a message. This is an interesting function that could be used with the Match data type to provide more complex message processing power. The following shows general use of receiveWait and match, where p and q are patterns that match with different types of messages.

```
receiveWait
  [ match $ \p -> do ...
  , match $ \q -> do ...
  ]
```

If we want to create a possible message handler, then we use the match primitive. Similar to the expect function, if there is no message that can be matched, then the process is blocked until it receives the needed message.

The echo server displays what the string receives. If the first message has no type String, then the evaluation is applied on the second match. So, if we have a t :: (ProcessId, String) pair, then the String constituent is sent backward to the sender. If there is no matching, then the echo server locks before another String comes, and performs another trial.

Serialization

A process can transmit data while it is implemented by the Serializable typeclass, whose definition is

```
class (Binary a, Typeable a) => Serializable a
instance (Binary a, Typeable a) => Serializable a
```

This definition says that Binary and Typeable can be used, because almost all of the main (primitives) data types are included here. For a custom data type, Typeable could be used, and Binary could be autogenerated.

```
{-# LANGUAGE DeriveDataTypeable #-}
{-# LANGUAGE DeriveGeneric #-}

data T = T Int Char deriving (Generic

instance Binary T
```

Starting and Locating Processes

To send actions, they need to be static and configured in a remote table.

The actions in the Process monad cause the behavior of a process. Unfortunately, Process and IO monad actions cannot be serialized. So, how are processes spawned in remote nodes?

The answer could be static actions and compositions. A closed expression, which is an expression that is evaluated at compiling because it does not depend on run-time parameters, is used for defining a static action whose type is Closure (Process a). A closure value is a combination of symbolic pointers and serializable values, thus it could be serialized. For example, actions whose type is Process () could not be sent, but instead we could send a value that contains a symbolic name for that action and has type Closure (Process ()). It is important that the remote node understands the same signification of the symbolic name. So, the remote spawn needs a static action that will be sent through the wire to a remote node.

Traditionally, static actions are difficult to create, but Cloud Haskell improves this issue with Template Haskell, as such as when we have a monomorphic function f::T1 -> T2 then $(mkClosure 'f) :: T1 -> Closure T2, provided that T2 is serializable.

mkClosure is a useful function that can make every top-level unary function in a Closure. In the case of curried functions, we need to make them uncurry (makes a tuple with its arguments). We mentioned the remote table, which stores the association between a value and the symbolic name of the function that generates it. This is used for assuring that all remote parts can interpret the obtained Closure. We know that spawning is successful when all remote nodes have the same remote table as the one from the local node.

The remote table should be configured by the library, which produces some code.

```
sampleTask :: (TimeInterval, String) -> Process ()
sampleTask (t, s) = sleep t >> say s

remotable ['sampleTask]
```

The end line represents a top-level Template Haskell . In the place where the spawn is called, a Closure could be created that is correlated with an implementation of sampleTask.

```
($(mkClosure 'sampleTask) (seconds 2, "foobar"))
```

Calling remoteTable automatically generates a remote table based on the insertion of a top-level definition in the module.

```
__remoteTable :: RemoteTable -> RemoteTable
```

This is used with other remote tables to obtain a final remote table for all the modules of the following program.

```
{-# LANGUAGE TemplateHaskell #-}

import Control.Concurrent (threadDelay)
import Control.Monad (forever)
import Control.Distributed.Process
import Control.Distributed.Process.Closure
import Control.Distributed.Process.Node
import Network.Transport.TCP (createTransport, defaultTCPParameters)

sampleTask :: (Int, String) -> Process ()
sampleTask (t, s) = liftIO (threadDelay (t * 1000000)) >> say s

remotable ['sampleTask]

myRemoteTable :: RemoteTable
myRemoteTable = Main.__remoteTable initRemoteTable

main :: IO ()
main = do
  Right transport <- createTransport "127.0.0.1" "10501" defaultTCPParameters
  node <- newLocalNode transport myRemoteTable
  runProcess node $ do
    us <- getSelfNode
    _ <- spawnLocal $ sampleTask (1 :: Int, "using spawnLocal")
    pid <- spawn us $ $(mkClosure 'sampleTask) (1 :: Int, "using spawn")
    liftIO $ threadDelay 2000000
```

In the previous example, sampleTask is spawned on the us node using two different methods.

- spawn needs a node identifier for spawning a process having Closure.

- spawnLocal is a particular type of spawn that is used when the node identifier is referring to the actual node (i.e., us).

Fault Tolerance

Processes can be linked to one another or to nodes or channels. The idea of linked processes came from the Actor model, where linked processes monitor each other.

A link is unidirectional. When a process wants to link to another, it should be sure that the other end exists. A handy method is to send a child process to the desired end, link it, and terminate. In the following example, two child processes are linked. They terminate after they receive a key message. If the subprocesses terminates OK, then the parent process terminates.

```
demo = do
  pid <- spawnLocal $ receive >>= return
  link pid
  send pid ()
  () <- receive
```

The preceding are also asynchronous exceptions. Note that we should not put the base on this fact, and the fact that the execution type is not sent further. We cannot directly catch the exit signals for links, but if we wanted to do that, we would use a monitor.

The link function aborts the link no matter the reason for exiting, but linkOnFailure (provided by distributed-process-extras) throws ProcessLinkException if the linked ends die unexpectedly (because of DiedReason or DiedNormal).

In general, monitors do not determine the processes that are listening to exit, only if the mailbox of the process receives ProcessMonitorNotification. The signal and the components are analyzed for deciding the action that needs to be taken by the receiver as a response for the termination of the monitored process. In the following, we use a monitor to find when and how a process terminates using linkOnFailure (from distributed-process-extras).

```
linkOnFailure them = do
  us <- getSelfPid
  tid <- liftIO $ myThreadId
  void $ spawnLocal $ do
    callerRef <- P.monitor us
    calleeRef <- P.monitor them
    reason <- receiveWait [
            matchIf (\(ProcessMonitorNotification mRef _ _) ->
                      mRef == callerRef) -- nothing left to do
                    (\_ -> return DiedNormal)
          , matchIf (\(ProcessMonitorNotification mRef' _ _) ->
                      mRef' == calleeRef)
                    (\(ProcessMonitorNotification _ _ r') -> return r')
          ]
    case reason of
      DiedNormal -> return ()
      _ -> liftIO $ throwTo tid (ProcessLinkException us reason)
```

In the example, monitors were used for observing the ends (processes) of the link, because a monitor uses a third spawned process. This approach is used to cover cases in which handling code is from the Node Controller. The route of the two matches is as follows: it goes to receiveWait, where it handles a ProcessMonitorNoritification, and the result is sent to matchIf. All of this is done to find out if the received notification should go to process that called, or to the other end of the link. When the former expires, there is nothing more to do because the links are in one direction. When it dies, we should check DiedReason and ProcessMonitorNotification to learn if the process expires in normal parameters (with DiedNormal). If the result is not DiedNormal, it throws a ProcessLinkException for the genuine caller.

Links and monitors are ways to supervise when working with a process that has many subprocesses.

As you have seen, exit signals from Cloud Haskell are different from asynchronous exceptions used in Haskell in other situation. Because the Process monad is a particular case of MonadIO, a process could use asynchronous exceptions. Links and exits could be used with asynchronous exceptions (like in the preceding example), but in this case, when a message is followed by an exit signal, we are sure that the message arrive first. As a good practice, we should avoid situations in which we use our own exceptions, but they terminate using exit, kill, or die.

Process Lifetime

A process executes while it evaluates something, or it is aborted, a crash occurs (which has not handled an exception), or it has instruction to terminate. When a process is programmed to stop, it used ProcessExitException or ProcessKillEception, which are usually sent asynchronously. Also, the exit and kill functions from distributed-process could be used to assure that remote processes are easily manipulated. Additionally, when a message is sent followed by an escape label, the message will be provided to the receiver until the exception is thrown. This behavior does not guarantee that the receiver could do something to the message until it terminates.

The ProcessExitException propagates to all processes, telling if the destination process should terminate. The processes could decide if it exits. For that die function it is used, which is a little different from exit, because exit needs that an inner signal to be sent inside into the local node controller. However, we need to pay attention that the node controller would process some other events, so it is possible to delay a little the exit signal for exit function. Still, in the thread that calls die if it throws the ProcessExitException by die itself, so actually there is no delay.

In reality, the two functions act a little differently at run-time.

```
-- this will never print anything...
demo1 = die "Boom" >> expect >>= say

-- this /might/ print something before it exits
demo2 = do
  self <- getSelfPid
  exit self "Boom"
  expect >>= say
```

In ProcessExitException, there is a field called reason, but it is serialized in the form of a raw Message. Because there is an export of this exception type, the exit signals can be caught and then handle them. Some primitives from distributed-process catch exit signals.

ProcessKillException is a signal that usually is not trapped; thus, the type is not sent further, so it could be handled just when whole exceptions are caught; but this is a bad habit.

Further, kill is used for terminating overseen processes that haven't terminated when they were asked, or shut down the processes that do not need particular cleanup code for running when exiting. Note that kill acts a little like exit when Node Controller is implied.

Receiving and Matching

The previous examples use the send function, which sends messages between processes. Let's summarize the use of send.

- It is asynchronous (i.e., the caller is not blocked).

- It never fails.

- When a message is sent, the time that it will be received is unknown.

- Nothing guarantees that the message will actually be received.

Asynchronous approach brings some advantages, because it is not really good that a process to be blocked or waiting for some data, or implementation of error handling to be done every time a message is sent. As an example, let's suppose that a pair of processes are communicating and the stream was a, b, c, and we can read c, then we know for sure that a and b were already seen.

In cloud Haskell is it guaranteed that the messages are sent in *First in First out (FIFO)* order between two concurrent processes, but this is not always true between an arbitrary numbers of processes.

When it uses expect for a message, then we actually ignore the order of messages because we need a message with content that is decoded into a certain type. If we want that message processing to be done in arriving order, we should delay the type check that leads to a mailbox traverse, and we need to get the raw message ourselves. For this, the functions that could be used are receive and matchAny, about we will talk later.

Next, let's talk about the expect and receive family of functions. They are used by the processes for unqueueing a message from its mailbox. After an optional timeout, they allow the expression to evaluate Nothing if there is no matching input.

The process is blocked by expect before a message that matches the awaited type of expression is discovered in the mailbox. When the mailbox is scanned and a match is found, the message is removed from the queue and returned. If there is no match, the process/thread that called is locked before a message with the expected type arrives. The following is an example.

```
demo :: Process ()
demo = do
    listener <- spawnLocal listen
    send listener "hello"
    getSelfPid >>= send listener
    () <- expect
  where
    listen = do
      third <- expect :: Process ProcessId
      first <- expect :: Process String
      second <- expectTimeout 100000 :: Process String
      mapM_ (say . show) [first, second, third]
      send third ()
```

After running the program, it displays hello, Nothing, and pid://.... In appearance order, the first expect (which has the label third because it comes third in the mailbox) is successful, because the parent transmits the string "hello" and its ProcessId, so the listener is locked before it removes ProcessId from the queue ahead of the string. Also, the next expect (labeled first) will be successful, which shows that the type of messages was more important for removing than the order in which they came. The evaluation of the last expect is Nothing because only one string is delivered to the listener, and the message at the last expect evaluation is yet removed from the mailbox. If the preceding program has not removed the messages, it will be blocked or will never complete.

The receive primitives has a list that contains Match objects as input, obtained through the evaluation of a match-style primitive. Matching messages is useful because the types of messages that can be handled are separated from the types of evaluations that receive an expression. Let's look at the following piece of code.

```
usingReceive = do
  () <- receiveWait [
      match (\(s :: String) -> say s)
    , match (\(i :: Int)    -> say $ show i)
    ]
```

The header of receiveWait :: [Match b] -> Process b says that all matches from the list should evaluate the same type.

There is another version called receiveTimeout that locks for a certain amount of time and then returns Nothing if there is no match during that time.

There are situations in which we need to get a message without explicitly specifying the type. It is a helpful characteristic, especially because it is the one method for processing messages in their order of arrival. Next, we use the relay function to show how it works. This primitive initiates a process that removes every message from the queue that arrives, and sends them to another process. For removing messages from the queue no matter the type, we use the matchAny function.

```
matchAny :: forall b. (Message -> Process b) -> Match b
```

The main approach in Cloud Haskell is to send messages in their raw form (i.e., they are not decoded before). For that, there is another useful function.

```
forward :: Message -> ProcessId -> Process ()
```

If we want to combine matchAny and forward, we should flip forward and apply the ProcessId, or use a lambda, like in the following.

```
relay :: ProcessId -> Process ()
relay !pid = forever' $ receiveWait [ matchAny (\m -> forward m pid) ]
```

This approach is helpful, but still there is a limit to what the operation can do with received messages, because matchAny works on the unprocessed Message type. If we want to examine the inside of the message, we need to know the message type.

When an expression works on a certain type, we could try decoding the message of that type and check the outcome to see if the decoding worked or not. To do this, we can use one of the primitives, unwrapMessage or handleMessage, which have the types.

```
unwrapMessage :: forall m a. (Monad m, Serializable a) => Message -> m (Maybe a)
handleMessage :: forall m a b. (Monad m, Serializable a) => Message -> (a -> m b) -> m (Maybe b)
```

The unwrapMessage primitive is easier and its input is an unprocessed Message. It evaluates Maybe a until it returns the result to the m monad. If it obtains the expected type, then the outcome will be Just a, else, it will be Nothing.

The other primitive, handleMessage, is less restrictive and takes a function like a-> m b. The result is Just b if the targeted message has type a, and Nothing if the type of the message is not compatible with the handler.

The following shows how handleMessage works. In the previous examples, we used the relay function, but now we will use a similar function called proxy. If it has a parameter as a predicate, then it is evaluating an input with type a, and the result is Process Bool. This allows running arbitrary Process code for deciding if a is suitable to be sent to process with ProcessId. The proxy has the following type.

```
proxy :: Serializable a => ProcessId -> (a -> Process Bool) -> Process ()
```

matchAny and handleMessage could be compounded for making a proxy server, because matchAny works on (Message -> Process b) and handleMessage works on a -> Process b. The messages whose predicate returns Just False or cannot evaluate because of type should not be sent. So, proxy is defined.

```
proxy pid proc = do
  receiveWait [
    matchAny (\m -> do
                next <- handleMessage m proc
                case next of
                  Just True  -> forward m pid
                  Just False -> return ()  -- explicitly ignored
                  Nothing    -> return ()) -- un-routable / cannot decode
  ]
  proxy pid proc
```

Monad Transformers Stack

Sometimes, an application may need a customized monad transformer stack with the Process monad as a base. As an example, the application could make requests to a network database. The solution for this could be creating a data access section with some configuration for connecting to a database server. The tool for an automatic configuration could be ReaderT.

The following uses the fetchUser function run in the AppProcess monad for configuring the connection to a database.

```
import Data.ByteString (ByteString)
import Control.Monad.Reader

-- imagine we have some database library
import Database.Imaginary as DB

data AppConfig = AppConfig {dbHost :: String, dbUser :: String}

type AppProcess = ReaderT AppConfig Process

data User = User {userEmail :: String}

-- Perform a user lookup using our custom app context
fetchUser :: String -> AppProcess (Maybe User)
fetchUser email = do
  db <- openDB
  user <- liftIO $ DB.query db email
  closeDB db
  return user

openDB :: AppProcess DB.Connection
openDB = do
  AppConfig host user <- ask
  liftIO $ DB.connect host user

closeDB :: DB.Connection -> AppProcess ()
closeDB db = liftIO (DB.close db)
```

Mainly, these are the things we need to do, but it is a little incomplete. When an exception occurs due to a query function, the database handle could remain open. For this, we use the bracket function from Control.Exception, defined as

```
bracket :: IO a        --^ computation to run first ("acquire resource")
        -> (a -> IO b) --^ computation to run last ("release resource")
        -> (a -> IO c) --^ computation to run in-between
        -> IO c
```

Using an IO action, it is acquired a resource, which is sent further using a bracket to a function that gets the resource and then runs another action. Moreover, provides a release function that assures that the bracket runs, even though an exception occurred in the initial action.

   Still, the function bracket could not be used in fetchUser, because openBD is running in the
AppProcess monad. Fortunately, distributed-process provides another implementation for the bracket.

```
-- | Lift 'Control.Exception.bracket'
bracket :: Process a -> (a -> Process b) -> (a -> Process c) -> Process c
bracket before after thing =
  mask $ \restore -> do
    a <- before
    r <- restore (thing a) `onException` after a
    _ <- after a
    return r

mask :: ((forall a. Process a -> Process a) -> Process b) -> Process b
mask p = do
    lproc <- ask
    liftIO $ Ex.mask $ \restore ->
      runLocalProcess lproc (p (liftRestore restore))
  where
    liftRestore :: (forall a. IO a -> IO a)
                -> (forall a. Process a -> Process a)
    liftRestore restoreIO = \p2 -> do
      ourLocalProc <- ask
      liftIO $ restoreIO $ runLocalProcess ourLocalProc p2

-- | Lift 'Control.Exception.onException'
onException :: Process a -> Process b -> Process a
onException p what = p `catch` \e -> do _ <- what
                                        liftIO $ throwIO (e :: SomeException)
```

   This is done by distributed-process to avoid many dependencies, but it is a little difficult to write all
the preceding code every time it uses a transformer stack in the application. But monad-control and lifted-
base free us from this inconvenience.

   monad-control provides some type classes and helper functions that help generalize the (un)wrapping
necessary for keeping transformer effects hidden while some actions are running in the base monad.
MonadBase and MonadBaseControl are a concern for the end user. If you are not familiar with the monad-
control package, please visit https://hackage.haskell.org/package/monad-control.

   The lifted-base brings improved versions of functions from Haskell base libraries using these type
classes. The following is the definition of bracket from Control.Exception.Lifted.

```
bracket :: MonadBaseControl IO m
        => m a         --^ computation to run first ("acquire resource")
        -> (a -> m b)  --^ computation to run last ("release resource")
        -> (a -> m c)  --^ computation to run in-between
        -> m c
```

   Mainly, it is the same as the classic bracket function, but adds the capability to operate with actions
that work with MonadBaseControl.IO. Even if monad-control creates instances for classical transformers, the
instances still need the original monad to have an instance from that class.

147

distributed-process-monad-control delivers instances of Process without any dependencies for MonadBaseIO and also MonadBaseControlIO. We will improve the preceding code by importing these libraries and using a bracket (from lifted-base) instead of fetchUser.

```
-- ...
import Control.Distributed.Process.MonadBaseControl ()
import Control.Exception.Lifted as Lifted

-- ...

fetchUser :: String -> AppProcess (Maybe User)
fetchUser email =
  Lifted.bracket openDB
                 closeDB
                 $ \db -> liftIO $ DB.query db email
```

lifted-base brings other benefits, like MVar, or other concurrent functions that work with MonadBaseIO. An advantage is that the code does not contain liftIO; however, MonadBaseControlIO does things, like lift withMVar.

Pay attention to the fact that these instances could allow the utilization of functions like forkIO, which would endanger the invariants from the Process monad, thus causing confusion or issues. In Cloud Haskell, it is recommended to use functions like spawnLocal.

Generic Processes

Sometimes there are situations in which bugs could occur when send and receive are directly evaluated. For example, when the destination is not monitored, when it expects a reply, in instances where binary was incorrectly created, or crashes from other reasons.

The /Managed Process/API deals with messages that are sent and received from the server process, and the code shows how the server process works when it gets a message written by the programmer. In the API there are some predefined actions with good semantics and failure approaches.

Managed processes are defined using record syntax, providing lists of Dispatcher objects describing how the server handles particular kinds of client interaction for specific input types. The ProcessDefinition record also provides hooks for error handling (in case of server code crashing *or* exit signals dispatched to the server process from elsewhere) and *cleanup* code to be run on termination/shutdown.

```
myServer :: ProcessDefinition MyStateType
myServer =
  ProcessDefinition {
      -- handle messages sent to us via the call/cast API functions
      apiHandlers = [
        -- a list of Dispatchers, derived by calling on of the various
        -- handle<X> functions with a suitable thunk, e.g.,
        handleCast myFunctionThatDoesNotReply
      , handleCall myFunctionThatDoesReply
      , handleRpcChan myFunctionThatRepliesViaTypedChannels
      ]

      -- handle messages that can only be sent directly to our mailbox
      -- (i.e., without going through the call/casts APIs), such as
      -- `ProcessMonitorNotification`
```

```
, infoHandlers = [
    -- a list of DeferredDispatcher, derived from calling
    -- handleInfo or handleRaw with a suitable function, e.g.,
    handleInfo myFunctionThatHandlesOneSpecificNonCastNonCallMessageType
  , handleRaw  myFunctionThatHandlesRawMessages
  ]

    -- what should we do about exit signals?
, exitHandlers = [
    -- a list of ExitSignalDispatcher, derived from calling
    -- handleExit with a suitable function, e.g.,
    handleExit myExitHandlingFunction
  ]

    -- what should I do just before stopping?
, shutdownHandler = myShutdownFunction

    -- what should I do about messages that cannot be handled?
, unhandledMessagePolicy = Drop -- Terminate | (DeadLetter ProcessId)
}
```

When it is defined as a client-server protocol, usually it specifies that some types are handled by the server, and maybe correspond to those that will be sent to the receiver. The following presents such an example. It is about a math server application, in which the client sends a triplet with a form (ProcessId, Double, Double), and the server sends back the sum of the two doubles. When the client waits for the result, but the process server was killed, then deadlock occurs on the client side. To avoid this problem, the client side should have a monitor that is waiting for a reply or for a monitor signal. Still, other problems could arise. For example, the facility expects the incorrect type. For this, there should be a typed channel, but a channel is unidirectional, so the client will receive messages, but not the server. It is a little unhandy to create more typed channels (for every type of message that is expected) to distribute to the clients. We will use call and cast, which helps us in this problem—for both client and server, providing a uniform API for the client.

```
module MathServer
  ( -- client facing API
    add
    -- starting/spawning the server process
  , launchMathServer
  ) where

import .... -- elided

-- We keep this data-type hidden from the outside world, and we ignore
-- messages sent to us that we do not recognise, so misbehaving clients
-- (who do not use our API) are basically ignored.
data Add = Add Double Double
  deriving (Typeable, Generic)
instance Binary Add where

-- client facing API

-- This is the only way clients can get a message through to us that
-- we will respond to, and since we control the type(s), there is no
```

```
-- risk of decoding errors on the server. The /call/ API ensures that
-- if the server does fail for some other reason however (such as being
-- killed by another process), the client will get an exit signal also.
--
add :: ProcessId -> Double -> Double -> Process Double
add sid = call sid . Add

-- server side code

launchMathServer :: Process ProcessId
launchMathServer =
  let server = statelessProcess {
      apiHandlers = [ handleCall_ (\(Add x y) -> return (x + y)) ]
    , unhandledMessagePolicy = Drop
    }
  in spawnLocal $ start () (statelessInit Infinity) server >> return ()
```

This approach is easy if in your previous applications you used send for clients and receive[match...] for the server. We have a great facility here, because we can implement the math server under a new type and avoid having messages sent to ProcessId in their entirely.

Even still, data type mismatches could occur because call and send have generic serializable data (for example, ErrorOnCodingFailure, IgnoreCodingFailure) when handling illegal sequences and constructing text encodings. The first error occurs when an illegal sequence appears, and the second function is used when we want to ignore an occurrence of an illegal sequence). This could be solved if we send a typed channel and reply directly to the server code. The code will not look very good, but at least it solved some run-time errors.

```
-- This is the only way clients can get a message through to us that
-- we will respond to, and since we control the type(s), there is no
-- risk of decoding errors on the server. The /call/ API ensures that
-- if the server does fail for some other reason however (such as being
-- killed by another process), the client will get an exit signal also.
--
add :: ProcessId -> Double -> Double -> Process Double
add sid = syncCallChan sid . Add

launchMathServer :: Process ProcessId
launchMathServer =
  let server = statelessProcess {
      apiHandlers = [ handleRpcChan_ (\chan (Add x y) -> sendChan chan (x + y)) ]
    , unhandledMessagePolicy = Drop
    }
  in spawnLocal $ start () (statelessInit Infinity) server >> return ()
```

It is not difficult to assure that the server receives only allowed types, because the client call is not directly used and the wrapper functions are written by us.

The cast function from the client-server protocol is not expecting a response, in contrast with the synchronous version of cast. It is more similar to send, but has the same supplementary type information, like call, and has a route to Dispatcher from apiHandlers filed from the process defining.

In the examples, cast is used with type Add for implementing a function that needs an add/request and displays the output, rather than returning it. We use this approach instead of a call function because in a call function there is nothing that distinguishes between the two Add instances, so the server would pick the first one as valid. Also, if the function is called in a test application, then the main thread should be blocked for some time from waiting for the server to get the message and display the result, because the client side is not waiting for a response.

```
printSum :: ProcessId -> Double -> Double -> Process ()
printSum sid = cast sid . Add

launchMathServer :: Process ProcessId
launchMathServer =
  let server = statelessProcess {
      apiHandlers = [ handleRpcChan_ (\chan (Add x y) -> sendChan chan (x + y) >> continue_)
                    , handleCast_ (\(Add x y) -> liftIO $ putStrLn $ show (x + y) >>
                        continue_) ]
    , unhandledMessagePolicy = Drop
    }
  in spawnLocal $ start () (statelessInit Infinity) server >> return ()
```

Client-Server Example

This section uses a type named BlockingQueue from the distributed-process-task library.

The tasks are executed on a generic node, and the caller is blocked while the remote job is executed. In addition, we need a maximum number of tasks that are concurrent, on which the server will accept.

ManagedProcess is used for implementing an arbitrary task server as described earlier. When the maximum number of tasks is achieved, the other tasks are organized in a queue to wait to be executed. Also, the asynchronous cast API is a good choice, because the client is blocked while the server is performing the tasks, or we could use callChan for typed channels.

First, we need to know the types from the client-server application (i.e., the tasks that will be performed). When a task is given, it submits an action to the process monad, encapsulated in a Closure. The Addressable type class will be used, which permits the clients to define the server location. So, the task has type Closure (Process a), and the server has two sides of returning: Left String (in case of failure) and Right (in case of success).

```
-- enqueues the task in the pool and blocks
-- the caller until the task is complete
executeTask :: forall s a . (Addressable s, Serializable a)
            => s
            -> Closure (Process a)
            -> Process (Either String a)
executeTask sid t = call sid t
```

Do not forget that in Cloud Haskell, communication with a process is done through its mailbox and typed channels, and it has two sides: synchronous from the receiver's side and asynchronous from the server's side.

On the server side, every request receives a response, but when call is handled, the replies could be different from those in an upper stage. While the server is working, the client is blocked, waiting for a response. Using call, there is no interference from other processes to the message sent by the server, because a call attaches a tag to the message and expects a particular response from the server with the same tag. This is useful because messages with type Either String could come in the mailbox, while the client is receiving. The tags used by the call are distinct for nodes, because MonitorRef's tag is an Identifier ProcessId and a local node's tag is the monitor reference counter for that node.

On the client side, there are no arbitrary messages with type signatures that arrive in the mailbox. If the call function crashes, then a ProcessExitException occurs.

On the server side, there are some internal states that need to be handled. Because the maximum numbers of tasks is known, the running tasks need to be tracked. As we said, every task will be registered as Closure (Process a), and asynchronously spawned. The output will be handled and the response will be sent to the initial sender. We need to specify what types of results are accepted by closures, so the state type is

```
data BlockingQueue a = BlockingQueue
```

Every task will be executed asynchronously using Control.Distributed.Process.Async, which also helps to give meaning to the result. If we want to use Async, we will need to use a reference. We need a manner in which the submitter is associated to the handle, so we have two fields: one for active tasks and one for the inactive tasks that are waiting in the queue to be resolved. Running tasks will be stored in MonitorRef, a reference of the sender and the handle async itself. The states will use a list of associations.

If the task cannot be executed right away, then holds the reference of the client and the closure, but does not hold the monitor reference. The data structure that is used in the example works on the FIFO principle.

```
data BlockingQueue a = BlockingQueue {
    poolSize :: SizeLimit
  , active   :: [(MonitorRef, CallRef (Either ExitReason a), Async a)]
  , accepted :: Seq (CallRef (Either ExitReason a), Closure (Process a))
  }
```

We make it act like a queue using Data.Sequence.

```
enqueue :: Seq a -> a -> Seq a
enqueue s a = a <| s

dequeue :: Seq a -> Maybe (a, Seq a)
dequeue s = maybe Nothing (\(s' :> a) -> Just (a, s')) $ getR s

getR :: Seq a -> Maybe (ViewR a)
getR s =
  case (viewr s) of
    EmptyR -> Nothing
    a      -> Just a
```

Closure is transformed into a evaluable thunk using the unClosure function. Next, the thunk is sent to async, and then to the handle, whose result is shown on the monitor.

```
proc <- unClosure task'
asyncHandle <- async proc
ref <- monitorAsync asyncHandle
```

The acceptTask function could be implemented, on which the server will use to deal with the registered tasks. The header of the function should fit with the API that handles the messages from ManagedProcess (i.e., handleCallFrom). This particular version of handleCall is used when it is more likely that the server will postpone the response than respond immediately. The arguments for this function is an expression that works with the state of the server—a CallRef that detects the sender and is used to respond, and a Closure (Process a).

```
storeTask :: Serializable a
          => BlockingQueue a
          -> CallRef (Either ExitReason a)
          -> Closure (Process a)
          -> Process (ProcessReply (Either ExitReason a) (BlockingQueue a))
storeTask s r c = acceptTask s r c >>= noReply_

acceptTask :: Serializable a
           => BlockingQueue a
           -> CallRef (Either ExitReason a)
           -> Closure (Process a)
           -> Process (BlockingQueue a)
acceptTask s@(BlockingQueue sz' runQueue taskQueue) from task' =
  let currentSz = length runQueue
  in case currentSz >= sz' of
    True  -> do
      return $ s { accepted = enqueue taskQueue (from, task') }
    False -> do
      proc <- unClosure task'
      asyncHandle <- async proc
      ref <- monitorAsync asyncHandle
      let taskEntry = (ref, from, asyncHandle)
      return s { active = (taskEntry:runQueue) }
```

In the function, a task is added to the accepted queue when the number of maximum running tasks is reached, or the task is started and monitored with async. The monitor reference, caller reference, and the async handle are in the active component.

A function that deals with the responses of the closures is needed. So, we have to do the following.

1. Discover the async handle for the monitor reference.

2. Get the result utilizing handle.

3. Transmit the result to the client.

4. Take the next task from the queue.

5. Continue the preceding steps.

The preceding mechanism can be summarized as wait >>= respond >> bump-next-task >>= continue.

To transmit the result to the client, we need a special API from ManagedProcess called replyTo because it sends a specific message to the client and responds to a specific call function.

The header of the function is similar to storeTask in the preceding, but the returned type is ProcessAction. It is not bound to a call or cast, because the monitor signal is sent by the node controller straight to the targeted mailbox. This approach is called an *info call* in the managed process API, and, because a response is not expected, it is returned as a ProcessAction, which tells the server the following step to be performed (i.e., continue to read from the mailbox).

```
taskComplete :: forall a . Serializable a
             => BlockingQueue a
             -> ProcessMonitorNotification
             -> Process (ProcessAction (BlockingQueue a))
```

```
taskComplete s@(BlockingQueue _ runQ _)
              (ProcessMonitorNotification ref _ _) =
  let worker = findWorker ref runQ in
  case worker of
    Just t@(_, c, h) -> wait h >>= respond c >> bump s t >>= continue
    Nothing          -> continue s

  where
    respond :: CallRef (Either ExitReason a)
            -> AsyncResult a
            -> Process ()
    respond c (AsyncDone       r) = replyTo c ((Right r) :: (Either ExitReason a))
    respond c (AsyncFailed     d) = replyTo c ((Left (ExitOther $ show d))  ::
                                              (Either ExitReason a))
    respond c (AsyncLinkFailed d) = replyTo c ((Left (ExitOther $ show d))  ::
                                              (Either ExitReason a))
    respond _ _                   = die $ ExitOther "IllegalState"

    bump :: BlockingQueue a
         -> (MonitorRef, CallRef (Either ExitReason a), Async a)
         -> Process (BlockingQueue a)
    bump st@(BlockingQueue _ runQueue acc) worker =
      let runQ2 = deleteFromRunQueue worker runQueue
          accQ  = dequeue acc in
      case accQ of
        Nothing             -> return st { active = runQ2 }
        Just ((tr,tc), ts) -> acceptTask (st { accepted = ts, active = runQ2 }) tr tc

findWorker :: MonitorRef
           -> [(MonitorRef, CallRef (Either ExitReason a), Async a)]
           -> Maybe (MonitorRef, CallRef (Either ExitReason a), Async a)
findWorker key = find (\(ref,_,_) -> ref == key)

deleteFromRunQueue :: (MonitorRef, CallRef (Either ExitReason a), Async a)
                   -> [(MonitorRef, CallRef (Either ExitReason a), Async a)]
                   -> [(MonitorRef, CallRef (Either ExitReason a), Async a)]
deleteFromRunQueue c@(p, _, _) runQ = deleteBy (\_ (b, _, _) -> b == p) c runQ
```

The apiHandler (from ProcessDefinition) contains the call and cast handler, whose type is Dispatcher s, where s is the type of the state for the process. We cannot create Dispatchers, but there are some functions in the ManagedProcess.Server that transforms functions similar to those written by us to the right type.

In order for the compiler to recognize it, a type signature needs to be placed at the location where storeTask is called.

```
handleCallFrom (\s f (p :: Closure (Process a)) -> storeTask s f p)
```

We do not need to do this for taskComplete in this case because there is no ambiguous type. The definition of the process becomes

```
defaultProcess {
    apiHandlers = [
            handleCallFrom (\s f (p :: Closure (Process a)) -> storeTask s f p)
          , handleCall poolStatsRequest
        ]
  , infoHandlers = [ handleInfo taskComplete ]
  }
```

It takes some work to start the server. ManagedProcess offers some functions for helping the spawned and running processes. The argument for the serve function is an initializer thunk, whose type is InitHandler, and its task is to engender the initial state and establish the receive timeout of the server, and then call the process definition from earlier.

```
run :: forall a . (Serializable a)
          => Process (InitResult (BlockingQueue a))
          -> Process ()
run init' = ManagedProcess.serve () (\() -> init') poolServer
  where poolServer =
            defaultProcess {
                apiHandlers = [
                    handleCallFrom (\s f (p :: Closure (Process a)) -> storeTask s f p)
                  , handleCall poolStatsRequest
                    ]
              , infoHandlers = [ handleInfo taskComplete ]
              } :: ProcessDefinition (BlockingQueue a)

pool :: forall a . Serializable a
    => SizeLimit
    -> Process (InitResult (BlockingQueue a))
pool sz' = return $ InitOk (BlockingQueue sz' [] Seq.empty) Infinity
```

To make the tasks remote-worthy, we proceed as follows.

```
sampleTask :: (TimeInterval, String) -> Process String
sampleTask (t, s) = sleep t >> return s

$(remotable ['sampleTask])
```

And to execute tasks, we do this.

```
tsk <- return $ ($(mkClosure 'sampleTask) (seconds 2, "foobar"))
executeTask taskQueuePid tsk
```

When a server starts locally or starts a local/remote node, we need to combine spawn or spawnLocal with start. If we want to add some security, we could use a nontransparent handle for communicating with the server. A consequence is that the client could send a Closure, whose return type is distinct from the one expected by the server. And, in this case, the server will respond with unhandeldMessagePolicy and will crash.

When it returns a handle to the server with parametrized type, just closures with a fitting type are delivered. Thus, a phantom type is used to hide the actual ProcessId into the new type. Further, an instance of Resolvable is defined, so that the handle is sent to the managed process call. Resolvable creates an instance of Routable, which is all that call needs.

```
newtype TaskQueue a = TaskQueue { unQueue :: ProcessId }

instance Resolvable (TaskQueue a) where
  resolve = return . unQueue
```

The last step is to write a start function that returns the handle and modifies the header of executeTask so that they match.

```
start :: forall a . (Serializable a)
      => SizeLimit
      -> Process (TaskQueue a)
start lim = spawnLocal (start $ pool lim) >>= return . TaskQueue

-- .......

executeTask :: (Serializable a)
            => TaskQueue a
            -> Closure (Process a)
            -> Process (Either ExitReason a)
executeTask sid t = call sid t
```

Matching Without Blocking

In practice, there are situations in which a function terminates until an expected message arrives at a particular process. This section shows you how this can be avoided.

Unexpected Messages

Using UnhandledMessagePolicy, the processes can handle unexpected messages, which is an important feature, because there could be many situations in which the mailbox of a process arrives unexpected messages, or messages that are not fitting in expected types of the server, or messages that do not respect some conditions of the message body.

There are methods to assure that some types of messages arrive in the process, but only by using monitors or other management systems, and only when node controller delivers the messages to the mailboxes. These methods are used with session types that belong to Cloud Haskell routes, but disconnect in managed processes.

Log writes an informational message in SystemLog about unforeseen messages. In production, we could choose between Drop or Terminate policies. Due to the nature of Cloud Haskell, unexpected messages could arrive, and the servers must have methods to handle them. Be careful when unexpected messages are received, particularly when using Drop policy, because it is possible for the server to reject messages unless the clients are notified, so deadlocks can occur.

Hiding Implementation Details

In real life, clients can send messages to a managed process, but this could be avoided if, for example, the id of the process was hidden. The server should be sure that the suitable client-server protocol is used. So, mainly, we need to compile to be sure that the communication between client and server is a classical one. Let's look to a previous example of the server.

```haskell
module MathServer
  ( -- client facing API
    MathServer()
  , add
    -- starting/spawning the server process
  , launchMathServer
  ) where

import .... -- elided

newtype MathServer = MathServer { mathServerPid :: ProcessId }
  deriving (Typeable)

-- other types/details elided

add :: MathServer -> Double -> Double -> Process Double
add MathServer{..} = call mathServerPid . Add

launchMathServer :: Process MathServer
launchMathServer = launch >>= return . MathServer
  where launch =
    let server = statelessProcess {
      apiHandlers = [ handleCall_ (\(Add x y) -> return (x + y)) ]
    , unhandledMessagePolicy = Drop
    }
    in spawnLocal $ start () (statelessInit Infinity) server >> return ()
```

From the previous example, the ProcessId is hidden, using another type and determining the client code to utilize the MathServer handler for calling the API functions. The new type MathServer, constructed around ProcessId, could be serialized and delivered to remote clients when it is necessary. Even if we changed the approach, we are not totally sure that informative messages will not arrive in the mailbox, because it is not 100% certain that the ProcessId is hidden because of APIs for managing or tracing from distributed-process. Also, the servers should be configured to accept monitor signals that come as informative messages.

The preceding approach (the server handles as an alternative to a native ProcessId) is also useful because the compatibility of the client-server is assured. Further, we will use Registry module, which is useful as general key/value store. Every Registry server has particular types of keys and values. We really need to avoid letting clients provide or get instructions for a registry server when we don't know exactly the types that were spawned to be handled by the server. This problem is avoided if we use phantom type parameters and store the correct ProcessId for communication with the server.

```haskell
data Registry k v = Registry { registryPid :: ProcessId }
  deriving (Typeable, Generic, Show, Eq)
instance (Keyable k, Serializable v) => Binary (Registry k v) where
```

To start the registry, we need to know the k and v types, but not necessarily their values.

```
start :: forall k v. (Keyable k, Serializable v) => Process (Registry k v)
start = return . Registry =<< spawnLocal (run (undefined :: Registry k v))

run :: forall k v. (Keyable k, Serializable v) => Registry k v -> Process ()
run _ =
  MP.pserve () (const $ return $ InitOk initState Infinity) serverDefinition
  -- etc....
```

Because ProcessId is incorporated by the new type, it is assured that the types with which the server was started are taken into consideration by clients. In the examples, the client is forced to work with the server (it does not just use the protocol), and needs to send the right types, such as a valid handle form.

```
addProperty :: (Keyable k, Serializable v)
            => Registry k v -> k -> v -> Process RegisterKeyReply
addProperty reg k v = ....
```

When we compel the user to communicate with the process through a nontransparent handle, it is a good thing, because ProcessId is hidden every time it is possible, so it would not send unexpected messages to the server. But sometimes ProcessId is needed, especially for monitoring, name registration, or other methods that work directly with ProcessId, or when informational messages are sent.

In such cases, Resolvable or Routable help. Using Resolvable, the ProcessId is seen only by those components that need them, which is handled in the client code.

```
instance Resolvable (Registry k v) where
  resolve = return . Just . registryPid
```

Further, Routable supplies a way to send messages in absence of knowing the implementation details. By default, every Resolvable instance contains an instance of Routable, which works pretty well. The explicit implementation for the Registry is presented next.

```
instance Routable (Registry k v) where
  sendTo       reg msg = send (registryPid reg) msg
  unsafeSendTo reg msg = unsafeSend (registryPid reg) msg
```

We can create type classes, for example, for kill or link, in the absence of ProcessId.

```
class Linkable a where
  -- | Create a /link/ with the supplied object.
  linkTo :: a -> Process ()

class Killable a where
  killProc :: a -> String -> Process ()
  exitProc :: (Serializable m) => a -> m -> Process ()
```

Messages Within Channels

Using Serializable is a very useful feature, but the correct interpretation of the types at run-time is the task of the programmer. Also, we need to pay attention to run-time overheads. Luckily, there are alternate variants for using send and receive, known as *typed channels*. We can interact with processes dissociated from the mailbox through a type-secure interface provided by abstraction resulted from using SendPort a (Serializable) and ReceivePort a (not Serializable) with different ends.

We use newChan :: Process (SendPort a, ReceivePort a) for creating channels, and sendChan :: SendPort a -> a -> Process() for sending messages. ReceivePort is used in receiveChan or with a receive (Wait, Timeout) that calls the matchChan function in combined mailbox scans with channel reads.

There are two different ways in which typed channels can be used: like an input for the server or like a reply channel for RPC-type interactions.

Reply Channels

When call is used in an application, it is possible that the server responds with data that does not have the expected type, which leads to deadlock or a timeout. This could be prevented by programmers because they write the code for both the server and the client, and should be careful of matching types.

Reply channels work in a simple manner: a new channel for a reply is created, and the SendPort with the input message is sent to the server. Then, the server should send to the SendPort its suitable ReceivePort. If there is no such correspondence, a reply will not exist, and it is possible that the server will collapse.

Typed channels are more suitable with client-server RCP calls than inter-process messaging. The basis for a call API is Async. The fail happens when AsyncFailed occurs, because of a certain ExitReason. On the other hand, if callTimeout is used leading to the time for message being overtaken, and another listening for getting the message is not working, then the client side should handle unexpected replies using flushPendingCalls. When typed channels are used for the reply, the preceding issues could be avoided after the RPC is started.

When it is necessary to wait for a reply after blocking, two block operations are used; one of them will return ExitReason in case it fails. This is the right thing to do when a call blocking runs, so the server is observed for a possible exit signal, which is done with awaitResponse from the Primitive module.

```
syncSafeCallChan server msg = do
  rp <- callChan server msg
  awaitResponse server [ matchChan rp (return . Right) ]
```

This is a nice advance related to the call/handleCall approach, because the programmer assures that there is always matching type. Using handleRcpChan functions is more restrictive than handleCall. In the following, we present how reply channels work.

```
-- two versions of the same handler, one for calls, one for typed (reply) channels

data State
data Input
data Output

-- typeable and binary instances ommitted for brevity

-- client code

callDemo :: ProcessId -> Process Output
callDemo server = call server Input

chanDemo :: ProcessId -> Process Output
chanDemo server = syncCallChan server Input

-- server code (process definition ommitted for brevity)
```

```
callHandler :: Dispatcher State
callHandler = handleCall $ \state Input -> reply Output state

chanHandler :: Dispatcher State
chanHandler = handleRpcChan $ \state port Input -> replyChan port Output >> continue state
```

Input (Control) Channels

For managing process servers, control channels are a good choice, having good influence over call, cast, and **reply** channels. It is based on efficiency and security, and the server can decide the priority of the received data.

Using typed channels is the best manner for enabling client-server communication, because internally, they use STM, so they supply another way to handle process definitions with high priority, determined by the apiHandlers list ahead of other senders. The messages that are sent using that channel will have a higher priority than others. This approach has the highest grade of efficiency, being very helpful when control messages need a higher priority than other data.

When a typed channel represents the input plane, it should communicate the SendPort to the clients in some way. A method implies the send function, which sends when it is requested. It is simpler to initialize a handler having all the necessary send ports and returning this data to a spawning process through a particular channel, MVar or STM. It is easy to forward them because SendPort is Serializable.

Because typed channels are unidirectional, there is no direct API assistance for RPC calls in situations in which they are used for sending data to the server. What we have to do is easy: codify a reply channel in the order/demand data, such that the server understands where to respond and with what type.

Next, we examine an example with only one control channel using the chanServe API. This approach, avoids the details of sending a control channel back to the initial process. We will use the Mailbox module because it provides a fire-and forget control channel with a nontransparent server handle.

```
-- our handle is fairly simple
data Mailbox = Mailbox { pid   :: !ProcessId
                       , cchan :: !(ControlPort ControlMessage)
                       } deriving (Typeable, Generic, Eq)
instance Binary Mailbox where

instance Linkable Mailbox where
  linkTo = link . pid

instance Resolvable Mailbox where
  resolve = return . Just . pid

-- lots of details elided....

-- Starting the mailbox involves both spawning, and passing back the process id,
-- plus we need to get our hands on a control port for the control channel!

doStartMailbox :: Maybe SupervisorPid
               -> ProcessId
               -> BufferType
               -> Limit
               -> Process Mailbox
```

```
doStartMailbox mSp p b l = do
  bchan <- liftIO $ newBroadcastTChanIO
  rchan <- liftIO $ atomically $ dupTChan bchan
  spawnLocal (maybeLink mSp >> runMailbox bchan p b l) >>= \pid -> do
    cc <- liftIO $ atomically $ readTChan rchan
    return $ Mailbox pid cc  -- return our opaque handle!
  where
    maybeLink Nothing    = return ()
    maybeLink (Just p') = link p'

runMailbox :: TChan (ControlPort ControlMessage)
           -> ProcessId
           -> BufferType
           -> Limit
           -> Process ()
runMailbox tc pid buffT maxSz = do
  link pid
  tc' <- liftIO $ atomically $ dupTChan tc
  MP.chanServe (pid, buffT, maxSz) (mboxInit tc') (processDefinition pid tc)

mboxInit :: TChan (ControlPort ControlMessage)
         -> InitHandler (ProcessId, BufferType, Limit) State
mboxInit tc (pid, buffT, maxSz) = do
  cc <- liftIO $ atomically $ readTChan tc
  return $ InitOk (State Seq.empty $ defaultState buffT maxSz pid cc) Infinity

processDefinition :: ProcessId
                  -> TChan (ControlPort ControlMessage)
                  -> ControlChannel ControlMessage
                  -> Process (ProcessDefinition State)
processDefinition pid tc cc = do
  liftIO $ atomically $ writeTChan tc $ channelControlPort cc
  return $ defaultProcess { apiHandlers = [
                          handleControlChan     cc handleControlMessages
                        , Restricted.handleCall handleGetStats
                        ]
                      , infoHandlers = [ handleInfo handlePost
                                       , handleRaw  handleRawInputs ]
                      , unhandledMessagePolicy = DeadLetter pid
                      } :: Process (ProcessDefinition State)
```

For the moment, we will not talk about mailbox initialization because it is a little complicated. What is important in the preceding code is the way chanServe is used and the needs for thunk in the initialization of ProcessDefinition. In the preceding code, the control port is sent through thunk to chanServe to the spawning process and init function, where we can see how broadcasting TChan is used for sharing some structures while initializing.

Next, we present another example with more typed control channels. It shows how control channels are created explicitly, how ControlPort is obtained for everyone (a method of sending them back to the process spawning the server), and how to use these features in the client code with typed reply channels. chanServe is not used because it works only with one control channel; instead, we use recvLoop. The main parts of the code are highlighted.

```haskell
type NumRequests = Int

data EchoServer = EchoServer { echoRequests :: ControlPort String
                             , statRequests :: ControlPort NumRequests
                             , serverPid    :: ProcessId
                             }
  deriving (Typeable, Generic)
instance Binary EchoServer where
instance NFData EchoServer where

instance Resolvable EchoServer where
  resolve = return . Just . serverPid

instance Linkable EchoServer where
  linkTo = link . serverPid

-- The server takes a String and returns it verbatim

data EchoRequest = EchoReq !String !(SendPort String)
  deriving (Typeable, Generic)
instance Binary EchoRequest where
instance NFData EchoRequest where

data StatsRequest = StatsReq !(SendPort Int)
  deriving (Typeable, Generic)
instance Binary StatsRequest where
instance NFData StatsRequest where

-- client code

echo :: EchoServer -> String -> Process String
echo h s = do
  (sp, rp) <- newChan
  let req = EchoReq s sp
  sendControlMessage (echoRequests h) req
  receiveWait [ matchChan rp return ]

stats :: EchoServer -> Process NumRequests
stats h = do
  (sp, rp) <- newChan
  let req = StatsReq sp
  sendControlMessage (statRequests h) req
  receiveWait [ matchChan rp return ]

demo :: Process ()
demo = do
  server <- spawnEchoServer
  foobar <- echo server "foobar"
  foobar `shouldBe` equalTo "foobar"

  baz <- echo server "baz"
  baz `shouldBe` equalTo baz
```

```
  count <- stats server
  count `shouldBe` equalTo (2 :: NumRequests)

-- server code

spawnEchoServer :: Process EchoServer
spawnEchoServer = do
  (sp, rp) <- newChan
  pid <- spawnLocal $ runEchoServer sp
  (echoPort, statsPort) <- receiveChan rp
  return $ EchoServer echoPort statsPort pid

runEchoServer :: SendPort (ControlPort EchoRequest, ControlPort StatsRequest)
              -> Process ()
runEchoServer portsChan = do
  echoChan <- newControlChan
  echoPort <- channelControlPort echoChan
  statChan <- newControlChan
  statPort <- channelControlPort statChan
  sendChan portsChan (echoPort, statPort)
  runProcess (recvLoop $ echoServerDefinition echoChan statChan ) echoServerInit

echoServerInit :: InitHandler () NumRequests
echoServerInit = return $ InitOk (0 :: Int) Infinity

echoServerDefinition :: ControlChannel EchoRequest
                     -> ControlChannel StatsRequest
                     -> ProcessDefinition NumRequests
echoServerDefinition echoChan statChan =
  defaultProcess {
     apiHandlers = [ handleControlChan echoChan handleEcho
                   , handleControlChan statChan handleStats
                   ]
  }

handleEcho :: NumRequests -> EchoRequest -> Process (ProcessAction State)
handleEcho count (EchoReq req replyTo) = do
  replyChan replyTo req  -- echo back the string
  continue $ count + 1

handleStats :: NumRequests -> StatsRequest -> Process (ProcessAction State)
handleStats count (StatsReq replyTo) = do
  replyChan replyTo count
  continue count
```

The preceding code is a didactic example. The client side works with ControlPort, not with ControlChannel, and the server is liable to reply to the client making use of the send ports given in the requested data.

Summary

Throughout the chapter, you saw that there are many ways for message matching.

- `match :: forall a b. Serializable a => (a -> Process b) -> Match b :` Matches with any message that has the type from the right.

- `matchIf :: forall a b. Serializable a => (a -> Bool) -> (a -> Process b) -> Match b :` Matches with any message that has the type from the right and meets the condition of the predicate.

- `matchUnknown :: Process b -> Match b :` Removes all messages from the queue.

- `matchAny :: forall b. (Message -> Process b) -> Match b :` Matches with an arbitrary message. It eliminates the first message that is available on the process mailbox.

- `matchAnyIf :: forall a b. Serializable a => (a -> Bool) -> (Message -> Process b) -> Match b :` Matches with an arbitrary message. A message is removed from the mailbox if it meets the supplied condition.

Also, you saw how processes and messages work in Cloud Haskell, how unexpected messages are handled, and how channels communicate.

CHAPTER 10

■ ■ ■

Haskell in Big Data

We have already discussed big data in Chapter 8. In this chapter, we provide a deeper overview of big data and its challenges. This chapter covers how data is generated, and presents some of the tools and methods used in big data. It also presents an example of MapReduce in Haskell.

More About Big Data

Usually, when we work with data, we need to accomplish mainly four steps: generation, collection, storage, and analysis of data (the latter is covered in the "MapReduce in Haskell" section).

Data Generation

The first stage in big data is the generation of data. The Internet is full of data. We can see it everywhere: searches, posts on different forums, registers of conversations, and much more. By analyzing data available on the Internet, we can learn much. Taken individually, we can discover the habits of a user, but taken as a whole, we can discover different trends, habits, or even emotional facts through sentiment analysis. The data is complex and diverse because it is obtained from different locations around the world and the sources are distributed. At this moment, the main origins of big data are operations and commercial data from companies, logistic and sensors data from the Internet of Things (IoT), social platforms, and data from the research fields, among others. This amount of data cannot be handled by traditional IT architectures and infrastructures. Moreover, it cannot be analyzed using traditional systems.

Data from Companies

In 2013, IBM published an analysis, called "The Applications of Big Data to the Real World," which concluded that an important source of big data is represented by companies, whose data refer to commercial or analysis data. Most of it is static and represents historical data, structured and handled by relational database management systems (RDBMS). An important quantity of it is internal data constituted by production, inventory, sales, and financial data.

A large amount of data has been generated in the last few years. It is predicted that the data generated by businesses doubles every 1.2 years, so there is a need for systems that performs data in real time, so that this data is valuable. A good example is Amazon, which performs a large number of terminal operations (millions of orders) and more than 500,000 queries daily. Other examples are Walmart or Akamai.

© Stefania Loredana Nita and Marius Mihailescu 2017
S. L. Nita and M. Mihailescu, *Practical Concurrent Haskell*, DOI 10.1007/978-1-4842-2781-7_10

IoT Data

The IoT is another important generator of data. The use of sensors has increased in the last few years. They generate a lot of data, provided by smart cities, in areas like industrial enterprises, agriculture, medical records, and so forth. Data generated by the IoT have the following characteristics.

- *Large scale*. The distributed deployment is used to handle large amounts of data.

- *Variated*. Data is collected from different devices (PCs, laptops, tablets, smartphones, etc.), so it is naturally diverse.

- *Time-space correlated*. Data generated by sensors can be geographically located and attaches the time it is generated. This is useful in statistics and analysis, and may provide accurate information about specific geographical areas.

Biomedical Data

Biological processes could be better understood by creating smart, effective, and precise models and theoretical environments. This data is very useful because it can be used for predictions, for determining the states of systems, or even decision making. Big data has many applications in the biomedical field; for example, in the Human Genome Project, where data generated by sequencing genes are exposed to special analysis, depending on the application requirements (the combination of different chemical products, diagnosis, individual treatment, etc.). The total amount of rough data collected from the sequencing of a human gene could reach 100,600 gigabytes.

Data Generation from Other Fields

Research areas have undergone many improvements through the development of techniques and technologies to acquire data that can be easily analyzed. The following are examples of science fields collecting large amounts of data.

- *Biology*. The GenBank database contains nucleotide sequences. New data is released every two months. According to the GenBank website (`https://www.ncbi.nlm.nih.gov/genbank`): "GenBank release 218.0 (2/13/2017) has 199,341,377 traditional records containing 228,719,437,638 base pairs of sequence data. In addition, there are 409,490,397 WGS records containing 1,892,966,308,635 base pairs of sequence data, 151,431,485 TSA records containing 133,517,212,104 base pairs of sequence data, as well as 1,438,349 TLS records containing 636,923,295 base pairs of sequence data. ... uncompressed GenBank Release 216.0 flat files require approximately 818 GB (sequence files only)."

- *Astronomy*. The Sloan Digital Sky Survey (SDSS), the biggest project in astronomy, has generated 25 TB (1 TB = 1 000 000 000 000 bytes) of data since 2008; but with improvements in the image quality of its telescope, it is expected that the amount of data collected every night to be greater than 20 TB.

- *Physics*. The Large Hadron Collider (2008 Atlas project) generated 2 PB (1 PB = 1 000 000 000 000 000 bytes) of data per second; in a year, it collected 10 TB of operated data.

Data Collection

After data is generated, the next step is to collect it from different sources. The following are data collection approaches.

- *Log files.* The system that represents the origin of data generates automatic log files at a certain time. Usually, the log files contain information about activities on that system. For example, web servers usually have three types of log files that contain information about users' behaviors: public format (NCSA), expanded format (W3C), and IIS format (Microsoft)—all in ASCII format. Sometimes, log information is stored in databases because the queries are more efficient. Also, log information could be financial data, or traffic from a network.

- *Detection.* Sensors are used to detect a certain type of data and to transmit it through a channel to a collecting site.

- *Techniques for collecting data.* Includes web crawlers (used in search systems when web pages are downloaded and stored), systems for word segmentation, tasks, and index systems.

We will not continue to talk about how data is transmitted to storage systems. Next, we discuss some of the tools for big data storage.

Data Storage

In big data, the main approach of data storage is distributed storage systems, which make use of more servers for data storage and copies of data. Commonly, data is fragmented into lower pieces that are stored on different servers. The storage systems need to have at least the following characteristics.

- *Consistency.* This ensures that all copies of the same original data are the same.

- *Availability.* This ensures that data is available anytime, even in the event of a server or virtual machine failure. This is the reason why data is fragmented and copies of the same data are stored at different locations.

- *Fault tolerance.* This ensures that the data is available and can be managed even if there is a network failure.

Big data storage systems have three levels on the top of the architecture.

- File systems represent the way in which files on a storage systems are named, the logical place of their storage, how they could be retrieved, and so on. Examples of file systems include GFS (Google File System) and Colossus from Google. HDFS (Hadoop Data File System) and Kosmosfs are open source and derived from GFS, Cosmos from Microsoft, Haystack from Facebook, and so forth.

- Traditional databases are collections of data organized (generally they are stored into tables) to be easily manipulated. In the last few years, however, NoSQL (Not Only SQL) databases, which are not relational, are being used more and more. Their targets are large sets of distributed data. You will see some examples of NoSQL databases in the next subsection.

- Programming models represent sets of concepts used for creating software applications. MapReduce is a well-known example of this programming model.

Database Technology

Because traditional database systems cannot handle big data, NoSQL database systems were developed to do it and they become the central part of big data. There are three categories of NoSQL databases.

- *Key-valued databases* are a basic data model, in which data is stored with corresponding keys. These keys are distinct and queries are based on their values. Examples of such databases include Dynamo, used by Amazon, and Voldemort, used by LinkedIn.

- *Column-oriented databases* are similar to traditional databases, but their focus is on queries of columns, rather than rows. Examples are BigTable from Google; Cassandra, initially developed by Facebook, now open source; and HBase and HyperTable, which are open source versions of BigTable. The HBase programming language is Java, and it represents a component of Apache Hadoop.

- *Document-oriented databases* allow you to store complex data, but also provide the facility to store keys for data. Examples include MongoDB, which stores data in the form of Binary JSON (BSON); SimpleDB; and Apache CouchDB written in Erlang.

Models and Tools

As you have seen, big data represents large volumes of complex data, stored in a distributed manner. The classical parallel models (Message Passing Interface (MPI), Open Multi-Processing (OpenMP)) cannot handle big data very well, so the development of another model was needed. The following are the most used models and systems in big data.

- *MapReduce.* This programming model is very simple, but also very useful in large-scale computing with many clusters of PCs. MapReduce has only two main functions: map and reduce, which need to be written by a programmer. The input for the map function is a list of pairs of key-value form, and the output is an intermediary list of such pairs. The next step is a combination of the values that have the same key, and transmitting to the reduce function, whose task is to reduce the dimension of the input, which results in a smaller list.

- *Dryad.* The main structure is a directional acyclic graph, with vertexes representing programs and edges representing channels. The operations are executed on nodes, and data is sent through channels.

- *All-Pairs.* This was developed especially for biometrics, bioinformatics, and datamining. In a few words, the main approach is to compare pair elements from different data sets according to a given function.

- *Pregel.* This was developed by Google with the purpose to process graphs with a high size. There are other differences between Dryad and Pregel, but the difference regarding parallelism is that in Pregel, the functions of users are executed concurrently over vertices within a super step; whereas in Dryad, vertices are executed concurrently over a stage.

MapReduce in Haskell

The examples in this section belong to authors of http://www.well-typed.com/blog. As you have seen, MapReduce works with pairs of key-value forms, which result after applying a compressed list of such pairs on both functions. In Haskell, the type of algorithm is

```
-- The type of Map-Reduce skeletons (provided by the user)
data MapReduce k1 v1 k2 v2 v3 = MapReduce {
    mrMap    :: k1 -> v1 -> [(k2, v2)]
  , mrReduce :: k2 -> [v2] -> v3
  }

-- A Map-Reduce skeleton by the driver
localMapReduce :: Ord k2 => MapReduce k1 v1 k2 v2 v3 -> Map k1 v1 -> Map k2 v3
```

In the beginning, a map is as key-value, where the keys have type k1 and the values have type v1. Using "Map" (i.e., mrMap), the pairs are transformed into a list of pairs, where keys have type k2 and values have type v2. An important observation is that the resulting list could contain more pairs with the same keys, which is very possible in practice. The MapReduce driver brings together all values for the same key, and then, "Reduce" (mrReduce) reduces the list of values whose type is v2 to a single value, whose type is v3.

Let's suppose that we want to count the number of words in more documents; that is, we want to turn the MapReduce FilePath Document into Word Frequency. Let's use the following.

```
{-# LANGUAGE TupleSections #-}
countWords :: MapReduce FilePath Document Word Frequency Frequency
countWords = MapReduce {
    mrMap    = const (map (, 1) . words)
  , mrReduce = const sum
  }
```

Next, we use a master-slave approach of Cloud Haskell, in which slaves nodes handle Map, and the tasks are distributed through work stealing. Reduce is performed only on a single machine, so it will not be distributed. In the following example of counting words, the implementation of MapReduce is monomorphic. So, the slave nodes require tasks that are executed using mrMap from the MapReduce skeleton.

```
mapperProcess :: (ProcessId, ProcessId, Closure (MapReduce String String String Int Int))
              -> Process ()
mapperProcess (master, workQueue, mrClosure) = do
    us <- getSelfPid
    mr <- unClosure mrClosure
    go us mr
  where
    go us mr = do
      -- Ask the queue for work
      send workQueue us

      -- Wait for a reply; if there is work, do it and repeat; otherwise, exit
      receiveWait
        [ match $ \(key, val) -> send master (mrMap mr key val) >> go us mr
        , match $ \()         -> return ()
        ]

remotable ['mapperProcess]
```

Let's observe that slaves need a `Closure` of MapReduce skeleton, which is not serializable because it has functions.

The following is the implementation for the master.

```
distrMapReduce :: Closure (MapReduce String String String Int Int)
                  -> [NodeId]
                  -> Map String String
                  -> Process (Map String Int)
distrMapReduce mrClosure mappers input = do
  mr     <- unClosure mrClosure
  master <- getSelfPid

  workQueue <- spawnLocal $ do
    -- Return the next bit of work to be done
    forM_ (Map.toList input) $ \(key, val) -> do
      them <- expect
      send them (key, val)

    -- Once all the work is done tell the mappers to terminate
    replicateM_ (length mappers) $ do
      them <- expect
      send them ()

  -- Start the mappers
  forM_ mappers $ \nid -> spawn nid ($(mkClosure 'mapperProcess) (master, workQueue,
  mrClosure))

  -- Wait for the partial results
  partials <- replicateM (Map.size input) expect

  -- We reduce on this node
  return (reducePerKey mr . groupByKey . concat $ partials)
```

The following is the rest of the implementation, in which the words are counted.

```
countWords_ :: MapReduce FilePath Document Word Frequency Frequency
countWords_ = countWords

remotable ['countWords_]

distrCountWords :: [NodeId] -> Map FilePath Document -> Process (Map Word Frequency)
distrCountWords = distrMapReduce ($(mkClosure 'countWords_) ())
```

Next, we present another example, which implements the k-means algorithm in a MapReduce approach. The k-means algorithm classifies a set of elements into n classes. It performs the steps a chosen number of times or until it converges.

- The algorithm has n cluster centers. Every point in the set choses a center to which the distance between the current point and the center is minimum.

- For every new cluster, compute the new center.

The initial centers could be randomly chosen.

Of course, the choice of initial centers has an impact on the results. Figure 10-3 applies the same k-means and over the same points, but with another initial center.

MapReduce is used for one iteration of k-means. The task for every node in the map is the first step of k-means. In the reduce step, the new centers of the clusters are implemented.

```haskell
type Point    = (Double, Double)
type Cluster  = (Double, Double)

average :: Fractional a => [a] -> a
average xs = sum xs / fromIntegral (length xs)

distanceSq :: Point -> Point -> Double
distanceSq (x1, y1) (x2, y2) = a * a + b * b
  where
    a = x2 - x1
    b = y2 - y1

nearest :: Point -> [Cluster] -> Cluster
nearest p = minimumBy (compare `on` distanceSq p)

center :: [Point] -> Point
center ps = let (xs, ys) = unzip ps in (average xs, average ys)

kmeans :: Array Int Point -> MapReduce (Int, Int) [Cluster] Cluster Point ([Point], Point)
kmeans points = MapReduce {
    mrMap    = \(lo, hi) cs -> [ let p = points ! i in (nearest p cs, p)
                              | i <- [lo .. hi]
                              ]
  , mrReduce = \_ ps -> (ps, center ps)
  }
```

The beginning is Map (Int, Int) [Cluster]. The input set contains the segmentation, which has corresponding keys in this map. For example, the key (20, 39) shows that clusters should be computed for [20..39] by the mapper. The current centers are just the values from this map.

Next, a list of type [(Cluster, Point)] that contains the association between points and clusters is obtained. In the reduce step, Map Cluster ([Point], Point) is created. It provides a set of points and the center for every cluster.

This implementation allows only a single iteration of k-means, but in reality, we need to iterate more than once. The following is a version in that allows more iterations.

```haskell
localKMeans :: Array Int Point
           -> [Cluster]
           -> Int
           -> Map Cluster ([Point], Point)
localKMeans points cs iterations = go (iterations - 1)
  where
    mr :: [Cluster] -> Map Cluster ([Point], Point)
    mr = localMapReduce (kmeans points) . trivialSegmentation
```

```
go :: Int -> Map Cluster ([Point], Point)
go 0 = mr cs
go n =  mr $ snd <$> (Map.elems $ go (n-1))

trivialSegmentation :: [Cluster] -> Map (Int, Int) [Cluster]
trivialSegmentation cs' = Map.fromList [(bounds points, cs')]
```

You have observed that the set of points remains the same in every iteration; but it should be spread out by map nodes. The following are the jobs of the master process in the example.

- Initialization of mappers

- Managing the MapReduce process

- Termination of mappers

The type of `distrMapReduce` is changed to

```
distrMapReduce :: Closure (MapReduce (Point, Point) [Cluster] Cluster
                                      Point ([Point], Point))
               -> [NodeId]
               -> ((Map (Point, Point) [Cluster] ->
                    Process (Map Cluster ([Point], Point))) -> Process a)
               -> Process a
```

In this piece of code, `distrMapReduce mrClosure mappers p`, the process p is used to manage map-reduce tasks.

This modification is useful, but the whole set of point is transmitted to all nodes, even when the nodes operates only on a subset. As a hint, the MapReduce driver needs generalization.

Polymorphic Implementation

Previously, we changed the type of `distrMapReduce`, because it was necessary that the type of the MapReduce skeleton be matched in the word-counting example. The type could be changed without changing the implementation. The following is the polymorphic version of `distrMapreduce`.

```
distrMapReduce :: (Serializable k1, Serializable v1, Serializable k2,
                   Serializable v2, Serializable v3, Ord k2)
               => Closure (MapReduce k1 v1 k2 v2 v3)
               -> [NodeId]
               -> ((Map k1 v1 -> Process (Map k2 v3)) -> Process a)
               -> Process a
```

Anyway, there is a little problem with the generalization. Let's think about mappers in the general form. What do they need to do? Well, at first sight, it should expect a message that has a specific type. For type matching, it should know something about the type (k1, v1). The next step is to send a list whose type is [(k2, v2)] to the master when a message comes. This is possible only when the map knows the way it could serialize the values with type [(k2, v2)].

`distrMapReduce` obtains this information from the `Serializable` type class's constraints. Unfortunately, in Haskell there is no explicit way such that the arguments to be handled, even more providing a way for serializing them for being shipped to the mapper nodes. We can define a type class constraint as an explicit dictionary, however.

```
data SerializableDict a where
    SerializableDict :: Serializable a => SerializableDict a
```

The objects whose type is SerializableDict cannot be directly serialized, but static SerializableDicts can. So, definition of serializing become:

```
distrMapReduce :: forall k1 k2 v1 v2 v3 a.
                   (Serializable k1, Serializable v1, Serializable k2,
                    Serializable v2, Serializable v3, Ord k2)
               => Static (SerializableDict (k1, v1))
               -> Static (SerializableDict [(k2, v2)])
               -> Closure (MapReduce k1 v1 k2 v2 v3)
               -> [NodeId]
               -> ((Map k1 v1 -> Process (Map k2 v3)) -> Process a)
               -> Process a
```

Maybe it is a little complicated, but the change is requiring static type information to ship this type of information to the mappers. We omitted the implementation. It could be found in distributed-process-demos package; the basic principles are explained in the documentation of the distributed-static package.

The polymorphic version of distrMapReduce has the same difficulty as monomorphic version; for example, "distributed word counting" can be implemented as follows.

```
dictIn :: SerializableDict (FilePath, Document)
dictIn = SerializableDict

dictOut :: SerializableDict [(Word, Frequency)]
dictOut = SerializableDict

countWords_ :: () -> MapReduce FilePath Document Word Frequency Frequency
countWords_ () = countWords

remotable ['dictIn, 'dictOut, 'countWords_]

distrCountWords :: [NodeId] -> Map FilePath Document -> Process (Map Word Frequency)
distrCountWords mappers input =
  distrMapReduce $(mkStatic 'dictIn)
                 $(mkStatic 'dictOut)
                 ($(mkClosure 'countWords_) ())
                 mappers
                 (\iteration -> iteration input)
```

Creating the necessary SerializableDicts is easy (there is only one constructor for SerializableDict, and it doesn't take any arguments!). Note that the word *counter* only calls the iteration function once; this will not be true for distributed k-means.

Distributed k-means

The following presents the distributed version of k-means. There are not very many modifications to the initial (local) implementation: go is added, and the rest (segments, dividePoints, pointsPerMapper, and numPoints) show where every segment needs to go to the corresponding node from map.

```haskell
dictIn :: SerializableDict ((Int, Int), [Cluster])
dictIn = SerializableDict

dictOut :: SerializableDict [(Cluster, Point)]
dictOut = SerializableDict

remotable ['kmeans, 'dictIn, 'dictOut]

distrKMeans :: Array Int Point
            -> [Cluster]
            -> [NodeId]
            -> Int
            -> Process (Map Cluster ([Point], Point))
distrKMeans points cs mappers iterations =
    distrMapReduce $(mkStatic 'dictIn)
                  $(mkStatic 'dictOut)
                  ($(mkClosure 'kmeans) points)
                  mappers
                  (go (iterations - 1))
  where
    go :: Int
       -> (Map (Int, Int) [Cluster] -> Process (Map Cluster ([Point], Point)))
       -> Process (Map Cluster ([Point], Point))
    go 0 iteration = do
      iteration (Map.fromList $ map (, cs) segments)
    go n iteration = do
      clusters <- go (n - 1) iteration
      let centers = map snd $ Map.elems clusters
      iteration (Map.fromList $ map (, centers) segments)

    segments :: [(Int, Int)]
    segments = let (lo, _) = bounds points in dividePoints numPoints lo

    dividePoints :: Int -> Int -> [(Int, Int)]
    dividePoints pointsLeft offset
      | pointsLeft <= pointsPerMapper = [(offset, offset + pointsLeft - 1)]
      | otherwise = let offset' = offset + pointsPerMapper in
                    (offset, offset' - 1)
                  : dividePoints (pointsLeft - pointsPerMapper) offset'

    pointsPerMapper :: Int
    pointsPerMapper =
      ceiling (toRational numPoints / toRational (length mappers))

    numPoints :: Int
    numPoints = let (lo, hi) = bounds points in hi - lo + 1
```

Summary

In this chapter, you saw

- the stages through which data (from structured and unstructured data sets) needs to pass to retrieve relevant information.

- two examples of the MapReduce programming model used in Haskell.

■ ■ ■

CHAPTER 11

Concurrency Design Patterns

In this chapter, we have chosen to present the most common problems that could occur in big data applications. One of best solutions to these problems is to use design patterns. Research contributions in functional programming continue to be made in this area, including attempts to make functional versions of OOP design patterns. Haskell is a very good programming language for big data, but some of patterns have implementations only in object-oriented programing languages. This is not an impediment for using both Haskell and design patterns, however, because they could be easily made interoperable, as you will see in this chapter. A good design pattern reference is *Design Patterns: Elements of Reusable Object-Oriented Software* by Erich Gamma, Richard Helm, Ralph Johnson, and John Vlissides (also known as the Gang of Four) (Addison-Wesley Professional, 1994).

The least difficult approach to portraying a pattern is to give a demonstrated solution for a typical issue separately archived in a reliable configuration and as a feature of a bigger collection. Patterns are now considered a principal part of daily existence. Without always recognizing it, we actually utilize design patterns to take care of basic problems every day.

Design pattern are very useful because they

- solve ordinary design issues.

- create projections based on standards and using intuitive formats.

- are used in designing applications by many IT professionals.

- assure consistency in systems.

- can be used as fundamentals for design standards.

- can be adapted in particular situations.

- can be used in collaboration with other design patterns in the same application.

Besides, because solutions are tested and their performance is demonstrated, their reliable application has a tendency to actually enhance the nature of framework outlines.

Despite the fact that design patterns give demonstrated solutions, this does not ensure that outline issues will always be resolved. There are many reasons to utilize design patterns, including constraints forced by the implementation platform, the competency of the specialists, wandering business necessities, and so forth. These aspects influence the degree to which the pattern is effectively used.

A *pattern language* is a suite of related patterns that go about creating blocks that can be used in at least one example application where every subsequent pattern expands upon the former. The thought of a pattern language began in building engineering as the expression "pattern sequence."

Big data design patterns are an open-ended, master pattern language. The degree to which diverse patterns are connected can change, yet are general enough to share a target, and interminable example successions can be investigated. This chapter provides implementation for patterns in Haskell, Java, and C++. Java or C++ code can be easily implemented in Haskell. This mechanism of integrating code written

© Stefania Loredana Nita and Marius Mihailescu 2017
S. L. Nita and M. Mihailescu, *Practical Concurrent Haskell*, DOI 10.1007/978-1-4842-2781-7_11

in another programming language than the base programming language used to develop an application, is called Foreign Function Interface (FFI).

Java code could be integrated using the inline-java package. The following is a short piece of code in which the message "Hello World!" is displayed in a message dialog control. For a comprehensive tutorial, please visit https://github.com/tweag/inline-java/.

```
{-# LANGUAGE DataKinds #-}
{-# LANGUAGE QuasiQuotes #-}
{-# LANGUAGE ScopedTypeVariables #-}
module Main where

import Data.Int
import Language.Java
import Language.Java.Inline

main :: IO Int32
main = withJVM [] $ do
    message <- reflect "Hello World!"
    [java| { javax.swing.JOptionPane.showMessageDialog(null, $message);
             return 0; } |]
```

The CPlusPlus library is used for integrating C++ in Haskell. For a comprehensive description, please visit https://wiki.haskell.org/CPlusPlus_from_Haskell.

Active Object

The active object design pattern separates a method execution from its invocation of the object, such that both invocation and execution have its own thread of control. The purpose is to use concurrency. This is done utilizing an asynchronous method invocation and a program to handle solicitations. The following lists the components of this pattern.

- The proxy (*resource*) that supplies an interface for users with public methods

- The *client interface* that establishes the method request applied over an active object

- The list (*message queue*) that contains awaiting requests from users

- The *scheduler* (program) that choses the next request that should be executed

- The implementation (*method representation*) of the active object method

- The variable used for the user to get the result

Now let's see what an active object is. We say that objects are active if their states depend on a clock. The state of an object is updated by a task encapsulated by that object. To avoid the corruption of the object's state, the methods should be synchronized with the task that updates the state.

The following is an implementation of active object pattern in Haskell.

```
data Set a = Empty | Add a (Set a)

pat Add' x _ =
  Add y s => if x==y then Add y s
             else let Add' x t = s
                  in Add x (Add y t)
```

```
delete x (Add' x s) = s
delete x s          = s
```

Next, we present an example that implements an active integrator object. It has an input that is set using the Input method, a function of time. The output is obtained by calling the Output method. As an example, if the input is $K(t)$ and the output is S, the object state S is modified in $S + (K(t1) + K(t0)) \times (t1 - t0) \div 2$; that is, it integrates K using the trapeze method. Initially, K is constant 0 and S is 0.

We will test the object as follows.

1. The input is $\sin(2\pi\,f\,t)$, with the frequency $f = 0.5$ Hz. The phase could be anything.

2. Wait for two seconds.

3. Reset the input to 0.

4. Wait for 0.5 seconds.

Now check if the output of the object is 0. Of course, the accuracy is dependent on the scheduler time of the operating system and the accuracy of the clock. The following is the implementation (also available at https://rosettacode.org/wiki/Active_object#Haskell).

```
module Integrator (newIntegrator, input, output, stop, Time, timeInterval)
 where
import Control.Concurrent (forkIO, threadDelay)
import Control.Concurrent.MVar (MVar, newMVar, modifyMVar_, modifyMVar, readMVar)
import Control.Exception (evaluate)
import Data.Time (UTCTime)
import Data.Time.Clock (getCurrentTime, diffUTCTime)

-- RC task
main = do let f = 0.5 {- Hz -}
          t0 <- getCurrentTime
          i <- newIntegrator
          input i (\t -> sin(2*pi * f * timeInterval t0 t)) -- task step 1
          threadDelay 2000000 {- µs -}                      -- task step 2
          input i (const 0)                                 -- task step 3
          threadDelay 500000 {- µs -}                       -- task step 4
          result <- output i
          stop i
          print result

---- Implementation ------------------------------------------------------

-- Utilities for working with the time type
type Time = UTCTime
type Func a = Time -> a
timeInterval t0 t1 = realToFrac $ diffUTCTime t1 t0

-- Type signatures of the module's interface
newIntegrator :: Fractional a => IO (Integrator a) -- Create an integrator
input  :: Integrator a -> Func a -> IO ()        -- Set the input function
output :: Integrator a          -> IO a          -- Get the current value
stop   :: Integrator a          -> IO ()         -- Stop integration, don't waste CPU
```

```
-- Data structures
data Integrator a = Integrator (MVar (IntState a)) -- MVar is a thread-safe mutable cell
  deriving Eq
data IntState a = IntState { func  :: Func a,       -- The current function
                             run   :: Bool,          -- Whether to keep going
                             value :: a,             -- The current accumulated value
                             time  :: Time }         -- The time of the previous update

newIntegrator = do
  now <- getCurrentTime
  state <- newMVar $ IntState { func  = const 0,
                                run   = True,
                                value = 0,
                                time  = now }
  thread <- forkIO (intThread state)  -- The state variable is shared between the thread
  return (Integrator state)           --   and the client interface object.

input  (Integrator stv) f = modifyMVar_ stv (\st -> return st { func = f })
output (Integrator stv)   = fmap value $ readMVar stv
stop   (Integrator stv)   = modifyMVar_ stv (\st -> return st { run = False })
  -- modifyMVar_ takes an MVar and replaces its contents according to the provided function.
  -- a { b = c } is record-update syntax: "the record a, except with field b changed to c"

-- Integration thread
intThread :: Fractional a => MVar (IntState a) -> IO ()
intThread stv = whileM $ modifyMVar stv updateAndCheckRun
  -- modifyMVar is like modifyMVar_ but the function returns a tuple of the new value
  -- and an arbitrary extra value, which in this case ends up telling whileM whether
  -- to keep looping.
  where updateAndCheckRun st = do
          now <- getCurrentTime
          let value' = integrate (func st) (value st) (time st) now
          evaluate value'                            -- avoid undesired laziness
          return (st { value = value', time  = now }, -- updated state
                  run st)                             -- whether to continue

integrate :: Fractional a => Func a -> a -> Time -> Time -> a
integrate f value t0 t1 = value + (f t0 + f t1)/2 * dt
  where dt = timeInterval t0 t1

-- Execute 'action' until it returns false.
whileM action = do b <- action; if b then whileM action else return ()
```

Balking Pattern

A balking pattern is used when we need to call a method of an object only when the object is in a particular state. This pattern is typically used on objects that could balk temporarily, but the time of balking is not known.

In most applications, a balking pattern is used with a single-threaded execution pattern. It is useful in helping coordinate an object's changes in a certain state. (A single-threaded execution pattern is used when many readers and many writers operate on a single resource).

The following is a general implementation (see https://en.wikipedia.org/wiki/Balking_pattern).

```
public class Example {
    private boolean jobInProgress = false;

    public void job() {
        synchronized(this) {
            if (jobInProgress) {
                return;
            }
            jobInProgress = true;
        }
        // Code to execute job goes here
        // ...
    }

    void jobCompleted() {
        synchronized(this) {
            jobInProgress = false;
        }
    }
}
```

If the jobInProgress variable has a false value, then no command is executed. job() simply returns, so the state of the object does not change. On the other hand, when jobInProgress has a true value, the Example object has the right state and it is able for executing the code from job().

This pattern is very useful when working with big data—namely, a large amount of data—because it can tell us if a job was correctly executed or not at certain time intervals. For example, a search for particular data in terabytes within an application would be useful to know if jobs were executed at certain intervals of time. Still, it should be used when the balking time is unknown. In situations where the time is known, a better choice would be a guarded suspension pattern.

Barrier

Concurrent and parallel programming could be very useful in many applications. You can do a lot with only a little number of threads, but what about if you increase the number of threads?

Well, this could lead to a disaster, because the performance could be dramatically decreased. The following could happen when there are too many threads: opening and closing threads could become more expensive than actually worthwhile, if the amount of work is relatively small; or, an overhead could occur when are shared fixed hardware resources.

Another type of overhead is virtual memory. Many systems have virtual memory, in which the processors contain an address space larger than the actual available memory. It lives on the disk and is used similarly to caches. Threads need virtual memory for the stack and private data structures. When there are a large number of threads, they "fight" for the actual memory, which decreases performance.

Another problem could occur when access to the shred memory is not synchronized, so the threads are in a continuous race, which leads to a deadlock.

In some applications, there are threads that need to have a higher priority than others. When memory is insufficient to run all threads, the threads with higher priorities get preference. Prioritizing threads could be useful, but you need to pay attention to a potential situation in which a thread with low priority blocks a thread with high priority.

A barriers is a solution to (some of) these problems. A barrier is a synchronization mechanism that lets you "corral" several cooperating threads (e.g., in a matrix computation), forcing them to wait at a specific point. All must finish before any one thread can continue.

The following is an example in which barriers are used to implement a matrix multiplication. implemented by Aliaksey Artamonau, also available at https://github.com/aartamonau/haskell-barrier/blob/master/examples/MatrixMultiplication.hs.

```
{-# LANGUAGE TupleSections #-}

import Control.Concurrent ( forkIO )
import Control.Monad ( mapM, mapM_, forM_ )
import Data.Array.IO ( IOUArray )
import Data.Array.MArray ( MArray (getBounds, newArray_),
                           readArray, writeArray, newListArray )

import Text.Printf ( printf )

--| This is from concurrent-barrier package
import Control.Concurrent.Barrier ( Barrier )
import qualified Control.Concurrent.Barrier as Barrier

-- | Matrix is just an unboxed mutable array of doubles.
type Matrix = IOUArray (Int, Int) Double

-- | Multiplies two matrixes. Spawns bunch of threads. Each thread computes one
-- element of a resulting matrix.
multiply :: Matrix -> Matrix -> IO Matrix
multiply a b = do
  (_, (ah, aw)) <- getBounds a
  (_, (bh, bw)) <- getBounds b

  result  <- newArray_ ((1, 1), (ah, bw))
  barrier <- Barrier.new (ah * bw + 1)

  let worker row col = do
        rs <- mapM (readArray a) (map (row,) [1 .. aw])
        cs <- mapM (readArray b) (map (,col) [1 .. bh])

        writeArray result (row, col) (sum $ zipWith (*) rs cs)

        Barrier.wait barrier

  mapM_ forkIO $ map (uncurry worker) [(i, j) | i <- [1 .. ah], j <- [1 .. bw]]

  Barrier.wait barrier

  return result

-- | Builds a matrix from list of lists.
matrix :: [[Double]] -> IO Matrix
matrix a = newListArray ((1, 1), (m, n)) (concat a)
```

```
  where m = length a
        n = length $ head a

-- | Dumps matrix to stdout.
dump :: String -> Matrix -> IO ()
dump heading a = do
  (_, (m, n)) <- getBounds a

  printf "%s:\n" heading

  forM_ [1 .. m] $ \i -> do
    forM_ [1 .. n] $ \j -> do
      v <- readArray a (i, j)

      printf "%10.2f " v
    printf "\n"

main :: IO ()
main = do
  a <- matrix [[1, 2, 3, 4, 5],
               [6, 7, 8, 9, 10]]
  b <- matrix [[1, 2],
               [3, 4],
               [5, 6],
               [7, 8],
               [9, 10]]

  dump "A" a
  dump "B" b

  r <- multiply a b

dump "Result" r
```

Disruptor

The disruptor pattern was developed by LMAX, a UK-based multilateral trading facility. It acts as a foreign exchange aggregator for trading. The LMAX team's studies shown that the classical approach of concurrent and parallel programming leads to a high level of latency in "Disruptor: High Performance Alternative to Bounded Queues for Exchanging Data Between Concurrent Threads" by Martin Thompson et al. (https://lmax-exchange.github.io/disruptor/files/Disruptor-1.0.pdf). This happens because many software applications require data from queues that need to be exchanged in different levels of processing. The more queues in the process, the more global latency is increased by hundreds of microseconds. Tests have shown that the latency is three times less in a pipeline with three stages using the disruptor pattern than the classical approach. Also, the throughput is eight times greater on the same configuration.

The concurrency is about running tasks in parallel, but also that tasks have access to the same resources. You have seen that it is characterized by reciprocal exclusion and the visibility of modifications, which include read/write operations. Of course, the write operation is the most expensive, and managing more threads that write on the same resource is very complex and costly. The traditional approach in this case is to use a lock.

The disruptor pattern is projected so that it maximizes the performance of memory allocation, and works in a cache-friendly way. The main component of the disruptor is a ring buffer that is a pre-allocated linked data structure. One or many producers add the data into the ring, and it is processed by one or many consumers. The concurrency in a disruptor pattern is handled through sequencing.

First, it creates a dependency graph. Then, through ProducerBarrier, the producers ask for entries in sequence. Next, the modifications are written in the asked entries, and the changes are saved through ProducerBarrier, available to all. The consumer just needs to implement BatchHandler, in which callbacks are received if a novel entry is disposable. The RingBuffer is the main component; it provides resources when data is exchanged without contention. ProducerBarrier is developed to handle concurrency when slots of ring buffers are asked; it prevents ring buffer congestion. The consumers, which belong to a graph of dependencies, are notified by ConsumerBarrier if a new entry is disposable. The original implementation is in Java.

The disruptor pattern was proven faster than traditional approaches. The original version of the disruptor pattern is written in Java. The following is an implementation from the original article (https://lmax-exchange.github.io/disruptor/files/Disruptor-1.0.pdf).

```
// Callback handler which can be implemented by consumers
final BatchHandler<ValueEntry> batchHandler = new BatchHandler<ValueEntry>()
{
    public void onAvailable(final ValueEntry entry) throws Exception
    {
        // process a new entry as it becomes available.
    }
    public void onEndOfBatch() throws Exception
    {
        // useful for flushing results to an IO device if necessary.
    }
    public void onCompletion()
    {
        // do any necessary clean up before shutdown
    }
};
RingBuffer<ValueEntry> ringBuffer = new RingBuffer<ValueEntry>(ValueEntry.ENTRY_FACTORY, SIZE,
                                    ClaimStrategy.Option.SINGLE_THREADED,
                                    WaitStrategy.Option.YIELDING);
ConsumerBarrier<ValueEntry> consumerBarrier = ringBuffer.createConsumerBarrier();
BatchConsumer<ValueEntry> batchConsumer = new BatchConsumer<ValueEntry>(consumerBarrier,
                                    batchHandler);
ProducerBarrier<ValueEntry> producerBarrier = ringBuffer.createProducerBarrier(batchConsumer);
// Each consumer can run on a separate thread
EXECUTOR.submit(batchConsumer);
// Producers claim entries in sequence
ValueEntry entry = producerBarrier.nextEntry();
// copy data into the entry container
// make the entry available to consumers
producerBarrier.commit(entry);
```

The following is Kim Altintop's implementation of RingBuffer in Haskell (for the complete project, please visit https://github.com/kim/data-ringbuffer).

```
{-# LANGUAGE RecordWildCards #-}

module Data.RingBuffer
    ( newMultiProducerRingBuffer
    , newSingleProducerRingBuffer
    , consumeWith
    , andAlso
    , andThen
    , start
    , stop
    , publish
    , publishMany
    )
where

import                Control.Concurrent
import                Control.Monad                (forM_, liftM, when)
import                Control.Monad.Catch          (finally)
import                Data.IORef
import                Data.RingBuffer.RingBuffer   (RingBuffer, elemAt,
                                                     mkRingBuffer)
import qualified      Data.RingBuffer.RingBuffer   as RB
import                Data.RingBuffer.Sequence
import                Data.RingBuffer.SequenceBarrier
import                Data.RingBuffer.Sequencer     ( SingleProducer
                                                    , MultiProducer
                                                    , mkMultiProducerSequencer
                                                    , mkSingleProducerSequencer
                                                    )

data Consumer m a s
    = Consumer (a -> IO ())
                -- ^ event processing action
               !Sequence
                -- ^ tracks which events were consumed by this 'Consumer'
               !(SequenceBarrier s)
                -- ^ barrier tracking producers and/or prerequisite handlers

data ConsumerGroup m a s = ConsumerGroup
    { rb :: RingBuffer a s
    , pr :: Maybe (ConsumerGroup m a s)
    , hs :: [Consumer m a s]
    }

data Disruptor a s = Disruptor (RingBuffer a s) [ThreadId] (IORef Bool)

newMultiProducerRingBuffer :: Int -> IO a -> IO (RingBuffer a MultiProducer)
newMultiProducerRingBuffer siz fill = do
    sqr <- mkMultiProducerSequencer siz []
    mkRingBuffer sqr fill
```

```haskell
newSingleProducerRingBuffer :: Int -> IO a -> IO (RingBuffer a SingleProducer)
newSingleProducerRingBuffer siz fill = do
    sqr <- mkSingleProducerSequencer siz []
    mkRingBuffer sqr fill

consumeWith :: (a -> IO ()) -> RingBuffer a s -> IO (ConsumerGroup m a s)
consumeWith f b = do
    h <- mkConsumer b f []
    return $ ConsumerGroup b Nothing [h]

andAlso :: (a -> IO ()) -> ConsumerGroup m a s -> IO (ConsumerGroup m a s)
andAlso f cg@ConsumerGroup{..} = do
    h <- mkConsumer rb f []
    return cg { hs = h : hs }

andThen :: (a -> IO ()) -> ConsumerGroup m a s -> IO (ConsumerGroup m a s)
andThen f cg@ConsumerGroup{..} = do
    h <- mkConsumer rb f (map consumerSequence hs)
    return cg { hs = [h], pr = Just cg }

start :: ConsumerGroup m a s -> IO (Disruptor a s)
start cg@ConsumerGroup{..} = do
    let rb' = RB.addGates rb (map consumerSequence hs)
    tids    <- startConsumers cg { rb = rb' }
    running <- newIORef True
    return $ Disruptor rb' tids running
  where
    startConsumers (ConsumerGroup rb' Nothing     cs) = mapM (run rb') cs
    startConsumers (ConsumerGroup rb' (Just prev) cs) = do
        t1 <- startConsumers prev { rb = rb' }
        t2 <- startConsumers $ ConsumerGroup  rb' Nothing cs
        return $ t1 ++ t2

stop :: Disruptor a s -> IO ()
stop (Disruptor _ tids ref) = do
    running <- atomicModifyIORef ref ((,) False)
    when running $
        mapM_ killThread tids

publish :: Disruptor a s -> (a -> IO ()) -> IO ()
publish (Disruptor rb _ _) = RB.publish rb

publishMany :: Disruptor a s -> Int -> (a -> IO ()) -> IO ()
publishMany (Disruptor rb _ _) = RB.publishMany rb

--------------------------------------------------------------------------------
-- internal
--------------------------------------------------------------------------------

mkConsumer :: RingBuffer a s -> (a -> IO ()) -> [Sequence] -> IO (Consumer m a s)
mkConsumer b f deps = do
    sq <- mkSequence
    return $ Consumer f sq (SequenceBarrier (RB.sequencer b) deps)
```

186

```
consumerSequence :: Consumer m a s -> Sequence
consumerSequence (Consumer _ s _) = s

run :: RingBuffer a s -> Consumer m a s -> IO ThreadId
run buf (Consumer f sq bar) = forkIO loop
  where
    loop = do
        next  <- (+1) `liftM` readSequence sq
        avail <- waitFor bar next

        forM_ [next .. avail] (f . (buf `elemAt`))
            `finally` writeSequence sq avail
loop
```

Double-Checked Locking

In some cases, the patterns used in concurrent software applications can be changed due to modifications in fundamental elements. There are situations in which certain tasks have a higher priority over the rest of the tasks, in which ordinary tasks are blocked to let those with higher priority be executed. Double-checked patterns (a.k.a. *lock hint patterns*) help with this. Is it used to optimize (reducing discord and synchronization costs if some sections of code is necessary to obtain locks one time), but it also should be thread-safe (thread-safe code works correctly when more threads execute in the same time) when they obtain locks. It is usually used with the singleton pattern.

The following are the elements of a double-checked locking pattern.

- *Only one critical section.* The code from here needs to be executed only one time (for example, the initialization of singleton, which occurs just one time).

- *Mutex.* A lock in which the access to the critical code is serialized.

- *Flag.* Shows if the critical section was executed.

- *Application thread.* The part in which the critical section is performed.

The following is the implementation in C++, from the original article *Double-Checked Locking* by Douglas C. Schmidt and Tim Harrison. The regular Singleton class is as follows.

```
class Singleton
{
public:
static Singleton *instance (void)
{
// Constructor of guard acquires
// lock_ automatically.
Guard<Mutex> guard (lock_);
// Only one thread in the
// critical section at a time.
if (instance_ == 0)
instance_ = new Singleton;
return instance_;
// Destructor of guard releases
// lock_ automatically.
}
```

```
private:
static Mutex lock_;
static Singleton *instance_;
};
```

Using a double-checked locking pattern, the singleton would be as follows.

```
class Singleton
{
public:
static Singleton *instance (void)
{
// First check
if (instance_ == 0)
{
// Ensure serialization (guard
// constructor acquires lock_).
Guard<Mutex> guard (lock_);
// Double check.
if (instance_ == 0)
instance_ = new Singleton;
}
return instance_;
// guard destructor releases lock_.
}
private:
static Mutex lock_;
static Singleton *instance_;
};
```

Guarded Suspension

The guarded suspension pattern is similar to the balking pattern. It administrates operations that need to acquire a lock, but a precondition needs to be met until the operation is executed. Its flow is simple: the method call and the calling thread are suspended before the precondition is accomplished. Usually, the time in which the precondition is accomplished is known.

This pattern uses try/catch blocks because an InterruptedException could occur when wait() is called. The rule is that wait() is called if the precondition is not satisfied. The notify() and notifyAll() are called for updating one thread or all threads, respectively, about what happened to the object. Usually, they notify that the state of the object was changed.

Let's look at the following code, from Drew Goldberg's *Executive Summary: Balking Design Patterns*.

```
public void guardedJoy() {
// Simple loop guard. Wastes
// processor time. Don't do this!
while(!joy) {}
System.out.println("Joy has been achieved!");
}
```

This code is actually wrong! Let's take an example where the guardedJoy() method should not continue before a common joy variable is established by another thread. A method like this would loop before the condition is met, a fact that will lose many CPU cycles.

```
public synchronized guardedJoy() {
    while(!joy) {
try {
wait();
} catch (InterruptedException e) {}
}
System.out.println("Joy and efficiency have been achieved!");
}
public synchronized notifyJoy() {
joy = true;
notifyAll();
}
```

Monitor Object

Some applications need an object to be accessed in a concurrent manner by more threads. In order for that application to work precisely, the threads need to be synchronized and scheduled for when they can access the object. Further, the following criteria should be accomplished.

- Synchronization limits need to correlate with the object methods.

- The synchronization should be done by objects.

- The schedule for the methods should be accomplished by the objects.

The solution for these inconveniences is the monitor object, in which the threads examine the defined services through synchronized methods.

The following are the elements of this pattern.

- *Monitor object*. It defines the methods that could be used by the clients, preventing the internal state of the object from being changed by unauthorized access. The methods are executed in client threads.

- *Synchronized methods*. These are used for implementing the thread-safe services on which the monitor object exports. Just one synchronized method should execute at a certain time in the monitor, no matter how many threads ask for the object's sync methods.

- *Monitor lock*. It is found in every monitor object, and it is used by synchronized methods to serialize method calls on a per-object basis. The rule is that when a method goes in or goes out, the monitor lock should be acquired or released, respectively.

- *Monitor condition*. The methods that are synchronized, but running on different threads, need to collaborate for scheduling their accession to the monitor. This is done by using notifications through conditions attached to the monitor object.

Reactor Pattern

The reactor pattern is used to manipulate the services requests, which are sent in a concurrent way to an application from multiple client threads. Services could have more methods and handled by a different event handler, whose task is to dispatch requests for a specific service. In this case, the server that hosts the application should perform demultiplexing, and then send every request that comes to the corresponding service provider. A performant server that accomplishes these mechanisms should have the following characteristics: availability, efficiency, programming simplicity, adaptability, and portability.

The following are the components of a reactor pattern.

- *Handles*. Recognizes resources that are overseen by an operating system. These resources regularly incorporate system associations, open documents, clocks, synchronization objects, and so forth. Logging servers use `Handles` for identifying socket endpoints such that the synchronous event demultiplexer expects the events that take place.

- *Synchronous event demultiplexer*. Blocks the events that wait for a suite of handles. It returns if a handles operation could be initiated without blocking.

- *Initiation dispatcher*. Describes an interface that is able to register, remove, and dispatch event handlers.

- *Event handler*. Describes an interface that contains a hook method for representing the dispatching operation for the events of a specific service.

- *Concrete event handler*. Implements the method from the event handler.

Scheduler Pattern

There are situations in which parallel implementation is not as efficient as we expect, but it could be made efficient under parallel composition. For this, work-stealing schedulers are used, which allows many parallel subprograms to run without oversubscription. Still, there are problems due to resources or the complexity of schedulers. A solution to this is a meta-scheduler based on the Par monad. It performs the following tasks.

- Creates worker threads, having work-stealing deque

- Detects nested `runPar` calls and prevents oversubscription

- Provides `Par` and `IVar` types that are used by all `Par` meta-schedulers and repacking

- Provides Par monad the GET operation

Resource could add data structures for storing work and operations similar to fork.

The following is a scheduler that combines two resources. It uses the meta-par package.

```
{-# LANGUAGE GeneralizedNewtypeDeriving #-}
module Control.Monad.Par.Meta.SMPGPU (Par, runPar) where
...
resource = SMP.mkResource 'mappend' GPU.mkResource

newtype Par a = Par (Meta.Par a)
           deriving (Monad, ParFuture Meta.IVar, ParIVar Meta.IVar, ParGPU Meta.IVar, ...)
runPar :: Par a -> a
runPar (Par work) = Meta.runMetaPar resource work
```

Thread Pool Pattern

A thread pool is a group of pre-instantiated, idle threads that stand ready to be given work. These are preferred over instantiating new threads for each task when there is a large number of short tasks to be done rather than a small number of long ones. This prevents having to incur the overhead of creating a thread a large number of times.

In Haskell, there is a specific library called `Control.ThreadPool`, whose functions work with `Control.Concurrent.Chan`. The thread pool library has only two functions.

- `threadPool :: Int -> (a -> b) -> IO (Chan a, Chan b)`. A trivial thread pool for pure functions (mappings). Simply specify the number of threads desired and a mutator function.

- `threadPoolIO :: Int -> (a -> IO b) -> IO (Chan a, Chan b)`. A trivial thread pool that allows IO mutator functions. Evaluation of output is not strict—force evaluation if desired!

An interesting example is Nicolas Tramgez's implementation of a worker threadpool using STM (https://gist.github.com/NicolasT/4163407).

```
{-# LANGUAGE CPP, FlexibleContexts, BangPatterns #-}

module Control.Concurrent.ThreadPool (
      createPool
    , destroyPool
    , withPool

    , pushWork
    , popResult
    , popResult'

    , hasPendingWork
    ) where

import Control.Applicative

import Control.Exception.Base (SomeException)
import Control.Exception.Lifted (bracket, try)

import Control.Monad (replicateM, replicateM_)
import Control.Monad.IO.Class (MonadIO, liftIO)
import Control.Monad.Trans.Control (MonadBaseControl)

import Control.Concurrent.Lifted
import Control.Concurrent.STM

#ifdef DEBUG
import System.IO (hPutStrLn, stderr)
#endif

type ThreadCount = Int
type QueueSize = Maybe Int
```

191

```
data Command c i = Execute !c !i
                 | Stop
type Result c o = (c, Either SomeException o)

type CommandQueue c i = Queue (Command c i)
type ReplyQueue c o = Queue (Result c o)

type Processor i m o = i -> m o

data ThreadPool c i o = ThreadPool { tpPending :: TVar Int
                                   , tpThreads :: [ThreadId]
                                   , tpChanIn :: CommandQueue c i
                                   , tpChanOut :: ReplyQueue c o
                                   }

data Queue a = Bounded (TBQueue a)
             | Unbounded (TQueue a)

newQueueIO :: QueueSize -> IO (Queue a)
newQueueIO l = case l of
    Nothing -> Unbounded <$> newTQueueIO
    Just l' -> Bounded <$> newTBQueueIO l'
{-# INLINE newQueueIO #-}

writeQueue :: Queue a -> a -> STM ()
writeQueue q = case q of
    Bounded q' -> writeTBQueue q'
    Unbounded q' -> writeTQueue q'
{-# INLINE writeQueue #-}

readQueue :: Queue a -> STM a
readQueue q = case q of
    Bounded q' -> readTBQueue q'
    Unbounded q' -> readTQueue q'
{-# INLINE readQueue #-}

tryReadQueue :: Queue a -> STM (Maybe a)
tryReadQueue q = case q of
    Bounded q' -> tryReadTBQueue q'
    Unbounded q' -> tryReadTQueue q'
{-# INLINE tryReadQueue #-}

createPool :: (MonadIO m, MonadBaseControl IO m) => ThreadCount
                                                 -> QueueSize
                                                 -> QueueSize
                                                 -> Processor i m o
                                                 -> m (ThreadPool c i o)
createPool count commandQueueSize replyQueueSize handler = do
    pending <- liftIO $ newTVarIO 0
    chanIn <- liftIO $ newQueueIO commandQueueSize
    chanOut <- liftIO $ newQueueIO replyQueueSize
    threads <- replicateM count $ fork $ worker handler chanIn chanOut pending
```

```
        return ThreadPool { tpPending = pending
                          , tpThreads = threads
                          , tpChanIn = chanIn
                          , tpChanOut = chanOut
                          }
{-# SPECIALIZE createPool :: ThreadCount
                          -> QueueSize
                          -> QueueSize
                          -> Processor i IO o
                          -> IO (ThreadPool c i o) #-}

atomically' :: MonadIO m => STM a -> m a
atomically' = liftIO . atomically
{-# INLINE atomically' #-}

destroyPool :: MonadIO m => ThreadPool c i o -> m ()
destroyPool pool =
    atomically' $ replicateM_ (length $ tpThreads pool) $ writeQueue (tpChanIn pool) Stop
{-# SPECIALIZE destroyPool :: ThreadPool c i o -> IO () #-}

pushWork :: MonadIO m => ThreadPool c i o -> c -> i -> m ()
pushWork pool !c !i = atomically' $ do
    writeQueue (tpChanIn pool) (Execute c i)
    modifyTVar' (tpPending pool) succ
{-# SPECIALIZE pushWork :: ThreadPool c i o -> c -> i -> IO () #-}

popResult :: MonadIO m => ThreadPool c i o -> m (Result c o)
popResult pool = atomically' $ readQueue (tpChanOut pool)
{-# SPECIALIZE popResult :: ThreadPool c i o -> IO (Result c o) #-}
popResult' :: MonadIO m => ThreadPool c i o -> m (Maybe (Result c o))
popResult' pool = atomically' $ tryReadQueue (tpChanOut pool)
{-# SPECIALIZE popResult' :: ThreadPool c i o -> IO (Maybe (Result c o)) #-}

-- This is... no good (for now)
hasPendingWork :: MonadIO m => ThreadPool c i o -> m Bool
hasPendingWork pool = atomically' $ (/= 0) <$> readTVar (tpPending pool)

worker :: (MonadIO m, MonadBaseControl IO m) => Processor i m o
                                             -> CommandQueue c i
                                             -> ReplyQueue c o
                                             -> TVar Int
                                             -> m ()
worker handler chanIn chanOut pending = loop
  where
    loop = do
        debug "Awaiting work"
        req <- atomically' $ readQueue chanIn
        case req of
            Execute c i -> do
                debug "Executing command"
                r <- try $! do
                    res <- handler i
                    return $! res
```

193

```
                    atomically' $ do
                        writeQueue chanOut (c, r)
                        modifyTVar' pending pred
                    loop
                Stop -> do
                    debug "Shutdown"
                    return ()
{-# SPECIALIZE worker :: Processor i IO o -> CommandQueue c i -> ReplyQueue c o -> TVar Int
-> IO () #-}

withPool :: (MonadIO m, MonadBaseControl IO m) => ThreadCount
                                               -> QueueSize
                                               -> QueueSize
                                               -> Processor i m o
                                               -> (ThreadPool c i o -> m a)
                                               -> m a
withPool count commandQueueSize replyQueueSize handler =
    bracket
        (createPool count commandQueueSize replyQueueSize handler)
        destroyPool
{-# SPECIALIZE withPool :: ThreadCount
                        -> QueueSize
                        -> QueueSize
                        -> Processor i IO o
                        -> (ThreadPool c i o -> IO a)
                        -> IO a #-}

debug :: MonadIO m => String -> m ()
#ifndef DEBUG
debug _ = return ()
#else
debug s = liftIO $ do
    tid <- myThreadId
    hPutStrLn stderr $ "[" ++ show tid ++ "] " ++ s
#endif
{-# INLINE debug #-}
```

Summary

In this chapter, you saw

- the most common problems that could occur in big data applications.

- design patterns and examples of design patterns that can be used in big data.

CHAPTER 12

■ ■ ■

Large-Scale Design in Haskell

There are approaches to manage the complexity of computations. We talked about some of them in previous chapters; here we will explain why they are used in large-scale design. We will also discuss new approaches and provide some examples.

The Type System

The type system is used to enforce abstractions and to simplify the interactions between the programmer and the environment. It imposes key invariants through types and ensures safety through checked exceptions (using Maybe/Either monads). The data types or data structures are not combined (Word, Int, Address). There are many useful data structures (as zippers).

Purity

The complexity of a program decreases if the state is removed. An advantage of pure functional code is scalability, due to its compositionality. Frege's principle states that the result of a complex expression is given by the results of expressions that constitute it and the rules that are applied to combine them. Another definition of complexity is "the meaning of a (syntactically complex) whole is a function only of the meanings of its (syntactic) parts together with the manner in which these parts were combined", provided by Francis Jeffry Pelletier in *The Principle of Semantic Compositionality* (available: https://link.springer.com/article/10.1007/BF00763644). A good practice is the model-view-controller programming style, which works in functional programming as follows: data is parsed externally in functional data structures that are pure, operations are made over the functional data structures, and in the last step, the data is rendered, flushed, or serialized. This way, the code remains as pure as possible. We discussed pure functions in Chapter 2.

Monads for Structuring

The key architectural designs are captured by monads and made into types, such that one part of the code is for accessing hardware, another part of the code is used for a session with a single user, and so on. We discussed monads in Chapter 2.

Type Classes and Existential Types

Type classes are used for abstraction. They hide the implementation behind a polymorphic interface. We discussed types in Chapter 2.

© Stefania Loredana Nita and Marius Mihailescu 2017
S. L. Nita and M. Mihailescu, *Practical Concurrent Haskell*, DOI 10.1007/978-1-4842-2781-7_12

Concurrency and Parallelism

Concurrency and parallelism are useful because they allow more tasks to run at the same time, which decreases the time to obtain a result. We also discuss concurrency and parallelism in other chapters.

Use of FFI

The Foreign Function Interface (FFI) works with code from other programming languages. It is very important to be careful with data that is returned by foreign code. We discussed FFIs in Chapter 11.

The Profiler

Profiling is a technique that analyzes other elements: the space complexity and time complexity, the use of specific instructions, and the rate and duration of function calls. Program heaps and time profiles can be tracked by a profiler. It is good practice to profile the heaps to make sure that memory is used as it is needed. GHC has its own tools for profiling. We can set the option so that a program is compiled with profiling by default. Profiling has three stages: compile the program to be profiled, run the program with specific profiling modes enabled, and check the resulting statistics.

Time Profiling

First, let's talk about time profiling. Consider an example in which we compute the mean of values from a list. To compile the program using profiling, we add the -prof flag. In addition, the profiling code needs to know which function we want to profile. This is done by adding cost centers that represent the code in our program that we want statistical information on. Some code is generated by GHC, which computes the cost of evaluation of the expression in every place. To add a cost center, use SCC pragma.

```
mean :: [Double] -> Double
mean xs = {-# SCC "mean" #-} sum xs / fromIntegral (length xs)
```

Another option for cost centers is letting the compiler add them on all functions at top levels. This could be done by compiling with the -auto-all option.

An important aspect of profiling in lazy languages is paying attention to values with no arguments, which should be computed once and their result is used later. Actually, the evaluation of these values is not made to every call, but we also need to know how expensive they are. They are called *constant applicative forms* (CAFs) and could be included in profiling using the -caf-all option.

Thus, the example is compiled as (-fforce-recomp option is used to forcing full recompilation).

```
$ ghc -O2 --make mean.hs -prof -auto-all -caf-all -fforce-recomp
[1 of 1] Compiling Main             ( mean.hs, mean.o )
Linking A ...
```

Space Profiling

Next, we will examine the example from a space profiling view, in which GHC generates graphs about memory usage during the program's lifetime. This is useful for discovering the locations in which memory is wrongly used leading to a heavy garbage collector. This is similar to time proofing (i.e., when we compile, we add -prof -auto-all -caf-all), but at execution time, the runtime system should collect some detailed statistics about heap use. This information could be broken down in many ways: through a cost center, through a module, through a constructor, or through a data type. The Haskell .hs file is profiled into an .hp file that contains raw data that is examined by the hp2ps tool, which finally generates a graphical visualization of the heap in time. In order to obtain a heap profile, we add the -hc option.

```
$ time ./mean 1e6 +RTS -hc -p -K100M
```

Different samples are retrieved at a regular time when the program is running. If we want to decrease the time between two samplings, we use -iN, where N represents the number of seconds. The more often samples are taken, the more accurate the result, but the program will be slower. Now let's take a look at the graph, as shown in Figure 12-1.

```
$ hp2ps -e8in -c mean.hp
```

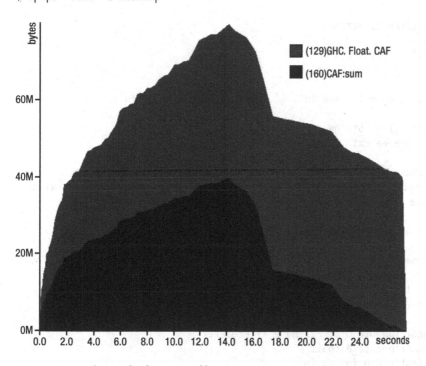

Figure 12-1. *The result of space profiling testing*

We can learn some things from the graph. The execution of the program has two stages: in the first, an increasingly large amount of memory is used for computing the sum of the values, and in the second, the values are cleaned.

QuickCheck

QuickCheck (https://hackage.haskell.org/package/QuickCheck) represents a library that can easily test our programs. In unit testing, particular cases are tested; while in property testing (the type of testing provided by QuickCheck), properties are tested. All we need to do is to write specifications for the code that describe invariant properties. QuickCheck generates random samples of data with which it will test if the properties that we defined are satisfied.

For the next example (from jasani.org, Testing Haskell with QuickCheck), we need to import some libraries.

```
> import Control.Monad ( liftM )
> import Data.List ( intersperse )
> import Test.QuickCheck.Gen
> import Test.QuickCheck.Arbitrary
> import Test.QuickCheck.Property
> import Test.QuickCheck.Test
```

Next, we write two simple functions that work with file names. The first is splitFN, in which the file name is separated into the name and the extension, and joinFN, in which a name and an extension are concatenated to obtain the file name.

```
> splitFN_0 :: String -> (String, String)
> splitFN_0 fn =
>   let fn' = span (/= '.') . reverse $ fn
>   in case (length (fst fn') == length fn) of
>       True  -> (fn, "")
>       False -> (reverse . drop 1 $ snd fn', ('.':) . reverse . fst $ fn')
>
> joinFN_0 :: (String, String) -> String
> joinFN_0 (name, ext) = name ++ ext
```

A property of the two functions is roundtripping (which we named prop_filenames_are_roundtrippable), because filename = joinFN(splitFN(filename)). Next, we want to generate file names, so we created a new type and an Arbitrary instance.

```
> newtype Filename = FN { unFN :: String } deriving Show
>
> instance Arbitrary Filename where
>   arbitrary = do name <- elements ["foo", "bar", "baz"]
>                  ext <- listOf $ elements ['a'..'z']
>                  return (FN (name ++ "." ++ ext))
>
> prop_filenames_are_roundtrippable_0 :: Filename -> Property
> prop_filenames_are_roundtrippable_0 fnStr =
>   property $ joinFN_0 (splitFN_0 fn) == fn
>   where fn = unFN fnStr
```

If we execute the code, we obtain

```
*Main> quickCheck prop_filenames_are_roundtrippable_0
+++ OK, passed 100 tests.
```

The test passed and the file names were successfully created, but we don't know how they look. If we want to see some samples, we can do the following.

```
*Main> sample' arbitrary :: IO [Filename]

[ FN {unFN = "baz.x"}, FN {unFN = "bar.v"}, FN {unFN = "foo.k"}, FN {unFN = "foo.s"},
FN {unFN = "baz.esra"}, FN {unFN = "baz.vkgg"}, FN {unFN = "bar.uln"}, FN {unFN = "bar.k"},
FN {unFN = "baz.crynhi"}, FN {unFN = "baz.ys"} ]
```

We can combine the property that we defined with collect to show the data that is used.

```
> prop_filenames_are_roundtrippable_1 :: Filename -> Property
> prop_filenames_are_roundtrippable_1 fnStr =
>    collect fn $
>    joinFN_0 (splitFN_0 fn) == fn
>    where fn = unFN fnStr
```

The following are some of the results.

```
*Main> quickCheck prop_filenames_are_roundtrippable_1

 1% "bar.tbgufhjxeqtfpn"
 1% "bar.rymnlegngyuzvl"
 1% "bar.ryddfkncgxdopxihkmb"
 1% "bar.rafel"
 1% "bar.qbrftss"
 1% "bar.pxwpbfovejqwiqslnrdboaluihlkjifawfiyerwwtdyuepynoejx"
 1% "bar.p"
 1% "bar.nyciiyidegiwpsxta"
 1% "bar.mtidqpnitvrseakbkppkjmqtlutkqtfuirlsmkrnsmxsvwhzhwfut"
 1% "bar.mogmmzl"
```

An alternative to the collect function is to classify the data.

```
> prop_filenames_are_roundtrippable_2 :: Filename -> Property
> prop_filenames_are_roundtrippable_2 fnStr =
>    classify (length ext == 0) "no ext" $
>    classify (length ext > 0 && length ext < 5) "normal ext" $
>    classify (length ext >= 5) "long ext" $
>    joinFN_0 (splitFN_0 fn) == fn
>    where fn = unFN fnStr
>          (name,ext) = splitFN_0 fn

*Main> quickCheck prop_filenames_are_roundtrippable_2
+++ OK, passed 100 tests:
72% long ext
21% normal ext
 7% no ext
```

We have seen the data that is generated, but we have not taken into consideration names like README, or foo.txt.old, or .emacs. Therefore, we will change the approach a little, writing a test generator for the property we defined.

```
> filenames :: Gen String
> filenames = do
>    name <- opt identifier
>    dot  <- opt (return ".")
>    ext  <- opt identifier
>    exts <- listOf identifier
>    oneof [ return $ name ++ dot ++ ext
>          , return $ name ++ "." ++ (concat . intersperse "." $ exts)]

> prop_filenames_are_roundtrippable_3 :: Property
> prop_filenames_are_roundtrippable_3 =
>    forAll filenames $ \fn ->
>    joinFN_0 (splitFN_0 fn) == fn
```

If we ask for some sample data, we note that they are diverse.

```
*Main> sample' filenames

[ ".K3", ".O.Va1", "1LAi.k", "rz.t", "41R8x.", ".wu.mi1kqh8.Y7PKH6.p86.O", "", ".",
"P214MM71fu.k4AyqnsOf", ".k.k9.Oo2e81n.d71ijpm7gh.XMNt" ]

*Main> quickCheck prop_filenames_are_roundtrippable_3
+++ OK, passed 100 tests.
```

Well, the results look better. But we haven't finish yet because we have a little problem with the file names that have no extension, such as README and .emacs. We will consider a particular generator for these types of files by adding a new property called prop_names_equal_filenames.

```
> noExtFilenames :: Gen String
> noExtFilenames = do
>    name <- identifier
>    dot  <- opt (return ".")
>    return ( dot ++ name )

> prop_names_equal_filenames_0 :: Property
> prop_names_equal_filenames_0 =
>    forAll noExtFilenames $ \fn ->
>    let (name,ext) = splitFN_0 fn
>    in name == fn
```

Now if we run the test for the new property, we get the following.

```
*Main> quickCheck prop_names_equal_filenames_0
*** Failed! Falsifiable (after 3 tests):
".i1"

*Main> splitFN_0 ".i1"
("",".i1")
```

We need to reconsider the split function. Then, let's put them in a library.

```
> splitFN_1 :: String -> (String, String)
> splitFN_1 fn =
>   let fn' = span (/= '.') . reverse $ fn
>   in case (length (fst fn') == length fn) of
>       True  -> (fn, "")
>       False | length (fst fn') == length fn - 1 -> (fn, "")
>             | otherwise -> (reverse . drop 1 $ snd fn'
>                            , ('.':) . reverse . fst $ fn')

> prop_names_equal_filenames_1 :: Property
> prop_names_equal_filenames_1 =
>   forAll noExtFilenames $ \fn ->
>   let (name,ext) = splitFN_1 fn
>   in name == fn

> prop_filenames_are_roundtrippable_4 :: Property
> prop_filenames_are_roundtrippable_4 =
>   forAll filenames $ \fn ->
>   joinFN_0 (splitFN_1 fn) == fn


> ---------------------------
> -- library functions

> iden0 :: Gen Char
> iden0 = oneof [ elements ['a'..'z'], elements ['A'..'Z']
>               , elements ['0'..'9'] ]
> idenN :: Gen String
> idenN = listOf iden0

> opt :: Gen String -> Gen String
> opt g = oneof [ g, return "" ]

> identifier :: Gen String
> identifier = iden0 >>= \i0 -> idenN >>= return . (i0:)
```

Finally, we see how QuickCheck works. It also helps us to keep the APIs clean for our modules. An intuitive conclusion is that if the properties of the code are complicated to state, a solution is to refactor it until we get clean code.

Refactor

Refactor can be used many times in Haskell, ensuring that large-scale changes are made safety, if the types are suitable. This is proper for code-base scale. You need to pay attention to type errors: they should not happen until refactoring is complete.

The following is a little tutorial from www.schoolofhaskell.com in which we compute the sum of the even numbers from a list. This is a first version of the solution.

```haskell
evenSum :: [Integer] -> Integer

evenSum l = accumSum 0 l

accumSum n l = if l == []
                    then n
                    else let x = head l
                             xs = tail l
                          in if even x
                                   then accumSum (n+x) xs
                                   else accumSum n xs
-- The trace of the execution
*Main> evenSum [1..5]
accumSum 0 [1,2,3,4,5]
1 is odd
accumSum 0 [2,3,4,5]
2 is even
accumSum (0+2) [3,4,5]
3 is odd
accumSum (0+2) [4,5]
2 is even
accumSum (0+2+4) [5]
5 is odd
accumSum (0+2+4) []
l == []
0+2+4
0+6
6
```

This code can be improved. We could generalize the type as follows.

```haskell
evenSum :: Integral a => [a] -> a
```

Next, we can use functions like where and let.

```haskell
-- Version 2
evenSum :: Integral a => [a] -> a

evenSum l = accumSum 0 l
    where accumSum n l =
            if l == []
                then n
                else let x = head l
                         xs = tail l
                      in if even x
                              then accumSum (n+x) xs
                              else accumSum n xs
```

Another improvement uses pattern matching and guards.

```
-- Version 3
evenSum l = accumSum 0 l
    where
        accumSum n [] = n
        accumSum n (x:xs) =
        | even x = accumSum(n+x)xs
        | otherwise = accumSum n xs
```

As you know, in Haskell, the definition of the functions could be eta-reduced by dropping arguments that appear at the end of both sides. So, the following could be a final improvement.

```
-- Version 4
evenSum :: Integral a => [a] -> a

evenSum = accumSum 0
    where
        accumSum n [] = n
        accumSum n (x:xs) =
            if even x
                then accumSum (n+x) xs
                else accumSum n xs
```

Haskell-tools is an automatic tool for refactoring in Haskell (www.haskelltools.org). It supports rename, generate type signature, generate exports, organize exports, extract binding, and inline binding. There is a simple demo on the official site.

Summary

In this chapter, you saw

- large-scale design techniques in Haskell.

- how time and space are profiled in Haskell.

- an example QuickCheck test.

- an easy example of refactoring in Haskell.

CHAPTER 13

■ ■ ■

Designing a Shared Memory Approach for Hadoop Streaming Performance

This chapter discusses Hadoop and Hadoop Streaming. It presents an improved model for streaming and examples of Hadoop Streaming.

Hadoop

Hadoop is an open source framework written in Java that implements simple programming models. It is used to process significant data sets over clusters in a distributed way. A Hadoop application is based on shared storage and computations on clusters. The Hadoop design allows you to scale up from one server to thousands, with every machine having its own local storage and computations.

The Hadoop architecture (see Figure 13-1) has the following components.

- *Hadoop Common*: Java libraries and tools necessary for other Hadoop modules. Also, the files that start Hadoop.

- *Hadoop YARN*: This framework schedules jobs and manages resources from the cluster.

- *Hadoop Distributed File System* (HDFS): This file system allows high throughput access to the application data.

- *Hadoop MapReduce*: This is the system based on YARN, which processes the data sets in parallel.

© Stefania Loredana Nita and Marius Mihailescu 2017
S. L. Nita and M. Mihailescu, *Practical Concurrent Haskell*, DOI 10.1007/978-1-4842-2781-7_13

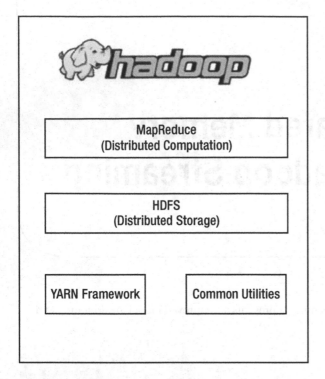

Figure 13-1. *Hadoop architecture (figure from* http://hadoop.apache.org)

More About MapReduce

Hadoop MapReduce is a part of the Hadoop software product, which allows you to write applications that process big data in parallel over extensive clusters with thousands of nodes. We already talked a little about MapReduce. There are only two programs that need to be performed.

- Map task, which converts the input into a set of (key, value) pairs.

- Reduce task, which has as input the output of a map task, and reduces the initial set of pairs into a smaller set of pairs.

You need to remember that map is always the first task, followed by reduce. Usually, the input and output are stocked in a file system. The framework schedules and monitors tasks, and when tasks fail, they are executed again.

In the MapReduce framework, there is one master, JobTracker, and one slave, TaskTracker, in every node of a cluster. JobTracker manages the resources, and schedules and monitors the job tasks of slaves. The slaves perform the tasks received from the master and send statuses of the tasks to the master at certain times. The JobTracker is the sensible point of MapReduce, because if it fails, its corresponding jobs are broken off.

Hadoop Distributed File System

Hadoop can work directly with many distributed file systems, but its specific file system is the Hadoop Distributed File System (HDSF). The base of HDFS is the Google File System (GFS). It is specifically created to run on clusters with thousands of nodes.

The architecture of HDFS is based on the master-slave model, in which the master has just one NameNode whose task is to manage the metadata of file system; but there is one or more slave DataNodes, where the data is actually stored. In HDFS, a file is broken into blocks that are stocked in more DataNodes. The NameNode establishes the spread of blocks to the DataNodes. It also sends instructions to DataNodes to create, delete, or replicate blocks. DataNodes read and write operations in the file system, and also create, delete, and replicate blocks based on the instructions it receives. If the option to have a SecondaryNameNode on a machine other than NameNode is not set, the file system goes offline; but DataNode is replicated on multiple servers. It is not recommended to host DataNode, JobTracker, and TaskTracker on the same system.

Like other file systems, HDFS provides a shell and commands through which the interaction between the user and HDFS is established. The following is an example in which a new directory is created, using the mkdir command.

- The following is a complete definition of mkdir, where -p option tells that the directory is a parent directory along the path.

  ```
  hadoop fs -mkdir46.8 pt [-p] <paths>
  ```

- The following are some examples (from official documentation).

  ```
  hadoop fs -mkdir /user/hadoop/dir1 /user/hadoop/dir2
  hadoop fs -mkdir hdfs://nn1.example.com/user/hadoop/dir
  hdfs://nn2.example.com/user/hadoop/dir
  ```

A complete list of shell commands is at https://hadoop.apache.org/docs/r2.7.2/hadoop-project-dist/hadoop-common/FileSystemShell.html.

How Hadoop Works

Hadoop works in three stages, as follows.

Stage 1

A Hadoop job client is submitted to Hadoop by a user or an application for a specific process, providing the following information.

- The location where input and output file are stored in HDFS.

- The Java classes that need to be provided in JAR format, where the map and reduce functions are implemented.

- The job configuration, which is obtained when different parameters for a specific job are set.

Stage 2

The job is submitted by the Hadoop job client. The job client provides the configuration for JobTracker, which works as described in the "More About MapReduce" section. JobTracker sends status and diagnostic information to the job client at certain intervals of time.

Stage 3

The tasks are executed by TaskTrackers as per MapReduce implementation. The output of reduce is stored in the output file on the file system.

Hadoop Streaming

Hadoop Streaming represents a collection of additional tools provided by Hadoop to develop applications in languages other than Java. Briefly, a MapReduce job is created by the utility, which is submitted to a suitable cluster. The utility also observes the evolution of the job, and while it runs, until it is completed. There is a streaming JAR (Java Archive) that acts as a bridge between code (from languages other than Java) and translates the scripts in MapReduce jobs.

Hadoop Streaming for mappers works as follows: the mappers receive a script, and then when every mapper is initialized, the script starts as a different process. When a mapper task is running, the inputs are converted into lines and then sent to the standard input (STDIN) of the process. At the same time, the line-oriented outputs are collected from the standard output (STDOUT). The collected lines are converted in a specific pair of map/reduce (key/value) and represent the output of the mapper. The convention is that, by default, the characters between the first character and the first tab represent the key, and the remaining characters of the line represent the value (the tab character is excluded). The special case in which there is no tab character means that there is no value, so the entire line is the key and the value is null. There is the option to customize this setting.

The reduce part of Hadoop Streaming works as follows: the reducers receive a script, then every reducer starts the script as a different process; after that, the reducer is initialized. The process is somewhat reversed: the pairs key/value are converted into lines and sent to the STDIN of the process, and at the same time, the line-oriented outputs of STDOUT are collected. The collected lines are converted into key/value pairs, which represent the output of the reducer. The default setting for mappers is as follows: the characters between the first character and the first tab represent the key, and the remaining characters represent the value. This could be customized.

In the process for the mappers, the jobs are launched and the communication is done from outside through pipes. `clientIn` and `clientOut` are used to accept or send data from/to external processes. The `map` function from Hadoop is called by `PipperMapper` from the Hadoop Streaming interface. The map works as we have explained. The scheme for reduce is very similar to the map scheme.

Hadoop Streaming is very useful, but its performance is not so good. A research paper stated that the poor performance is due to the pipe technique. It was discovered that while the size of input increases, the performance dramatically decreases.

The work of Hadoop is very intensive. For example, in one streaming job, the system needs to make calls of read and write to pipes in a number proportional to the number of key/value pairs. So, the number of reads and write is very high, which leads to decreasing performance.

An Improved Streaming Model

There is an improved model streaming called `ShmStreaming`, proposed and implemented by Longbin Lai et al. in "ShmStreaming: A Shared Memory Approach for Improving Hadoop Streaming Performance" a paper from the 2013 IEEE 27th International Conference on Advanced Information Networking and Applications (AINA).

For the `ShmStreaming`, the source code of Hadoop is minimally changed, such that bugs and unexpected behavior are avoided. Also, the changes in the external programs are minimal.

When you use `ShmStreaming`, all you need to do is to change the configuration file a little by setting `stream.map(reduce).input=shm`, and `stream.map(reduce).output=shm`.

The difference between the traditional approach and `ShmStreaming` is that the programs create a `SMStream` object, using it for read and write, instead of using `stdin` and `stdout`. The following is an example of `SMStream`.

```
1: class SMStream {
2: public :
3: //Initialize shared memory with buffer size
4: SMStream(intbufSize =4096) ;
5: ~ SMStream () ;
6: //write buffer shared memory
7: int write (char_buf, int size);
8: // read data from shared memory into a buffer
9: int read (char_buf, int size);
10: };
```

In the preceding piece of code, SMStream is a class, which has all public elements (they could be accessed by anybody). On fourth line there is the constructor of the class, which is called anytime that STMSTream is instantiated (i.e., an object is created), while on fifth line there is the destructor of the class, which is called anytime an SMStream object is no longer used, to release the resources allocated for the object. Next, there is the write function, which writes a particular number of elements on the shared memory buffer, and then, its opposite read function, which reads a particular number of elements from the buffer.

Access to the shared memory needs to be synchronized, and usually there are used locks, using semaphores that need system calls and switches of context. This approach is more expensive than pipe implementation, because every time the memory is accessed, there are two necessary operations: lock and unlock. Remember that every time the memory is accessed, only one read or write of one key/value pair is done. Because the streaming communication follows a single read—the single write (SRSW) model. A natural choice for the queue is FIFO (First In, First Out) for storing the positions of reader and writer. When a writer pushes n bytes of data into the FIFO, the pointer goes forward with n. This is similar to reader: when it finishes reading, the other pointer is moving. There is no need for locks here. The following is the proposed algorithm, in which read and write are implemented using *busy wait*. readFIFO and writeFIFO try to read/write certain bytes from/on FIFO and return actual completed bytes.

```
function READ(buf, n)
      while n > 0 do
read =  readFIFO(buf, n)
n =  n - read;
      end while
end function

function WRITE(buf, n)
      while n > 0 do
written = writeFIFO(buf, n)
n =  n - written;
      end while
end function
```

Using FIFO, the locks are avoided, but synchronization is still necessary. The busy wait approach could also lead to decreased performance, because the reader cannot read data when the buffer is not empty. Similarly, the writer cannot write if the buffer is full. For Hadoop, this means that mappers are used many times for writing, and reducers wait for reads. So, it is a necessary technique that blocks and resumes execution at a later time. When there is no data for reading, the reader is blocked while the writer pushes data in the FIFO. Alternatively, the writer is blocked when the buffer is full, and in this time, the reader reads data from the FIFO, and the writer can resume its work. To do this, a semaphore is used. The following is the pseudo-code of this approach.

```
// Global variables
int batch_size = CONSTANT
semaphore sem_full(0), sem_empty(0)
// flag of FIFO's status
bool empty = 1, full = 0
// # of FIFO's is full/empty
int times_full = 0, times_empty = 0
// functions testing whether the FIFO is empty or full
is empty(), is full()

function READ_WAIT(buf, n)
        if not compare_and_swap(empty, 0, is empty()) then
                if compare_and_swap(full, 1, 0) then
                        times_full = 0
                        sem_post(sem_full) // wake up writer
                end if
                sem_wait(sem_empty) // wait for writer
end if
READ(buf, n)
  if full then
          times_full = times_full + 1
          if times_full > batch_size then
                  times_full = 0
                  sem_post(sem_full)
          end if
   end if
end function

function WRITE_WAIT(buf, n)
        if not compare_and_swap(full, 0, is full()) then
            if compare_and_swap(empty, 1, 0) then
                    times_empty = 0
                    sem_post(sem_empty) // wake up reader
            end if
            sem_wait(sem_full) // wait for reader
end if
WRITE(buf, n)
        if empty then
              times_empty = times_empty + 1
              if times_empty > batch_size then
                      times_empty = 0
                      sem_post(sem_empty)
              end if
          end if
end function
```

Hadoop Streaming in Haskell

This section presents some tools that could be used in Haskell to integrate with Hadoop Streaming.

Haskell-Hadoop Library

There are several ways in which Hadoop Streaming can be accomplished in Haskell. One method is to use Haskell-Hadoop, a Haskell interface proposed by Paul Butler for Hadoop Streaming jobs (https://github.com/paulgb/haskell_hadoop). It is easy to install. All you need to do is run the cabal install command in the command prompt window. It is imported as Hadoop.MapReduce.

Of course, the programmer needs to write map and reduce functions, whose signatures are as follows.

```
type Map = String -> [String]
type Reduce = String -> [String] -> [String]
```

As you can see, the input and the output are strings, so the programmer needs to do some parsing.

When we run the program with Hadoop, the streaming JAR should be used, as well as the program that has been compiled with options -m and -r for mappers and reducers.

```
/path-to-hadoop/bin/hadoop
    jar /path-to-hadoop/contrib/streaming/hadoop-[version]-streaming.jar
    -input /path-to-input/
    -output /path-to-output/
    -mapper "/path-to-mapreduce/mapreduce-program -m"
    -reducer "/path-to-mapreduce/mapreduce-program -r"
```

You have seen how Hadoop works and you know that you need to provide the files for input and output.

The author of the library remarks that the tab character separates the key from its value and the newline character separates records.

The following is a very simple example of the author of the Haskell-Hadoop library.

```
module Main where

import Hadoop.MapReduce (mrMain, Map, Reduce)

wfMap :: Map
wfMap = words

wfReduce :: Reduce
wfReduce key values =
    return $ key ++ " " ++ (show $ length values)

main = mrMain wfMap wfReduce
```

In the example, the frequencies of the words from a document are counted. The words are all non-spaces characters separated by a space character. The output contains a list of pairs, one per line, in which there is a word followed by the number of times it occurs in the document.

Hadron

Another Haskell approach to Hadoop Streaming is a project called Hadron (https://github.com/Soostone/hadron), which was proposed by researchers from Soostone. It is more complex than Haskell-Hadoop, but at the same time, it is easier to use. This section presents examples provided by Ozgun Ataman in his talk "Conquering Hadoop with Haskell" (https://vimeo.com/90189610).

The following are some of Hadron's characteristics.

- It bounds Haskell to Hadoop through the Streaming interface.

- It orchestrates Hadoop jobs in multiple steps, so the programmer does not need to call Hadoop manually.

- The programmer can interact with input or output on every system that Hadoop supports.

- MapReduce steps are fully typed.

- It contains combinators for different tasks in the Controller module.

- It has built-in support for different types of joins.

It has three modules: Hadron.Basic (one-step MapReduce), Hadron.Controller (MapReduce jobs with multiple stages), and Hadron.Protocol (defines strategies for encoding and decoding of data through the Protocol type).

Now let's talk a little about some of Hadron's elements.

Lenses are very important to Hadron developing. They are available on the lens package and can be imported as Data.Lens. A comprehensive description of lenses is in Simon Peyton Jones' talk, "Lenses: Compositional Data Access And Manipulation," and Alejandro Serrano Mena's book *Beginning Haskell: A Project-Based Approach* (Apress, 2014). In short, lenses represent functional references that allow you to look at, construct, and use functions over complex data types. As a simple definition, a lens is a value that represents a mapping between a complex type and one of the components. As an analogy to object-oriented programming, they can be seen as the getters and setters of Haskell, but much more powerful. They are important because they let the programmer focus deeply into a complex data structure. They are grouped into a combinator library that is sensible. And they have general behavior regarding composition, failure, multiplicity, transformation, and representation. A very simple example of lens is _1, which works only with the first element of a pair.

When we have a lens, we can do the following things: view the subpart, change the whole through changing the subpart, and combine the lens with another lens for looking in more depth. A good example of the use of lenses in a large-scale application is lens-aeson, which is used for querying and modifying JSON data.

Before continuing with Hadron, let's look at some of the operations using lenses.

Let's define the following types by using an employee as an example.

```
data ShortAddress = ShortAddress {
  _nameOfStreet :: String,
  _no :: Int
} deriving (Eq, Show)

data Employee = Employee {
  _nameOfEmp :: String,
  _salaryOfEmp :: Int,
  _addressOfEmp :: ShortAddress
} deriving (Eq, Show)

employee = Employee "Alice" 1000 (ShortAddress "Broadway" 10)
```

If we want to focus on a field of a structure, we need two functions: one to get/return the value of a field, and another one to update the focused field. The following function takes as an argument a structure and a focused field, and makes two operations of the focused field.

```
data LensRecord structure field = LensRecord {
  viewField :: structure -> field,
  setField :: field -> structure -> structure
}
```

Let's define a lens that focuses on the name of an employee.

```
nameOfEmployee :: LensRecord Employee String
nameOfEmployee = LensRecord {
  viewField = nameOfEmp,
  setField = \a s -> s {nameOfEmp = a}
}
```

Now we use it.

```
setField nameOfEmployee "Bob" employee
```

Now, let's focus on the street field and the short address of the employee.

```
street :: LensRecord ShortAddress String
street = LensRecord {
  viewField = nameOfStreet,
  setField = \a s -> s { nameOfStreet = a}
}
```

```
addressOfEmployee :: LensRecord Employee ShortAddress
addressOfEmployee = LensRecord {
  viewField = _addressOfEmp,
  setField = \a s -> s { addressOfEmp = a}
}
```

Next, let's look at how to compose lenses. Let's say we want to change the street of the employee.

```
composeRecords :: LensRecord s1 s2 -> LensRecord s2 a -> LensRecord s1 a
composeRecords (LensRecord v1 s1) (LensRecord v2 s2) = LensRecord {
  viewField = v2 . v1,
  setField = \a s -> s1 (s2 a (v1 s)) s
}
```

Here are some examples.

```
viewField (composeRecords addressOfEmployee street) employee
"Broadway"
```

```
setField (composeRecords addressOfEmployee street) "Fifth Avenue" employee
Employee {_nameOfEmp = "Bob", _salaryOfEmp = 1000, _addressOfEmp = ShortAddress
{nameOfStreet = "Fourth Avenue", _no = 120}}
```

213

Now let's take a look at Hadron.Basic, which takes just one MapReduce step. The types are

```
type Mapper a k b = Conduit a IO (k, b)
type Reducer k a r = Conduit (k, a) IO r
```

The idea is as follows: As the input comes in, we want to be able to take it row by row, and then resolve the write to collect a few of those until we want to meet a key/value pair. We might take a row or 10 rows, or 15, so we need flexibility with each input to meet a certain key/value pair. This is the reason for which Conduit is used. If they are changed, the authors prevents the program from having unexpected behaviors during the time its running.

Conduit (https://hackage.haskell.org/package/conduit) takes input items of type a until it meets a key/value pair, with the key k and the value b. The reducer takes key type k and the input with type a, which results in type of r.

This does not happen on the same physical nodes. It could be thousands of nodes, on which mappers are running and giving results that will be processed further by reducers on other nodes from the cluster.

There are a few MapReduce options for communicating with Hadoop.

```
-- | Options for a single-step MR job.
data MROptions = MROptions {
_mroPart :: PartitionStrategy
-- ^ Number of segments to expect in
incoming keys.
, _mroComparator :: Comparator
, _mroNumMap :: Maybe Int
-- ^ Number of map tasks;
, _mroNumReduce :: Maybe Int
-- ^ Number of reduce tasks;
, _mroCompress :: Maybe String
-- ^ Whether to use compression
, _mroOutSep :: Maybe Char
-- ^ Output separator
}
```

At the very lowest level is the mapReduce combinatory which takes a Prism (a serialization of the lens library, which basically translates the incoming into a ByteString a, and then goes back from a to a ByteString; essentially it is an encoder coupled with a decoder). The input of type a from Haskell is encoded into a ByteString, which is shuffled through the nodes. The final result is transformed from ByteString back to type a. Besides Prism, the other parameters are a map function, a reduce function, and two IO functions.

```
mapReduce
:: MROptions
-> Prism' B.ByteString a
-- ^ Serialization for data between map and reduce stages
-> Mapper B.ByteString CompositeKey a
-> Reducer CompositeKey a B.ByteString
-> (IO (), IO ())
mapReduce mro mrInPrism f g = (mp, rd)
where
  mp = mapperWith mrInPrism f
  rd = reducerMain mro mrInPrism g
```

All of this is for a single step of MapReduce. As you can see, there is no type safety here, because we mostly work with ByteString. The next step is to resolve the input/output type safety problem. The answer to this problem is the Protocol type, which basically is a record that knows how to transform type a into type b and vice versa. The conduits operate over IO, so it can do arbitrary conversion, and even handle binary files.

```
data Protocol b a = Protocol {
protoEnc :: Conduit a IO b
, protoDec :: Conduit b IO a
}
type Protocol' a = Protocol B.ByteString a
instance Category Protocol
```

The following are some of the out-of-the-box protocols.

- idProtocol is the id of the protocol

  ```
  idProtocol :: Protocol' B.ByteString
  idProtocol = id
  ```

- linesProtocols parses lines

  ```
  linesProtocol :: Protocol' B.ByteString
  ```

- base64SerProtocol: takes a Haskell object, it serializes it (with cereal library), encodes it in base 64, and change line protocol in order to become a ByteString blob.

  ```
  base64SerProtocol :: Ser.Serialize a => Protocol' a
  ```

- protocols for archives or CSV files:

  ```
  gzipProtocol :: Protocol B.ByteString B.ByteString
  csvProtocol :: (CSV b a) => CSVSettings -> Protocol b a
  ```

A little more about Protocol...

- Through a serialization, a protocol knows to read/write from/into a destination.

- prismToProtocol makes the conversion from a lens' prisms.

- They can be extended to different proprietary data formats when the data does not contain a newline character.

Next, the distinct primitive operations that the interface is allowed to do should be defined. The operations will be presented as data type (i.e., using a *generalized algebraic data types* approach). A data declaration is a method through which a type constructor and data constructors are both declared. Let's take an example.

```
data Either a b = Left a | Right b
```

The preceding is declared an Either type constructor and two data constructors, Left and Right. In Haskell, classical functions use data constructors.

```
isLeft (Left a) = True
isLeft (Right b) = False
```

This is the same as

```
type X a = Either a a
```

An a type function called X is declared; it has a parameter called a that needs to be of some type, and X returns some type. The function is not used on data values, but it could be used on type values. A mix between using type constructors declared as "data" and functions declared as "type" is very good for defining complex types. In this approach, the type constructors are like basic values, and type functions are ways in which they are processed. For more information, please visit https://wiki.haskell.org/GADTs_for_dummies.

The interface defined by the ConI type takes a MapReduce program, and connects it with input and output files, using Connect. It is then given a Protocol, resulting in a new Tap, which means that temporary files are created using MakeTap. Next, the main purpose of BynaryDirTap is to clear damaged files. It takes a file path and a filter function, does some intelligent work, and results in a clean Tap that could be read by other nodes. SetVal and GetVal are quite simple—a master node could set a value that could be read by the other nodes.

```
data ConI a where
Connect :: forall i o. MapReduce i o
-> [Tap i] -> Tap o
-> Maybe String
-> ConI ()
MakeTap :: Protocol' a -> ConI (Tap a)
BinaryDirTap :: FilePath -> (FilePath -> Bool) -> ConI (Tap B.ByteString)
ConIO :: IO a -> ConI a
SetVal :: String -> B.ByteString -> ConI ()
GetVal :: String -> ConI (Maybe B.ByteString)

newtype Controller a = Controller { unController :: Program ConI a }
```

In the preceding, Program belongs to the operational package, and allows programs as sequences of primitive instructions.

We mentioned Tap, but let's discuss what it is. A Tap is a protocol with a file location that allows operations on a file from a specific path, using a specified protocol.

```
data Tap a = Tap
{ location :: [FilePath]
, proto :: Protocol' a
}
```

These are the underlying types.

```
data MapReduce a b = forall k v. MRKey k => MapReduce {
_mrOptions :: MROptions
-- ^ Hadoop and MapReduce options affecting only this job.
, _mrInPrism :: Prism' B.ByteString v
-- ^ A serialization for values between the map-reduce steps.
, _mrMapper :: Mapper a k v
, _mrReducer :: Reducer k v b
}
```

The preceding code uses the `forall` keyword, which explicitly brings new type variables into scope. Let's take a look at the following example.

```
data Toy a = forall x. Toy x (x -> a)

example1, example2 :: Toy Int
example1 = Toy "Hello world!" length
example2 = Toy 5 (+1)
```

In example1, String is an instance of x, but in example2, Int is an instance of x. Still, example1 and example2 have the same type—namely Toy Int—because x is not a parameter of Toy. Existentials permit defining a unitary type that has values with heterogeneous-type components.

Thus, MapReduce is encapsulated as a data record; all operations that put together MapReduce programs are captured, and data endpoints are captured as "Taps."

The following connects MapReduce programs.

```
— | Connect a MapReduce program with observable input and output (and give it a name)
connect
:: MapReduce a b -> [Tap a] -> Tap b -> Maybe String -> Controller ()

— | Connect a MapReduce program with input and write into a temporary output Tap
connect
' :: MapReduce a b -> [Tap a] -> Protocol' b -> Maybe String -> Controller (Tap b)

— | Create a tap on the fly (randomly named)
makeTap
:: Protocol' a -> Controller (Tap a)

— | Set a value to run-local storage (but all nodes will be able to access this state)
setVal
:: String -> B.ByteString -> Controller ()

— | Read a value from run-local storage (even during run inside of a remote node)
getVal
:: String -> Controller (Maybe B.ByteString)

— | Perform IO (Caveat: Only for side effects)
io:: IO a -> Controller a
```

A controller application could be interpreted in many ways: orchestrate the MapReduce chain or just perform the computations.

```
Orchestrate :: (MonadIO m) => Controller a -> HadoopEnv -> RerunStrategy -> ContState -> m ()
```

This runs on the central command-line node and initiates the MapReduce program on Hadoop, starting the CLI commands. It also handles everything about Hadoop Streaming execution. Importantly, it retains the local state in every step of execution and makes it available to all nodes, ensuring that they access the same state while the relevant MapReduce step is running.

```
runMR :: (MonadIO m) => Controller a -> HadoopEnv -> RerunStrategy -> m ()
```

The alternate code-path is interpreted just by the remote nodes, which executes the MapReduce job. The same executable automatically detects if it is running on a map node or on a reduce node.

Briefly stated, this is how Hadron works. To compile and run the program, all we need to use are the following commands, where cabal-meta is a wrapper for cabal with more facilities (for more information, please visit https://hackage.haskell.org/package/cabal-meta).

```
cd emr-bundle
cabal-meta install
~/emr-bundle$ hadron-demo
```

Now, let's look at an example of MapReduce using Hadron from the official examples available on the Hadron GitHub web page. The following example is a local counting frequency of words in a document.

```
{-# LANGUAGE BangPatterns              #-}
{-# LANGUAGE FlexibleContexts          #-}
{-# LANGUAGE NoMonomorphismRestriction #-}
{-# LANGUAGE OverloadedStrings         #-}
{-# LANGUAGE TupleSections             #-}

module Main where


-------------------------------------------------------------------------------
import           Control.Category
import           Control.Lens
import qualified Data.ByteString.Char8 as B
import qualified Data.Conduit          as C
import qualified Data.Conduit.List     as C
import           Data.CSV.Conduit
import           Data.Default
import           Prelude               hiding (id, (.))
-------------------------------------------------------------------------------
import           Hadron.Controller
-------------------------------------------------------------------------------


main :: IO ()
main = hadoopMain [("app", app)] (LocalRun def) RSReRun

-- notice how path is a file
source :: CSV B.ByteString a => Tap a
source = tap "data/sample.csv" (csvProtocol def)

-- notice how path is a folder
target :: CSV B.ByteString a => Tap a
target = tap "data/wordFrequency" (csvProtocol def)

truncated :: CSV B.ByteString a => Tap a
truncated = tap "data/truncated.csv" (csvProtocol def)

-- notice how output is a file
wordCountTarget :: CSV B.ByteString a => Tap a
wordCountTarget = tap "data/wordCount.csv" (csvProtocol def)
```

```
mr1 :: MapReduce (Row B.ByteString) (Row B.ByteString)
mr1 = MapReduce def pSerialize mapper' Nothing (Left reducer')
```

```
-------------------------------------------------------------------------------
mapper':: Mapper (Row B.ByteString) B.ByteString Int
mapper' = C.concatMap (map (\w -> (w, 1 :: Int)) . concatMap B.words)

reducer' :: Reducer B.ByteString Int (Row B.ByteString)
reducer' = do
  (!w, !cnt) <- C.fold (\ (_, !cnt) (k, !x) -> (k, cnt + x)) ("", 0)
  C.yield [w, B.pack . show $ cnt]


-------------------------------------------------------------------------------
-- | Count the number of words in mr1 output
mr2 :: MapReduce (Row B.ByteString) (Row B.ByteString)
mr2 = MapReduce def pSerialize mapper Nothing (Left r)
    where
      mapper :: Mapper (Row B.ByteString) String Int
      mapper = C.map (const $ ("count", 1))

      r :: Reducer (String) Int (Row B.ByteString)
      r = do
          cnt <- C.fold (\ !m (_, !i) -> m + i) 0
          C.yield ["Total Count", (B.pack . show) cnt]

mr3 :: MapReduce (Row B.ByteString) (Row B.ByteString)
mr3 = MapReduce opts pSerialize mapper Nothing r
  where
    opts = def & mroNumReduce .~ Just 0

    mapper = C.map (\ v -> ((), map (B.take 5) v) )

    r = Right (C.map id)

app :: Controller ()
app = do
    let src = source
    connect mr1 [src] target (Just "Counting word frequency")
    connect mr2 [target] wordCountTarget (Just "Counting words")
connect mr3 [target] truncated (Just "Truncating all fields")
```

The next example does the same thing as the previous, but uses Cloudera services.

```
{-# LANGUAGE BangPatterns                #-}
{-# LANGUAGE FlexibleContexts            #-}
{-# LANGUAGE NoMonomorphismRestriction #-}
{-# LANGUAGE OverloadedStrings           #-}
{-# LANGUAGE TupleSections               #-}
```

```haskell
module Main where

-------------------------------------------------------------------------
import qualified Data.ByteString.Char8      as B
import           Data.Conduit ((=$=), yield)
import qualified Data.Conduit.List          as C
import           Data.CSV.Conduit
import           Data.Default
-------------------------------------------------------------------------
import           Hadron.Controller
-------------------------------------------------------------------------


main :: IO ()
main = hadoopMain [("count", app)] (HadoopRun clouderaDemo def) RSReRun

source :: Tap B.ByteString
source = tap "hdfs://localhost/user/cloudera/full_meta_4.csv.gz" idProtocol

target :: CSV B.ByteString a => Tap a
target = tap "hdfs://localhost/user/cloudera/wcOut1" (csvProtocol def)

mr1 :: MapReduce B.ByteString (Row B.ByteString)
mr1 = MapReduce def pSerialize mapper' Nothing (Left reducer')

mapper' :: Mapper B.ByteString CompositeKey Int
mapper' = intoCSV def =$= C.concatMap f
    where
        f :: [B.ByteString] -> [([B.ByteString], Int)]
        f ln = concatMap (map (\w -> ([w], 1 :: Int)) . B.words) ln

reducer' :: Reducer CompositeKey Int (Row B.ByteString)
reducer' = do
  (!w, !cnt) <- C.fold (\ (_, !cnt) ([k], !x) -> (k, cnt + x)) ("", 0)
  yield $ [w, B.pack . show $ cnt]

app :: Controller ()
app = connect mr1 [source] target (Just "Counting words")
```

Summary

In this chapter, you saw

- Hadoop's architecture and how it works.

- examples of Hadoop Streaming in Haskell.

■ ■ ■

CHAPTER 14

Interactive Debugger for Development and Portability Applications Based on Big Data

In computer programming and engineering, debugging represents a process with multiple steps through which a problem is identified, and the source of the problem is isolated and it is corrected. In the last step of debugging, the programmer needs to test the modification to make sure that it works as expected.

In software development, debugging means that code errors from a computer program are located and corrected. It also represents a part of a testing process; an integrated part of the whole software development life cycle. The programmer could begin to debug as she writes code and the process is kept in gradual stages of developing software product. If the program is complex, the code could be more easily debugged through unit testing (in the first part of debugging), code reviewers, pair programming, or other types of testing.

When an unexpected behavior is discovered, the programmer has to identify the code that generated this error. In this step, it could be useful to inspect the logs of the code and to use a debugger tool or the default debugging component of the IDE.

A common approach is to set a breakpoint in the code that is suspected to generate the error, and to run the code line by line in debugging mode. The debugger of an IDE usually lets the programmer examine the memory and variables, running the program to the next breakpoint or to the next line. Some debuggers provide the capability to change a variable's values while the program is in debugging mode, or even to change a line of code.

As a funny fact, the term *debugging* is actually named after a moth. In 1940, while Admiral Grace Hopper was working a Mark II Computer at Harvard University, she found a moth stuck in a relay, so she said that she and her team were "debugging" the system.

As you saw in previous chapters, big data applications can be integrated into Haskell; so for the moment, it is not necessary to create a dedicated debugger for big data application written in Haskell. In this chapter, we present a debugger incorporated into GHCi, proposed and implemented by Simon Marlow et al. in "A Lightweight Interactive Debugger for Haskell" (https://pdfs.semanticscholar.org/f718/caebfb4b70212b8553ae0d865a9e6702f041.pdf).

S. L. Nita and M. Mihailescu, *Practical Concurrent Haskell*, DOI 10.1007/978-1-4842-2781-7_14

Approaches to Run-Time Type Reconstruction

Type reconstruction means that the data type of an expression is determined automatically. It is also known as *type inference*. For debuggers for functional programming like Haskell, there are two fundamental ways to do run-time type reconstruction.

- *Backward traversal of the call stack*. All typed values that are polymorphic are generated in calls to polymorphic functions, but in the call place, the arguments are actually monomorphic. Let's take an example: `c = map ord [1, 2, 3]`. Inside the definition of map, there is no information about the type of the elements. When a map function is called inside the body of c, the type of elements is determined, so an x element has type `Integer`. This manner becomes the default approach for all cases. The debugger needs to have access to the function call stack and to the chain with binding-time calls for every variable of scope. The type of the function could also inform the arguments, like having f `:: (Int -> Int) -> Int` and calling f `(\x -> x)`. The x needs to be type `Int`.

- *Decoding the types*. This is done through inspection of heap representations. In this approach, information should be added to the code, such as specific type tags; but it is less portable than the first one.

Run-Time Type Inference

To evaluate arbitrary expressions, a run-time type inference could be invoked at any point, started by the programmer when it is needed, upon an established run-time term t. Run-time type inference occurs in two phases.

First, a type T for t is deduced, where the term represents a structure that contains only constructor applications.

```
Terms t ::= □ cₙt̄      function or non-value
          |               constructor application
```

In this definition, □ means that the expressions and functions were not evaluated in the run-time term.

Before continuing, note that in computer science, unification represents an algorithm through which an equation between symbolic expressions is solved. In the second phase, T and T' are unified, where T' represents the type of t determined at compile time. Note that T' could require type variables. A refined type for t is achieved through substitution obtained from unification between T and T' applied on T'. This process is applied to all types in other run-time terms. If type variables still exist after the two stages, the substitution is corresponding to an unknown run-time type.

There is a difference between a run-time type inference and a compile time inference. In a standard type inference, a more specific type should be deduced (instead of the main type) because the program will work fine, although it is possible for a type check failure to occur. In run-time, it is usually not safe to assume a type that is not the most general. In a run-time type inference, the type variables need to be considered from an existential point of view, not a universal point of view, because they are actually a specific type.

The debugger proposed by Simon Marlow et al. combines these two types of type inference to obtain as much as possible data about types, but assuring the safety.

A difficult operation is when the user creates its own type (with newtype), because at run-time, they could not be deduced. Let's take the following example: `newtype T = T Int`. If we declare a variable with type T `Int`, it could not be differentiated by a variable of type `Int`. This problem arises because GHC represents both types in the same way under the hood, and that no type tags are kept at run-time (in contrast to JVM or .NET run-times).

The debugger that Simon Marlow et al. created improved the type for these: a source term that corresponds to the run-time term, which is displayed to the user. The source term could have gaps in the sense that there are expressions that could not be evaluated, but the user will not see the gaps; instead, they are allocated new variable names, which is useful because it could be used in further expressions.

As an example, the following term is partially evaluated at run-time.

```
t=Just □:(Just (1: □) : □)
```

In Figure 14-1, the term t is shown in the heap, in which the dark rectangle means that the expression is not evaluated. Let's assume that we obtain that term t is of partial type [a].

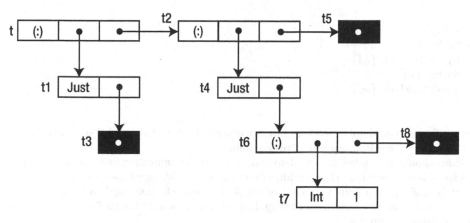

Figure 14-1. *Heap representation for the example*

In the run-time type inference, a constraint is generated for every closure in which the convention is that the data constructor type is placed on the right side, and the left side is constructed based on the subterms' types of the heap. The constructors have the following signatures.

```
(:) :: a -> [a] -> [a]
[] :: [a]
Just :: a -> Maybe a
```

All subterms are visited, generating the constraints in Figure 14-1.

```
t = [a1]
t1 -> t2 -> t = a2 -> [a2] -> [a2]
t3 -> t1 = a3 -> Maybe a3
t4 -> t5 -> t2 = a4 -> [a4] -> [a4]
t6 -> t4 = a5 -> Maybe a5
t7 -> t8 -> t6 = a6 -> [a6] -> [a6]
t7 = Int
```

The primal equation is obtained from information about the type at compiling time. The equations are solved using a classical technique of unification and, as whole result, is obtained a substitution for the solution, where are included the types for every closure, inclusive t :: [Maybe [Int]]. What it is obtained, it is unified with the type of t :: [a] from compilation time, and finally, the result is the substitution a -> Maybe [Int] that will be applied in the runtime environment for refining the types for what is inner it.

RTTI and New Types

RTTI is the abbreviation for Runtime Type Information. After the compiler checks the types, it eliminates the new types. New types constructors are not tracked in the heap, but they still shown up on the right side of constraints and in the signature of type at compile time. In this case, more implicit equations are needed to solve the constraints. When a new type is declared as newtype Set a = Set [a], it leads to the equation Set a = [a].

Reconsider the previous example with a minor modification, such that t :: Set a represents the information about the type of t from compile time. The constraints for types are obtained through inspecting the heap. The term t has the same representation in the heap.

```
t = [a1]
t1 -> t2 -> t = a2 -> [a2] -> [a2]
t3 -> t1 = a3 -> Maybe a3
t4 -> t5 -> t2 = a4 -> [a4] -> [a4]
t6 -> t4 = a5 -> Maybe a5
t7 -> t8 -> t6 = a6 -> [a6] -> [a6]
t7 = Int
```

In this case, the unification could not be made because in one equation for t is type Set $\alpha 1$, and in the other, it is [$\alpha 1$], even though there is isomorphism between them.

New type equations should be applied, if needed, to make a successful unification between static and run-time types in as few places as possible. The algorithm for the proposed debugger does the following: the constraints generated through inference attempt to be unified; if they cannot be unified, then there new type equivalencies for the terms that failed in unification are applied. This approach is a little difficult, but the heuristic works fine on classical examples.

Termination and Efficiency

The number of closures that are processed are proportional to the number of constraints generated by the RTTI algorithm; it is finite, so the unification applied on a suite of closures will terminate. The constraints are generated at the same time as the unification, but it is possible that the process through which they are generated will not terminate if it is applied on cyclic data structures. A solution to this could be keeping a log for the nodes that were visited to recover the termination.

For this debugger, the creators have talked about two improvements that are based on availability for an entire re-created type.

The constraints are solved in a breadth manner first, and unification is realized in a series of stages. When a full type is met, the process stops and returns it. Even if this solution is strange, we need to remember that this it is not the same thing as a type inference problem. In this case, we need to concentrate only on the term from the top level in the context in which many engendered constraints are used in typing subterms. This approach also improves termination that works on cyclic data structures. Some exceptions are cases in which cyclic structures have a fully unrolled spine and suspended contents.

The second approach focuses on situations in which the type for each subterm needs to be recovered, and it is based on walking in depth-first through all tree subterms. When the fully homomorphic type is retrieved, it is spread through the tree and the unification is replaced by matching. This process needs attention, because there is the possibility that the type variables will appear deep in the tree.

Practical Concerns

In the previous sections, you saw how a partial type is reconstructed. In practice, there are some issues. One of them is the inspection of a structure from a run-time term that is not totally evaluated in a Haskell program and obtaining the type signatures for constructors utilized in the term.

The system supplies an operation called unpackClosure# whose purpose is to inspect closures. Essentially, a closure has two components: an *info pointer* (used to point to a structure) and an *info table* that

- depicts the closure's layout and the code that should inspect it.

- contains *payload* where the fields of the closure are stored.

The data constructor that is corresponding to a closure is determined by looking in the information table, and then the type signature needs to be retrieved. At this step, the information from the table is completed with a special field that contains the fully qualified name of the constructor. Due to the uniqueness of the name of a program, the information about data constructor from internal GHC data structures could be easily retrieved.

The authors made this change to the technique of compiling GHC to allow debugging. The space complexity is small because there are only some data constructors.

In some situations, the fields from a heap data structure do not match the data constructors in the source code.

- Additional type-class dictionaries could be stored in the constructor due to existential quantification (called *existential dictionaries*).

- It is possible that strict fields are not unpacked. As an example, a strict field with type (a, b) is seen as two fields with types a and b, instead of as a single field.

In GHC, every constructor is managed as a record that contains the types of fields from the source code representation of the constructor. When types are reconstructed, it should be used last to match types to type values.

Implementation in Haskell

The debugger should consume as few resources as possible, and it needs to be integrated with GHCi for two reasons.

- The connection between the representation of the source code for a data constructor and the representation in the heap could be complicated while heap is traversed. To know how to represent in run-time, it is necessary to know how GHC makes the derivation of the representation.

- A fully interactive Haskell evaluation is necessary when the debug is done.

Accessibility is a characteristic of the debugger. It needs to operate with everything and to be accessible all the time. Profiling libraries are included in the debugger, which includes cost-center stacks that are very useful to a debugger.

The implementation of the debugger does not depend on the user interface being available through GHC API. The compiling and dynamic evaluation of GHC uses a programmatic interface from the GHC API. The GHCi interface is based on text, and it is created on the peak of the GHC API. GHC API is useful in the interoperability of product systems, in which different programming languages could be combined. This is the case with big data, where different tools are used for every stage through which data passes until becoming relevant knowledge. If Haskell is one of the programming languages used in one of these stages, then the GHC API could be called to build the Haskell code.

A light version of the API for debugging is shown here.

```
runStmt :: Session -> String -> IO RunResult
resume :: Session -> IO RunResult
data RunResult
= RunOk
| RunFailed
| RunException Exception
| RunBreak BreakInfo
getResumeContext :: Session -> IO [Resume]
data Resume
resumeStmt :: Resume -> String
resumeBreakInfo :: Resume -> BreakInfo
abandon :: Session -> IO ()
```

An interactive statement is started by calling runStmt by the client of GHC API. The result returned by the runStmt could be RunBreak, which means that a breakpoint has stopped the execution. Next, the client could request getResumeContext (using the :show context command) for finding the place where the breakpoint was. The getResumeContext function returns a list of Resume, because it is possible that a list of breakpoints actually exists; when the program is in a breakpoint, it could run a statement that leads to another breakpoint, and so on.

For every Resume, information about breakpoints could be requested through resumeBreakInfo, which returns a value whose type is BreakInfo, which stores information about the module or the placement of the source code with a breakpoint.

An execution could be resumed with the resume command or with the abandon command, which exits the execution. There are more options regarding breakpoint: list, enable/disable, single-step (:step command), trace (:trace command) and history (:history, :back, :forward).

A common challenge for every debugger is the way compiled code and source code are related. Intuitively, it is needed to manage a relation between the original source code and the compiled one in every step of compiling. The good news is that the problem is already solved by the Haskell Program Coverage tool (https://wiki.haskell.org/Haskell_program_coverage). To determine coverage, you need to find out if the expression was introduced at run-time for every targeted place in the initial source code. If an expression that is introduced at run-time has a secondary impact, this should be mentioned in a table that contains information about coverage in the current run. When coverage information about an expression E from the source code needs to be retrieved, it is replaced by a tick with some parameters. In this step, a tick is just an annotation, and the corresponding source code is easy to find, based on a list of mapping ticks.

Breakpoints are similar to coverage ticks. A tick technique is used for annotating the program with breakpoint sites. Still, there are differences between ticks used for breakpoint and those used for coverage.

- The way in which locations of ticks are discovered is different.

- Breakpoint places are annotated using a set of free variables, but this information is not needed with coverage.

When a breakpoint is found while evaluating, the debugger should do the following.

- The interpreter verifies if the place of breakpoint is empowered by :break or if it is in a single step execution. If none of this happens, then the execution goes on normally.

- If one of these happens, then GHCi takes control, but it permits the computation to be done later and the values of the free variables can be accessed.

Remember that runStm starts executing a new statement, which fails (RunFailed), successfully completes (RunOk), throws an exception (RunException), or meets a breakpoint (RunBreak). resume retakes the newest computation in the breakpoint. The following is the implementation of runStmt.

```
runStmt stmt = do
status_mvar <- newEmptyMVar
break_mvar  <- newEmptyMVar
let  on_break info = do
putMVar status_mvar (Break info)
takeMVar break_mvar
forkIO $ withBreakAction on_break $ do
result <- try stmt
putMVar status_mvar (Complete result)
result <- takeMVar status_mvar
case result of
Complete (Left ex) -> return (RunException ex)
Complete (Right r) -> return RunOk
Break info -> do
setResume session (break_mvar, status_mvar)
return (RunBreak info)
```

Threads and MVars are used in implementing breakpoints. A new thread is used to run the computation, and the result is stored in status_mvar. The on_break action could be invoked when a breakpoint occurs, depending on the result of the withBreakAction function. The status_mvar is used by the thread to store the result. When a breakpoint is met, on_break is run by the interpreter, which communicates through status_mvar to the principal thread that a breakpoint has occurred and is waiting for break_mvar. The principal thread retains the necessary data for resuming the actual computation in Session when it receives Break and the thread returns RunBreak to the caller.

If an exception occurs, the debugger could stop the execution, no matter if it arises in the compiled code (for example, an evaluation of head [] will throw an exception at compiling time). This is a natural choice, because exceptions could be thrown by a primitive of the compiler (raise#), in whose implementation the breakpoint handler is invoked if it is set. The breakpoint handler represents IO actions sent to withBreakAction. The behavior is the same as when a breakpoint occurs, except that a location for the breakpoint does not exist. There is an issue when the user hits the Ctrl+C keyboard combination, because it raises an asynchronous exception that does not work with #raise. A solution is to catch this exception and throw it again as a synchronous exception.

The following briefly shows how the debugger works, implementing a simple example of Data.List.lines.

```
lines    :: String -> [String]
lines "" = []
lines s  =  let (l, s') = break (=='\n') s
in  l : case s' of
[]      -> []
(_:s'') -> lines s''
```

To compile a program, just load it as normal. Let's look at how lines behave for leading and trailing newline.

```
*Main> lines "\na"
["","a"]
*Main> lines "a\n"
["a"]
```

We can place a breakpoint somewhere in the program. This represents a place where the execution will be interrupted, such that it is allowed to check the values of the local variables. The breakpoint could be placed on a line with an expression, or on the top-level function.

```
*Main> :break lines
Breakpoint 1 activated at lines.hs:(4,0)-(8,24)
```

Execution is interrupted when the breakpoint is met in lines.

```
*Main> lines "a\n"
Stopped at lines.hs:(4,0)-(8,24)
_result :: [String]
[lines.hs:(4,0)-(8,24)] *Main>
```

The user is notified that a breakpoint has occurred and the prompt is changed to show the actual source location. The _result variable is linked with the value of the expression from the breakpoint, which permits the user to work with it. The parameters can be checked only if pattern matching occurs. The :step command is used to debug step by step.

```
[lines.hs:(4,0)-(8,24)] *Main> :step
Stopped at lines.hs:(6,10)-(8,24)
_result :: [String]
s' :: [Char]
l :: [Char]
[lines.hs:(6,10)-(8,24)] *Main>
```

The execution is interrupted in the second equation in the program, at the extreme expression in the body of let. Using the :list command, the source code around the actual breakpoint is shown with the actual expression highlighted. The values for s' and l could be checked, bounded in let expression:

```
[lines.hs:(6,9)-(8,23)] *Main> (l,s')
("a","\n")
```

The lines were divided as expected. If a step-by-step approach is further used, the next piece of code will be executed.

```
[lines.hs:(6,13)-(8,23)] *Main> :step
Stopped at lines.hs:8:15-23
_result :: [String]
s" :: [Char]
```

We can show the value of s".

```
[lines.hs:8:15-23] *Main> s"
""
```

Clearly, the recursive call will now enter the base case of lines, returning the empty list. This explains why lines drop a trailing newline from the input.

In Haskell, programs run using the laziness strategy. Laziness is useful, but in many cases, it decreases performance because it adds overhead to everything. To avoid the issue of laziness, Haskell uses strict analysis, which tries to identify arguments of the function that are always evaluated, and thus they could be evaluated by the caller instead. This approach could bring big improvements.

In Haskell, type inference occurs at compile time, when all the types are checked. Implementations may erase types at run-time, as they have compile-time proof of type safety.

Summary

This chapter provided a short description how GHC works. Due to its modularity and compositionality, it is more suitable to big data than other programming languages. When large volumes of data are involved, it is useful that a program system's tools are able to automatically support modularity of the interactions between components. Haskell has the capability to manage software complexity very well.

As Don Stewart claims in its presentation "Haskell in the Large" for Google Tech Talk, Haskell is also useful in big data applications because

- the errors are caught earlier.

- accidental interactions between components is limited

- pieces in isolation could be easily changed.

- it provides strong and expressive types that lead to machine-checkable and modular software.

- it is impossible that values be combined in nonsenses ways.

- phantom types could be used. Augments types with origin/security/other metadata makes it possible to prove security properties, information flow properties, very lightweight, but high power/expressiveness, and first steps down the road to GADTs and type level programs.

- algebraic data types could be used. For example, we need to create only JSON (JavaScript Object Notation) data. For this, we define JSON grammar as a (recursive) data type.

```
data JSValue
= JSNULL
| JSDouble Double
| JSString String
| JSRecord [(String, JSValue)]
           | JSArray [JSValue]
```

- Abstract data types could contain primitives as new variants. For example, a key value store.

```
data Query
= MetadataKey Is Key
| MetadataValue Is Value
| Size Is Integer [Integer]
| SizeRange Is Integer Integer
| IngestTime Is Datetime
| Custom Is String

data Is = Is | IsNot
```

- Interfaces between Haskell and extern systems are done by interpreters and compilers. For example, we want to compile a Query:

```
compile :: [Query] -> QueryString
compile [] = "*:*"
compile qs = String.intercalate " " (map compileQuery qs)

compileQuery :: Query -> String
compileQuery (MetadataKey is k) =
    implode [compileIs is, "(", "customMetadataContent:" , "\"k.",
    escape k , "\"", ")"]
compileQuery(MetadataValue is v) =
    implode [compileIs is, "(", "customMetadataContent:" , "\"v.",
    escape v , "\"", ")"]C
compileQuery (Size is s ss) =
    implode [compileIs is, "(", "size:" , "("
        , String.intercalate " " (map compileInteger (s:ss)) , ")" , ")"
]
...
```

■ ■ ■

CHAPTER 15

Iterative Data Processing on Big Data

We know that a computer application/product is scalable if it works as expected, even when its size or volume (or the size or volume of its environment) regarding data and computations has changed to improve the user's computation necessities. In most situations, rescaling means increasing the volume or size of the computation capabilities. This is an important characteristic of cloud computing, which for big data in particular, helps because large amounts of data need to be manipulated, processed, cleaned, and analyzed; in many situations, increased computation capabilities are needed. Also, it is very important that the system run normally, even when, for example, a cluster node is down.

MapReduce is very powerful when the platform that implements it is part of a large scalable cluster. As you saw in previous chapters, in algorithms such as PageRank, data processing is done iteratively and the computations do not meet a specific stopping rule. This is not the case with MapReduce, which does not directly support iterative steps. But programmers could manually use this approach by emitting more MapReduce jobs and manipulating the executions through a driver program.

This chapter presents a nice solution to this Hadoop issue, proposed and implemented by Yingyi Bu et al in the original article *HaLoop: Efficient iterative data processing on large clusters*. It is called HaLoop.

Programming Model

Even if an iterative approach could be used in MapReduce, there are two impediments: the same data could be processed on more iterations (because data remains unchanged) and the stopping condition that checks whether a fixed point occurred (namely, to check if the same data is processed on two successive iterations).

The main architecture and functionalities of Hadoop are kept in HaLoop, which works as follows: the input and the output of the jobs are stored in HDFS. There is a master node that coordinates the slave nodes. When the client sends its jobs, the master node allocates a particular number of parallel tasks that need running over the slave nodes. In each slave node, a tracker monitors the execution of the jobs and communicates with the master node. There could be a map task or a reduce task. Figure 15-1 illustrates the similarities and differences between Hadoop and HaLoop.

© Stefania Loredana Nita and Marius Mihailescu 2017
S. L. Nita and M. Mihailescu, *Practical Concurrent Haskell*, DOI 10.1007/978-1-4842-2781-7_15

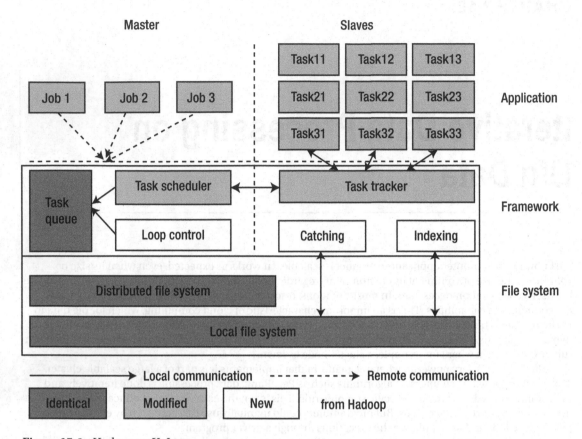

Figure 15-1. *Hadoop vs. HaLoop*

MapReduce programs are optimized by HaLoop through catching the intermediary results between MapReduce jobs. This ends if a fixed point is achieved (i.e., two consecutive iterations have the same result).

In HaLoop it is possible to have an approximate fixed point in which the difference between the outputs of two successive iterations is less than a value given by the user, or the maximum number of iterations is achieved. The two types of approximate fixed points are useful in machine learning applications.

In HaLoop programs, the work of the programmer is to specify the loop body (i.e., one or more map-reduce steps). Specifying the termination rule and the data invariant for the loop is optional. The map and reduce functions are similar to those of standard MapReduce. In a HaLoop program, the following functions should be used.

- The map function takes as input a pair (key, value) and outputs an intermediate pair (in_key, in_value);

- The reduce function takes as input the intermediate pair (in_key, in_value) and outputs the final pair (out_key, out_value). There is a new parameter used for cached invariant values corresponding to in_key.

- AddMap and AddReduce contain a loop body in which there are multiple map-reduce steps. Every map/reduce function has a corresponding integer that shows the order of the step associated with AddMap/AddReduce.

HaLoop's default state is dedicated to testing if the current iteration is equal with the previous iteration. In this way it is determined when the computation should be terminated. To specify a specific point as a condition, the programmer should use these functions.

- The SetFixedPointThreshold function fixes a bound on the distance that is situated between the current iteration and the next iteration. The computation continues while the threshold is not excedeed and the fix point is not reached.

- The ResultDistance function computes the distance between out_values sets that share the same out_key. v_i is an out_value set from the reducer output of the current iteration. v_{i-1} an out_value set from the previous iteration's reducer output. The distance between the reducer outputs of the current iteration, I, and the last iteration, i-1, represents the sum of ResultDistance for each of the keys.

- The SetMaxNumOfIterations function provides further control of the loop termination condition. HaLoop terminates the job if the maximum number of iteration has been executed, taking into consideration the current and previous iteration's outputs. SetMaxNumOfIterations acts as guidance to implement a simple for-loop.

To specify the control inputs, the programmer has to acknowledge the following:

- The SetIterationInput function associates an input source with a specific iteration, since the input files to different iterations may be different. Figure 15-2 illustrates that at each iteration, i+1, $R_i \cup L$ is the input.

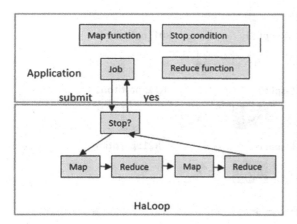 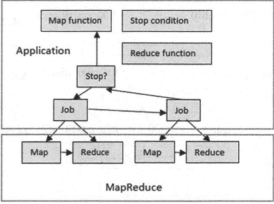

Figure 15-2. *The boundary between an iterative application and the framework illustrated in Figure 15-1. HaLoop knows and controls the loop, while Hadoop only knows jobs with one map-reduce pair.*

- The AddStepInput function associates an additional input source with an intermediate map-reduce pair situated in the body of the loop. The output resulted from the preceding map-reduce pair is always in the input of the next map-reduce pair.

- The AddInvariantTable function specifies an input a table (under the form of HDFS file) that is loop-invariant. After the code executes, HaLoop caches this table on cluster nodes.

The current programming interface is sufficient to express a variety of iterative applications. Figure 15-2 depicts the main difference between HaLoop and Hadoop, from the application's point of view. With HaLoop, the user of the application specifies the loop settings and the framework that controls the loop execution; but in Hadoop, it is the application's responsibility to control the loops.

Loop-Aware Task Scheduling

From this point, we focus on the HaLoop task scheduler. The scheduler provides potentially better schedules for iterative programs, which Hadoop's scheduler is not capable of offering.

Inter-Iteration Locality

The high-level goal of HaLoop's scheduler is to place the maps and to reduce the tasks that can occur on the same physical machines in different iterations, but access the same data. Using this approach, data can be more easily cached and reused between the respective iterations.

The scheduling of iteration 1 is no different than it is in Hadoop. In the join step of the first iteration, the input tables are L and R_0. Three map tasks are executed, each of which loads a part of one or the other input data file (e.g., file split). As in Hadoop, the mapper output key is hashed to reduce the task to which it should be assigned. After this, three reduce tasks are executed, each of which loads a partition of the collective mapper output. In Figure 15-3, the reducer denoted with R_{00} processed the mapper output keys whose hash value is 0. The R_{10} reducer processes the keys with hash value 1, and the R_{20} reducer will process the keys with hash value 2.

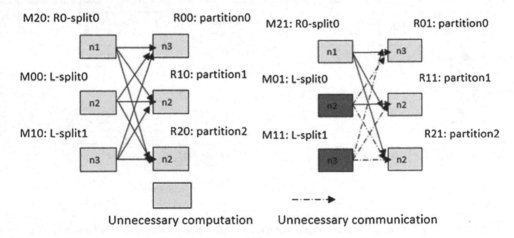

Figure 15-3. A schedule exhibiting inter-iteration locality. Tasks processing the same inputs on consecutive iterations are scheduled to the same physical nodes.

The scheduling of the join step of iteration 2 has the advantage of *inter-iteration locality*, which means that the task (either a mapper or a reducer) that processes specific data partition D is scheduled on the physical node that D is processed in iteration 1.

The schedule in Figure 15-5 provides the feasibility to reuse loop-invariant data from past iterations. Because L is loop invariant, mappers M_{01} and M_{11} would compute identical results to M_{00} and M_{10}. There is no need to recompute these mapper outputs or to communicate them to the reducers. In iteration 1, if reducer input partitions 0, 1, and 2 are stored on nodes n3, n1, and n2, respectively, then in iteration 2, L need not be loaded, processed, or shuffled again. In that case, in iteration 2, only one mapper M_{21} for R_1-split 0 needs to be launched, and thus the three reducers will only copy intermediate data from M_{21}. With this strategy, the reducer input is no different, but it now comes from two sources: the output of the mappers (as usual) and the local disk.

We refer to the property of the schedule in Figure 15-3 as the inter-iteration locality. Let d be a file split (mapper input partition) or a reducer input partition. Let T_d^i be a task consuming d in iteration i. Then we say that a schedule exhibits inter-iteration locality if for all $i > 1$, and T_d^i and T_d^{i-1} are assigned to the same physical node if T_d^{i-1} exists. The goal of task scheduling in HaLoop is to achieve inter-iteration locality.

To achieve this goal, the only restriction is that HaLoop requires that the number of reduce tasks should be invariant across iterations, so that the hash function assigning mapper outputs to reducer nodes remains unchanged.

Experimental Tests and Implementation

HaLoop supports iterative and recursive data analysis tasks as mainly recursive joins. These joins could be map joins (for example, they are used in a k-means algorithm) or reduce joins (for example, they are used in a PageRank algorithm). The key to HaLoop is caching loop-invariant data to slave nodes, and reutilizing them between iterations.

HaLoop is available at `http://haloop.googlecode.com/svn/trunk/haloop`.

To configure a cluster in HaLoop, we take the same steps as in Hadoop. The difference between clusters in Hadoop and HaLoop is that local mode and the pseudo-distributed mode are not supported by HaLoop, but it is supports real distributed mode.

To run the examples, first compile them.

```
% ant -Dcompile.hs=yes examples
```

And then copy the binaries to `dfs`.

```
% bin/hadoop fs -put examples
```

Create an input directory with text files.

```
% bin/hadoop fs -put my-data in-dir
```

Now, as practice, modify the word count examples in Chapter 13 (see the "Hadron" section), adding `AddMap` and `AddReduce` as described earlier, and run the word-count example as follows.

```
% bin/hadoop pipes -conf pathfile/word.hs \ -input in-dir -output out-dir
```

Summary

This chapter presented HaLoop, an improvement for Hadoop proposed and implemented by Yingyi Bu et al. It supports iterative and recursive data analysis tasks, which brings

- a loop-aware task scheduler
- loop-invariant data caching
- caching for efficient fixpoint verification

CHAPTER 16

■ ■ ■

MapReduce

This chapter's goal is to present the importance of using techniques for incremental and iterative processes applied in development applications for the cloud. Intelligent applications such as PageRank perform iterative computations on data sets that are constantly changing. We will point out that iterative computation are too expensive in order to realize an entirely new large-scale MapReduce iterative job which will make the desired changes on the datasets.

We present the main elements that characterize the changes in data sets by implementing solutions based on incremental and iterative computation. You will see how these changes are impacting only a very small fraction of data sets.

Incremental and Iterative Techniques

Iterative computations are important elements in cloud applications used in many areas. A good example is the PageRank algorithm in search engines on the Web. Gradient descent for optimization is another example. These algorithms are intensely used, especially in recommendation systems or link predictions. Searching data within large amounts of data (which could be unstructured) is a great challenge because it could take hours, or even days, to get results. Data is also very dynamic, and it could change every minute, so fast results are needed so that we can say what we obtained is accurate. If algorithms run on data that isn't up-to-date, it is very possible that the outcomes are too old or inaccurate. Frequent refresh of iterative computations of data is very important in receiving accurate results. Unfortunately, this is very expensive, so the capability of performing incremental processing over unstructured data is needed. As we discussed in previous chapters, MapReduce is the most used platform in data analysis in a cloud environment.

An algorithm that is iterative makes the same computations to a given data set in each iteration, which always leads to improved results. The algorithm stops when the difference between the results from two successive iterations is sufficiently small. There are two types of data involved here: the static data (i.e., the input data set) and dynamic data (i.e., the output of every iteration).

The result of the current iteration is just a little different from the result of the previous iteration. The outputs of two consecutive iterations rarely depend on one another. An element that is updated in its current iteration will influence just a small number of elements from the next iterations, so there are parts that converge faster than the others do. These techniques have applications in graph theory, especially in cases in which changes from a vertex (node) affects its neighbors. For some algorithms, the update could be done asynchronously, which eliminates the barriers between iterations.

Due to slow converging, many iterative algorithms are not suitable for current systems. The iterative algorithms presented and developed in the last few years—such as HaLoop, Twister (proposed by J. Ekanayake, H. Li, B. Zhang, T. Gunarathne, S. H. Bac, J. Qiu, and G. Fox in article titled Twister: a runtime for iterative mapreduce), Stateful Bulk Processing (proposed by D. Logothetis, C. Olston, B. Reed, K. C. Webb, and K. Yocum in article titled Stateful bulk processing for incremental analytics), Naiad, and Incoop—are

© Stefania Loredana Nita and Marius Mihailescu 2017
S. L. Nita and M. Mihailescu, *Practical Concurrent Haskell*, DOI 10.1007/978-1-4842-2781-7_16

developed to further support incremental and iterative techniques, but not all of the are reliable. All of these algorithms are very lightweight when they are implemented. The efficiency of iterative computations will be improved if we focus on the task scheduler loop and consider caching mechanisms. The system will also need other specific analysis and transformation tasks. For large data sets, the processing will be realized on many systems that need to manage their work through workflow frameworks. In MapReduce (but also in other models where large data sets are trained), it is necessary to monitor the data flow that pre-processes the data, to have a specific system for a training algorithm, and to have a specific system for post-processing.

There are some reasons for which iterations should be integrated with data flow, instead of creating specialized systems for different jobs.

- The managing frameworks will not be needed anymore, because integrating iterations directly in data flow allows analytical pipelines to be viewed as a unique element.

- Data flows can be easy optimized.

- Data flows are suitable for distributed algorithms and become widely used in machine learning.

Some algorithms are asynchronous iterative computations, especially machine learning and data-mining algorithms that update large sets of parameters. Synchronous algorithms are based on graphs; updates depend on the values of parameters. For example, in the working paper "i^2 MapReduce: Incremental Iterative MapReduce," the authors, Yanfeng Zhang and Shimin Chen, propose and implement a model called Map-Reduce Bipartite Graph (MRBGraph) to illustrate iterative and incremental computations, which contain a loop between mappers and reducers. In synchronous approaches, all parameters are updated in parallel at the same time and the input is from the parameter values from the previous iteration. In an asynchronous approach, parameters are updated based on the most recent value of parameter input. Studies show that many times an asynchronous approach is more efficient than a synchronous approach.

Iterative algorithms are mainly based on update functions. An update function represents a procedure without a state that changes the data within the scope of a vertex V (i.e., data stocked in the V and into all neighbor vertices and corresponding edges) and sets up the subsequent executions of the update function on another vertex.

Make sure that the scope of update functions that are running concurrently are not overlapping. This leads to fully consistent models based on iterative algorithms. This is a good thing, but it has its inconveniences: parallelism is limited because update functions need to run with a difference of at least two vertices. In most cases, the update function does not use all the data from a scope. A benefit of edge consistency is that access to the update function's vertex and adjacent edges is represented by read and write operations; but for adjacent vertices, the access is read-only. This increases the parallelism because one update function will have a little overlapping of scopes to safely run in parallel. It also permits all functions to run in parallel, so maximum parallelism will be achieved.

We mentioned the PageRank algorithm many times in this section. Behind this algorithm, there are concepts based on probability theory and linear algebra. It is used by Google to display relevant links regarding some keywords introduced by the user. The following is a Haskell implementation of this algorithm. It is available for download at https://github.com/derekchiang/Haskell-Page-Rank/blob/master/pagerank.hs. The solution and idea are proposed and implemented by Derek Chiang.

```
import        Data.Map    (Map, empty, insert, insertWith, lookup,
                           mapWithKey, member, size)
import        Data.Maybe  (fromJust)
import        Debug.Trace (trace)
import        Prelude     hiding (lookup)
import        Text.Printf (printf)
```

```
type Node = Int
type PRValue = Double
type PageRank = Map Node PRValue
type InboundEdges = Map Node [Node]
type OutboundEdges = InboundEdges

parseLine :: (InboundEdges, OutboundEdges, Node) -> String -> (InboundEdges, OutboundEdges,
             Node)
parseLine (iEdges, oEdges, maxNode) line =
    let ws = words line
        (from, to) = (read $ ws !! 0, read $ ws !! 1)
        in (insertWith ++ plusNode to [from] iEdges,
            insertWith ++ plusNode from [to] oEdges,
            max to (max maxNode from))
    where
        plusNode :: [Node] -> [Node] -> [Node]
        plusNode new_node old_node =
            new_node ++ old_node


newPageRank :: Int -> PageRank
newPageRank n =
    let v :: Double = 1 / fromIntegral n
        in go n v empty
    where
        go :: Int -> Double -> PageRank -> PageRank
        go 0 _ pr = pr

        go n v pr =
            go (n-1) v $ insert (n-1) v pr


-- The goal of postProcess is to deal with the nodes that have no outbound
-- edges, in which case they should be treated like they have outbound edges
-- to every other node.
postProcess :: (InboundEdges, OutboundEdges, Node) -> (InboundEdges, OutboundEdges)
postProcess (iEdges, oEdges, maxNode) =
    let numNodes = maxNode + 1
        newIEdges = addAllNodes (numNodes-1) iEdges
        in loop (numNodes-1) newIEdges oEdges


    where
        loop :: Int -> InboundEdges -> OutboundEdges -> (InboundEdges, OutboundEdges)
        loop n iEdges oEdges
            | n < 0 = (iEdges, oEdges)
            | otherwise =
                if member n oEdges then
                    loop (n-1) iEdges oEdges
                else
                    let numNodes = maxNode + 1
                        newOEdges = insert n (filter (/= n) [0..maxNode]) oEdges
                        newIEdges = mapWithKey (\k v -> if k /= n then v ++ [n] else v) iEdges
                        in loop (n-1) newIEdges newOEdges
```

239

```
        -- This function makes sure that every node is a key in the InboundEdges map
        addAllNodes :: Int -> InboundEdges -> InboundEdges
        addAllNodes n iEdges
            | n < 0 = iEdges
            | otherwise =
                addAllNodes (n-1) $ insertWith (\new old -> new ++ old) n [] iEdges

parseGraph :: String -> (InboundEdges, OutboundEdges, PageRank)
parseGraph input =
    let ls = lines input
        (iEdges, oEdges) = postProcess $ foldl parseLine (empty, empty, 0) ls
        numNodes = size iEdges
        in (iEdges, oEdges, newPageRank numNodes)

loopProcess :: Int -> Double -> InboundEdges -> OutboundEdges -> PageRank -> PageRank
loopProcess 0 _ _ _ pageRank = pageRank
loopProcess n dampingFactor iEdges oEdges pageRank =
    let newPageRank = loop' ((size pageRank) - 1) empty
        in loopProcess (n-1) dampingFactor iEdges oEdges newPageRank


    where
        loop' :: Int -> PageRank -> PageRank
        loop' n pr
            | n < 0 = pr
            | otherwise =
                let inbounds = fromJust $ lookup n iEdges
                    newPrValue = (+)
                        ((1 - dampingFactor) / (fromIntegral $ size iEdges))
                        (dampingFactor * (foldl calc 0 inbounds))
                    in loop' (n-1) $ insert n newPrValue pr


                where
                    calc acc node =
                        let outbounds = fromJust $ lookup node oEdges
                            prValue = fromJust $ lookup node pageRank
                            in acc + prValue / (fromIntegral $ length outbounds)

process :: String -> Int -> Double -> PageRank
process input numIters dampingFactor =
    let (iEdges, oEdges, pageRank) = parseGraph input
        in loopProcess numIters dampingFactor iEdges oEdges pageRank

main :: IO ()
main = do
    putStrLn "How many iters?"
    numIters <- getLine
    f <- readFile "input.txt"
    -- damping factor defaults to 0.85
writeFile "output.txt" $ show $ process f (read numIters :: Int) 0.85
```

This shows how an iterative algorithm works. Haskell also provides an implemented version of PageRank that can be used by importing the `Data.Graph.PageRank` module, which is in the `graph-utils` package. You can use

```
pageRanks :: Graph gr => gr a b -> Double -> Double -> RankDic
```

to compute a rank for every page of Graph, where the following is stored PageRank data.

```
type RankDic = Map Node Double
```

Iterative Computation in MapReduce

Now, let's look at how iterative computation works in MapReduce.

A user sends a set of MapReduce jobs to the iterative algorithm. An iteration must have at least one job. In every iteration, the map function is processing the result from the previous iterations and the initial data input (i.e., both static and dynamic data), and the reduce function is combining the intermediary data to output the dynamic data of the current iteration. With distributed environments, this is stocked in the distributed file system, and it is the input for the next iteration. Usually, every iteration is done through a job. This is the reason why iterative computation is not very efficient in native MapReduce. MapReduce extensions improve its efficiency in iterative computation. Mainly, there are two directions.

- Direction is based on creating an intern data flow on a single MapReduce job, where all computations are done. For this approach, the result of the reduce function is sent directly to the map function. This leads to a lower start-up cost (because, dynamic data does not need to be read from a file system).

- Caching iteration-invariant data, namely input data, leads to one read of the input data in the first iteration.

An interesting application of iterative techniques in MapReduce is an extension of the GraphLab framework for distributed computing proposed by Yucheng Low et al. The data from the graph is in the first step over partitioned through domain specific knowledge or through a distributed graph partitioning heuristic. The number of elements (an element is called an *atom*) of partition is k, which is much larger than the number of machines. Every atom is stored in a distinct file in the form of a binary compressed list of graph generation commands (for example, AddVertex or AddEdge). In every atom, there is information about vertices and edges adjacent to the partition frontiers. An atom index file contains the connections between vertices and the locations for the other atom files. The information in this index file could be considered as a metagraph in which the vertices are the k atoms and the edges are the connections between the atoms.

The user constructs the atom graph on a distributed file system. Hashed partitioning is the technique suitable for MapReduce. The construction of the graph needs to perform a map function on every vertex and edge, and every reduce function collects an atom file. The benefit of atom files is that modifications can be done without retaking the whole process from the beginning.

Data Parallel Haskell (DPH) is a good Haskell example of iterative computation (examples in this section could also be found at https://wiki.haskell.org/GHC/Data_Parallel_Haskell). It is an extension of GHC that contains libraries for nested data parallelism (i.e., applying a function in parallel on every item of a set and nesting parallel calls), using CPUs with multiple cores. Currently, DPH is not maintained by the community. The last update was in 2012. The current version offers the main benefits of creating applications based on iterative computation.

DPH is an add-on. Its focus is on vectorization and parallel execution on systems with multiple cores. Vectorization is characterized by applying an elaborate transformation to the DPH code, which turns the nested into flat data parallelism. This transformation is very useful for the code that is executed in parallel, and for dramatically simplifying load balancing. The degree of nesting is fixed and the user cannot create its own data types. The main approach is irregular parallelism. If you want to get this library, run the following commands in a command prompt window.

```
$ cabal update
$ cabal install dph-examples
```

Among the packages, there are also some examples installed.

DPH introduces a new data type in Haskell—namely parallel arrays, and also the operations on the arrays. If you want to define a parallel array, use [: and :] instead of [and].

- [:e:] represents the type of parallel array, containing elements with type e.

- [: x,y,z:] represent a parallel array with three elements: x,y,z.

- [:x+1 | x <- xs :] represents an array comprehension.

The following are differences between lists and parallel arrays.

- Parallel arrays have a strict data structure, in the sense that if one element is used, then all the others elements are required. From here, the elements are processed in parallel.

- Parallel arrays could not be inductively defined. To assure the parallelism, they are seen in entirety. This is the reason why they cannot be defined inductively.

- Parallel arrays are always finite. They have the foldP function, which is undirected and needs that the input function to be associative. Some aggregate functions (e.g., permuteP) are not implemented in the standard library.

The following is an example in which the dot product of two parallel arrays is implemented. The parallel list array comprehension is used.

```
dotp :: Num a => [:a:] -> [:a:] -> a
dotp xs ys = sumP [:x * y | x <- xs | y <- ys:]
```

This is another version of implementation.

```
[:x * y | (x, y) <- zipP xs ys:]
```

The preceding version of dotP is very simple, but it cannot be compiled and run in this version right now, so we need to change it. GHC needs to apply some transformations through a technique called *vectorization* over DPH in order to transform it from nested to flat data parallelism.

Because type classes are not available, we should not use overloaded operations in parallel code. Due to this restriction, dotP is implemented only on Double.

```
dotp_double :: [:Double:] -> [:Double:] -> Double
dotp_double xs ys = sumP [:x * y | x <- xs | y <- ys:]
```

Because there are data type limitations, vectorization cannot be applied on certain language constructs, so Prelude cannot be used in its entirety. But DPH contains a limited version of Prelude available on Data.Array.Parallel.Prelude, and additional modules for these numeric types: Data.Array.Parallel. Prelude.Int, Data.Array.Parallel.Prelude.Double, Data.Array.Parallel.Prelude.Float, Data. Array.Parallel.Prelude.Word8, and Data.Array.Parallel.Prelude.Bool. Actually, the modules contain the same operations, but they are implemented specifically for one data type. To use the same operation on arrays that have different types of elements, all the corresponding modules need to be imported. If the programmer needs a function that is not contained in these modules, then he needs to implement and vectorize them.

In order to compile and run dotp_double, we need to add the following qualified imports.

```
import qualified Prelude
import Data.Array.Parallel
import Data.Array.Parallel.Prelude
import Data.Array.Parallel.Prelude.Double
```

We need to pay attention to the interaction with vectorized and non-vectorized code. Simple types can be used in both of them and passed through them. Parallel arrays could not be passed, but the PArray type could be passed, on which a special Prelude will export with fromPArrayP, which is a conversion function specific to the type of elements in a parallel array. Next, we need to create a wrapper for our product, which will be exported and used in non-vectorized code.

```
 dotp_wrapper :: PArray Double -> PArray Double -> Double
{-# NOINLINE dotp_wrapper #-}
dotp_wrapper v w = dotp_double (fromPArrayP v) (fromPArrayP w)
```

The wrapper should be NOINLINE, because it should not be inlined in the non-vectorized code.

To use the syntax of parallel arrays, we need to enable it with ParallelArrays. We should tell the compiler that we will vectorize a module by adding the -fvectorise option. Either the code will be vectorized into one module, or it will not be vectorized at all, so it is highly recommended that vectorized and non-vectorized code be kept in separate modules. So, for dotP example, we get the following.

```
{-# LANGUAGE ParallelArrays #-}
{-# OPTIONS_GHC -fvectorise #-}

module DotP (dotp_wrapper)
where

import qualified Prelude
import Data.Array.Parallel
import Data.Array.Parallel.Prelude
import Data.Array.Parallel.Prelude.Double

dotp_double :: [:Double:] -> [:Double:] -> Double
dotp_double xs ys = sumP [:x * y | x <- xs | y <- ys:]

dotp_wrapper :: PArray Double -> PArray Double -> Double

{-# NOINLINE dotp_wrapper #-}

dotp_wrapper v w = dotp_double (fromPArrayP v) (fromPArrayP w)
```

This code is stored in a file called DotP.hs. It is compiled as shown in the following, using -Odph, which enables some optimizations for DPH, and -fdph-par, which picks the standard DPH back-end library.

```
ghc -c -Odph -fdph-par DotP.hs
```

The last step is to create a main module in which the vectorized code is called. This module is not vectorized, which allows inputs and outputs. Further, two lists are converted into parallel arrays, and then their dot product is computed, and finally, the result is displayed.

```
import Data.Array.Parallel
import Data.Array.Parallel.PArray (PArray, fromList)

import DotP (dotp_wrapper)  -- import vectorised code

main :: IO ()
main
  = let v      = fromList [1..10]    -- convert lists...
        w      = fromList [1,2..20]  -- ...to parallel arrays
        result = dotp_wrapper v w    -- invoke vectorised code
    in
    print result                     -- print the result
```

The module is compiled as you saw previously.

```
ghc -c -Odph -fdph-par Main.hs
```

Then the two modules are linked into an executable called dotp.

```
ghc -o dotp -threaded -fdph-par -rtsopts DotP.o Main.o
```

The -threaded option links with GHC run-time based on multithreading. -fdph-par links to the DPH back-end. -rtsopts determines the number of threads involved in code execution.

Parallel execution is very efficient on very large data sets, and the benefits are easily seen. We can generate a larger input data, as follows.

```
import System.Random (newStdGen)
import Data.Array.Parallel
import Data.Array.Parallel.PArray (PArray, randomRs)

import DotP (dotp_wrapper)  -- import vectorised code

main :: IO ()
main
  = do
      gen1 <- newStdGen
      gen2 <- newStdGen
      let v = randomRs n range gen1
          w = randomRs n range gen2
      print $ dotp_wrapper v w   -- invoke vectorized code and print the result
  where
    n     = 10000        -- vector length
    range = (-100, 100)  -- range of vector elements
```

To use the data that we have generated, we just need to follow the preceding steps.

Incremental Iterative Processing on MRBGraph

You have seen that sending the result of a reduce function directly to a map function improves performance. This loop will be modeled as MapReduce Bipartite Graph (MRBGraph). The map function works with a state data record and a structure data record. The reduce function works with intermediary data leading to another state data record that will be sent to a corresponding mapper. In this type of graph, we find two types of nodes: mapper nodes and reducer nodes. The shuffled intermediary data is represented by edges from mappers to reducers (MR-Edge), and the iterated state data is represented by reducers to mappers edges (RM-Edge). The state of the MRBGraph is improved with every iteration, and the algorithm stops only when the state of the MRBGraph is stable (converged state).

Incremental iterative processing on MRBGraph consists of using the last converged state data. The performance in incremental iterative performance will increase. Starting with a converged state, the data resulted from the first iteration is different from the input data just with a small degree ΔD. The changes in ΔD could be insertion, alteration, or removal from initial data D. So, in MR-Edge, states are affected because only mappers make these operations over data.

Only D(0) and D(2) are influenced by ΔD, so only mapper0 and mapper2 should be performed. Their performance is followed by reducers at the end of MR-Edge mapper0 and mapper2. The reducers that are running combine the last converged MR-Edge state of the MR-Edges corresponding to reducers that are not running with the up-to-date MR-Edge state. When the reducers send results to corresponding mappers, the first iteration is completed. As expected, some parts of dynamic state data from RM-Edges could be modified according to the previous iteration; therefore, only the mappers that correspond with modified RM-Edges need to run. Until the last iteration, there will be a certain number of RM- and MR-Edges that will change, which will lead to another MRBGraph state.

The purpose of this approach is to avoid computations that are not needed. The map function is running only when the input state or the data structure is changed from the previous iteration, and the reduce function is running only when the state of a corresponding MR-Edge is changed.

To implement MRBGraph, the reducers' outputs are sent back to the right mappers. According to Zhang and Chen, the behavior is modeled as a MRBGraph. From a theoretical point of view, the mapper will take action on the state data record $r^k(i)$ and a structure data record $S(i)$. The reducer takes action on the intermediate data and it produces an update on the state of the data records $r^{k+1}(i)$, which is sent back to the right mappers and replicated on several mappers for the next iteration.

You have to consider that in MRBGraph, there are two types of vertices: the mapper vertices and the reducer vertices.

Summary

This chapter discussed the following aspects of and techniques for incremental and iterative strategies.

- The importance of using MapReduce in the application, including the main advantages and disadvantages

- The incremental and iterative techniques and how integrate in the process of development

- Incremental iterative processing using MRBGraph

- Iterative computation in MapReduce

- Data Parallel Haskell (DPH), which focuses on nested data parallelism

CHAPTER 17

■ ■ ■

Big Data and Large Clusters

MapReduce represents a simple programming model, used in applications that generate and process large sets of data. All what the programmer needs to do is to implement the map and the reduce functions, as follows: map function processes a (key, value) pair, resulting an intermediary list of (key, value) pairs, and the reduce function takes as parameter the list resulted from map and merges all intermediary values that correspond to the same intermediary key.

Programs that adopt this programming model, are by default implemented in parallel and cloud be run on a large cluster of nodes. The way in which data is partitioned, the schedule of the program's execution in the cluster, handled failures, and communications between nodes of the cluster are managed by the runtime system.

In this way, the resources provided by a distributed system could be used by any programmer, even if there is no experience in parallel and distributed programming. Adopting MapReduce model, the application is scalable, because terabytes of data are processed on a large number of nodes. By its appearance, thousands of MapReduce jobs are implemented and executed in Google's clusters every day.

For a better understanding of MapReduce, this chapter includes some technical details from the original implementation proposed by Jeffrey Dean, et al., in a working paper available at https://static. googleusercontent.com/media/research.google.com/en//archive/mapreduce-osdi04.pdf.

Programming Model

As mentioned in the other chapters that worked with MapReduce, the input is represented by a list of pairs (key/value), and the output is another set of such pairs. The programmer needs to implement only the map and reduce functions. As a reminder, a map function takes as input the initial set of the pairs, and outputs an intermediary list of such pairs in which the values that have the same keys are grouped, which become the input for the reduce function that outputs the final set of pairs. A reduce function calling usually outputs one value or no value. It receives intermediary values through an iterator, which is useful when working with large data lists that cannot fit into memory.

Master Data Structures

The master stores just a few data structures: for every map step and every reduce step, the state of the task is retained (which has one of the following types: idle, in progress, completed) and an id for worker machines if they are not in the idle state. Also, the master manages the paths of intermediary files and makes them available for map or reduce tasks. If a completed map task outputs R intermediary file paths, the master stores the location and the size of each file. They are updated just when map tasks are completed, and notifications are sent incrementally to reduce tasks that are in progress.

Fault Tolerance

Due to the large amount of data that needs to be processed, MapReduce ensures that the work will not be affected in the event of failures.

Worker Failures

Every worker is checked from time to time by the master. If it is not responding on time, the worker is marked as failed. When a task is completed by a worker, its state becomes idle, which means that it could be scheduled to another worker. When a task is running, but the worker has failed, it is reset to an idle state and becomes available to other workers. When a worker fails, the completed map task is run again, because their output is stored locally on the worker, and thus, in the event of a failure, the output is not be accessible; but

Reduce tasks do not need re-executing because their results are stored globally. When a map task is re-executed because of a failure, all reducers tasks that are running are notified about this situation, and they begin reading data from the new worker on which the map task is currently running (if they haven't already read from the worker that failed).

Master Failures

The master occasionally writes about its state in the master data structure, registering checked points. If a master task is down, then a copy of it is started, retaking the work beginning at the last registered checked points. If there is just one master task available, then the entire MapReduce process is cancelled. The user can check if this has happened; there is the possibility to restart the MapReduce process.

Locality

Network bandwidth does not influence the computing environment much. Network bandwidth is preserved through the fact that input data is stored on local workers. Every file is divided into blocks of size 64MB by the Google file system. More copies (typically three) are stored on different machines for every block. The data is transferred on demand. All locations are made known to the master, which plans a map task (to run on a worker) that contains a copy of the all input data. If this worker fails, the task is run by a close worker (for example, a worker in the same network as the one that failed). Usually, the input data for more map tasks is read locally, so bandwidth is not used.

Task Granularity

The map is divided into M components. The reduce part is divided into R components. M and R are larger than the number of workers. Load balancing is improved by the fact that a worker executes several tasks at the same time.

The speed of recovery in the event of failure is increased: if a worker fails, its tasks are distributed across other workers. The performance of the system is described as follows: the master takes a number of scheduling operations proportional to M+R and keeps the MR states in the memory. (The space complexity is small, because O(MR) piece of states contains about 1 byte of data for every map task and reduce task.)

Moreover, usually the user constrains R, because every reduce task "writes" its result in a different output file. In practice, M is chosen such that every single task has approximately 16 – 64 MB of input data (this leads to the conclusion that local optimizations has a greater effect). R is a small multiple of the number of worker machines that we expect to use. MapReduce computations are often performed as M = 200000 and R = 5000, using 2,000 worker machines.

Backup Tasks

The reason behind the total time extended for a MapReduce action is a "struggler" machine consuming a significant amount of time to reduce the final tasks in the computation.

On the cluster system, you can schedule different tasks, which could result in a slow execution of MapReduce code due to the CPU, memory, local disk, or worse, network bandwidth. There could also be bugs such as in the machine initialization code, bug that disables the processor cache.

There is a general mechanism to reduce stragglers. When a MapReduce operation is at a state of completion, the execution of master schedules backs up the remaining tasks in progress. When the primary or backup execution is completed, the task is marked as finished. You can refine the mechanism in such way that it will typically increase the resources used in the computational process used by the operation. This stratetgy reduces the time to complete big operations based on MapReduce.

Partitioning Function

As a initial setup, the user choses a number of reduce tasks and output files that need to be achieved (R). Data is partitioned across these tasks by applying a partitioning function that uses hashes to intermediate key (for example, "hash (key) mod R"). This seems to be well partitioned. Of course, there are situations in which data is partitioned using another functions of the key. For such special situations, MapReduce library contains special partitioning functions. An example is when the outputs are URLs and the user wants that all inputs for the same host to be in the same file. For this, "hash (Hostname(urlkey)) mod R" could be used to partition data such that all output URLs for the same host to be in the same file.

Implementation of Data Processing Techniques

This section presents the implementation of a MapReduce monad for Haskell. It is also available at `https://git://github.com/Julianporter/Haskell-MapReduce.git`. The following example implements the MapReduce in memory, taking into consideration and applying the best solution to distribute the tasks and to serve them in the shortest time possible using advanced threads and traditional mappers at the end.

```
-- | Module that defines the 'MapReduce' monad and exports the necessary functions.
--
--   Mapper / reducers are generalised to functions of type
--   @a -> ([(s,a)] -> [(s',b)])@ which are combined using the monad's bind
--   operation.  The resulting monad is executed on initial data by invoking
--   'runMapReduce'.
--
--   For programmers only wishing to write conventional map / reduce algorithms,
--   which use functions of type @([s] -> [(s',b)])@ a wrapper function
--   'liftMR' is provided, which converts such a function into the
--   appropriate monadic function.
module Parallel.MapReduce.Simple (
-- * Types
        MapReduce,
-- * Functions
--
```

```haskell
-- ** Monadic operations
      return, (>>=),
-- ** Helper functions
      run, distribute, lift) where

import Data.List (nub)
import Control.Applicative ((<$>))
import Control.Monad (liftM)
import Control.DeepSeq (NFData)
import System.IO
import Prelude hiding (return,(>>=))
import Data.Digest.Pure.MD5
import Data.Binary
import qualified Data.ByteString.Lazy as B
import Control.Parallel.Strategies (parMap, rdeepseq)

-- | The parallel map function; it must be functionally identical to 'map',
--    distributing the computation across all available nodes in some way.
pMap :: (NFData b) => (a -> b)             -- ^ The function to apply
        -> [a]                             -- ^ Input
        -> [b]                             -- ^ output
pMap = parMap rdeepseq

-- | Generalised version of 'Monad' which depends on a pair of 'Tuple's, both
--    of which change when '>>=' is applied.
class MonadG m where
        return :: a                        -- ^ value.
                -> m s x s a               -- ^ transformation that inserts the value
                                           --   by replacing all
                                           --   the key values with the specified
                                           --   value, leaving the data unchanged.

        (>>=)  :: (Eq b,NFData s'',NFData c) =>
                m s a s' b                 -- ^ Initial processing chain
                -> ( b -> m s' b s'' c )    -- ^ Transformation to append to it
                -> m s a s'' c             -- ^ Extended processing chain

-- | The basic type that provides the MapReduce monad (strictly a generalised monad).
-- In the definition
-- @(s,a)@ is the type of the entries in the list of input data and @(s',b)@
-- that of the entries in the list of output data, where @s@ and @s'@ are data
-- and @a@ and @b@ are keys.
--
-- 'MapReduce' represents the transformation applied to data by one or more
--    MapReduce staged.  Input data has type @[(s,a)]@ and output data has type
-- @[(s',b)]@ where @s@ and @s'@ are data types and @a@, @b@ are key types.
--
--    Its structure is intentionally opaque to application programmers.
newtype MapReduce s a s' b = MR { runMR :: [(s,a)] -> [(s',b)] }
```

```
-- | Make MapReduce into a 'MonadG' instance
instance MonadG MapReduce where
        return = ret
        (>>=)  = bind

-- | Insert a value into 'MapReduce' by replacing all the key values with the
--   specified value, leaving the data unchanged.
ret :: a                                         -- ^ value
        -> MapReduce s x s a                     -- ^ transformation that inserts the value
                                                 --   into 'MapReduce' by replacing all
                                                 --   the key values with the specified
                                                 --   value, leaving the data unchanged.
ret k = MR (\ss -> [(s,k) | s <- fst <$> ss])

-- ^ Apply a generalised mapper / reducer to the end of a chain of processing
--   operations to extend the chain.
bind :: (Eq b,NFData s'',NFData c) =>
                  MapReduce s a s' b             -- ^ Initial state of the monad
        -> (b -> MapReduce s' b s'' c)           -- ^ Transformation to append to it
        -> MapReduce s a s'' c                   -- ^ Extended transformation chain
bind f g = MR (\s ->
        let
                fs = runMR f s
                gs = map g $ nub $ snd <$> fs
        in
        concat $ pMap (`runMR` fs) gs)

-- | Execute a MapReduce MonadG given specified initial data.  Therefore, given
--   a 'MapReduce' @m@ and initial data @xs@ we apply the processing represented
--   by @m@ to @xs@ by executing
--
--   @run m xs@
run :: MapReduce s () s' b                        -- ^ 'MapReduce' representing the required
processing
                  -> [s]                          -- ^ Initial data
                  -> [(s',b)]                      -- ^ Result of applying the processing to
                                                  --   the data
run m ss = runMR m [(s,()) | s <- ss]

-- | The hash function.  Computes the MD5 hash of any 'Hashable' type
hash :: (Binary s) => s                           -- ^ The value to hash
        -> Int                                    -- ^ its hash
hash s = sum $ map fromIntegral (B.unpack h)
        where
        h = encode (md5 $ encode s)

-- | Function used at the start of processing to determine how many threads of processing
--   to use.  Should be used as the starting point for building a 'MapReduce'.
--   Therefore a generic 'MapReduce' should look like
--
```

```
--    @'distribute' '>>=' f1 '>>=' . . . '>>=' fn@
distribute :: (Binary s) => Int              -- ^ Number of threads across which to
                                                  distribute initial data
                 -> MapReduce s () s Int      -- ^ The 'MapReduce' required to do this
distribute n = MR (\ss -> [(s,hash s `mod` n) | s <- fst <$> ss])

-- | The wrapper function that lifts mappers / reducers into the 'MapReduce'
--   monad.  Application programmers can use this to apply MapReduce transparently
--   to their mappers / reducers without needing to know any details of the implementation
--   of MapReduce.
--
--   Therefore the generic 'MapReduce' using only traditional mappers and
--   reducers should look like
--
--    @'distribute' '>>=' 'lift' f1 '>>=' . . . '>>=' 'lift' fn@
lift :: (Eq a) => ([s] -> [(s',b)])          -- traditional mapper / reducer of signature
                                             -- @([s] -> [(s',b)]@
       -> a                                  -- the input key
       -> MapReduce s a s' b                 -- the mapper / reducer wrapped as an
                                                instance
                                             -- of 'MapReduce'
lift f k = MR (\ss -> f $ fst <$> filter (\s -> k == snd s) ss)
```

Summary

This chapter presented a MapReduce solution that can be used in large clusters and big data environments. We discussed specific ideas that need to be taken into consideration when developing solutions for environments, such as

- Creating a conceptual programming model
- Advanced master data structures
- Fault tolerance
- Locality and where workers are stored
- Task granularity
- Backup tasks
- Partitioning techniques
- Impementing data processing techniques

Bibliography

[1]   Algehed, Maximilian, and Patrik Jansson. "VisPar: Visualising dataflow graphs from the Par monad." (2017).

[2]   Andersson, Oscar, and Jin, Yanling. "A Tutorial on Parallel Strategies in Haskell", 2014.

[3]   Ankner, Johan, and Josef David Svenningsson. "An EDSL approach to high performance Haskell programming." ACM SIGPLAN Notices. Vol. 48. No. 12. ACM, 2013.

[4]   Aswad, M. KH, and Philip W. Trinder. "Architecture aware parallel programming in Glasgow Parallel Haskell (GPH)." Procedia Computer Science 9 (2012): 1807-1816.

[5]   Armbrust, Michael, et al. Above the clouds: A berkeley view of cloud computing. Vol. 17. Technical Report UCB/EECS-2009-28, EECS Department, University of California, Berkeley, 2009.

[6]   Aswad, M. KH, and Philip W. Trinder. "Architecture aware parallel programming in Glasgow Parallel Haskell (GPH)." Procedia Computer Science 9 (2012): 1807-1816.

[7]   Bekki, Daisuke, and Ai Kawazoe. "Implementing Variable Vectors in a CCG Parser." International Conference on Logical Aspects of Computational Linguistics. Springer, Berlin, Heidelberg, 2016.

[8]   Bird, Richard. "Thinking functionally with Haskell". Cambridge University Press, 2014.

[9]   Bu, Yingyi, et al. "HaLoop: Efficient iterative data processing on large clusters." Proceedings of the VLDB Endowment 3.1-2 (2010): 285-296.

[10]   Burke, John. "A Haskell Implementation of MapReduce."

[11]   Cavalheiro, Gerson GH, and Renata HS Reiser. "Concurrent Hash Tables for Haskell." Programming Languages: 20th Brazilian Symposium, SBLP 2016, Maringá, Brazil, September 22-23, 2016, Proceedings. Vol. 9889. Springer, 2016.

[12]   Chen, Hsinchun, Roger HL Chiang, and Veda C. Storey. "Business intelligence and analytics: From big data to big impact." MIS quarterly 36.4 (2012).

[13]   Chen, Yu-Fang, et al. "An executable sequential specification for Spark aggregation." International Conference on Networked Systems. Springer, Cham, 2017.

© Stefania Loredana Nita and Marius Mihailescu 2017
S. L. Nita and M. Mihailescu, *Practical Concurrent Haskell*, DOI 10.1007/978-1-4842-2781-7

[14]   Church, James. "Learning Haskell Data Analysis". Packt Publishing Ltd, 2015.

[15]   Dean, Jeffrey, and Sanjay Ghemawat. "MapReduce: simplified data processing on large clusters." Communications of the ACM 51.1 (2008): 107-113.

[16]   Dean, Jeffrey, and Sanjay Ghemawat. "MapReduce: a flexible data processing tool." Communications of the ACM 53.1 (2010): 72-77.

[17]   Dittrich, Jens, and Jorge-Arnulfo Quiané-Ruiz. "Efficient big data processing in Hadoop MapReduce." Proceedings of the VLDB Endowment 5.12 (2012): 2014-2015.

[18]   Doets, H. C., and Jan Eijck. "The Haskell road to logic, maths and programming." Texts in Computing (2012).

[19]   Duarte, Rodrigo Medeiros, et al. "Concurrent Hash Tables for Haskell." Brazilian Symposium on Programming Languages. Springer, Cham, 2016.

[20]   Ekanayake, Jaliya, et al. "Twister: a runtime for iterative mapreduce." Proceedings of the 19th ACM international symposium on high performance distributed computing. ACM, 2010.

[21]   Epstein, Jeff, Andrew P. Black, and Simon Peyton-Jones. "Towards Haskell in the cloud." ACM SIGPLAN Notices. Vol. 46. No. 12. ACM, 2011.

[22]   Fischer, Christian. "Haskell vs. JavaScript for Game Programming." USCCS 2017: 55.

[23]   Fritsch, Joerg. Functional Programming Languages in Computing Clouds. Diss. Cardiff University, 2016.

[24]   Gantz, John, and David Reinsel. "The digital universe in 2020: Big data, bigger digital shadows, and biggest growth in the far east." IDC iView: IDC Analyze the future 2007.2012 (2012): 1-16.

[25]   Glushenkov, Mikhail. "A Cross-Platform Scalable I/O Manager for GHC: Improving Haskell Networking on Windows." (2016).

[26]   Hage, Jurriaan. "Haskell in the Large." (2013).

[27]   Haven, Drew, and Eric Stratmann. "Web-based Data Analytics in Haskell."

[28]   Hayes, Brian. "Cloud computing." Communications of the ACM 51.7 (2008): 9-11.

[29]   Hinze, Ralf, Johan Jeuring, and Andres Löh. "Comparing approaches to generic programming in Haskell." Datatype-Generic Programming. Springer, Berlin, Heidelberg, 2007. 72-149.

[30]   Holmes, Alex. Hadoop in practice. Manning Publications Co., 2012.

[31]   Hutton, Graham. Programming in Haskell. Cambridge University Press, 2016.

[32]   Jain, Akshat, and Megha Gupta. "Evolution and Adoption of programming languages." Evolution 5.1 (2017).

[33]   John Walker, Saint. "Big data: A revolution that will transform how we live, work, and think." (2014): 181-183.

[34]   Jones, Simon Peyton, Andrew Gordon, and Sigbjorn Finne. "Concurrent haskell." POPL. Vol. 96. 1996.

[35]   Jost, Steffen, et al. "Type-Based Cost Analysis for Lazy Functional Languages."
       Journal of Automated Reasoning 59.1 (2017): 87-120.

[36]   Juchli, Marc, et al. "Mining motivated trends of usage of Haskell libraries."
       Proceedings of the 1st International Workshop on API Usage and Evolution. IEEE
       Press, 2017.

[37]   Kusakabe, Shigeru, and Yuuki Ikuta. "Large Scale Random Testing with
       QuickCheck on MapReduce Framework." Functional and (Constraint) Logic
       Programming: 131.

[38]   Lai, Longbin, et al. "ShmStreaming: A shared memory approach for improving
       Hadoop streaming performance." Advanced Information Networking and
       Applications (AINA), 2013 IEEE 27th International Conference on. IEEE, 2013.

[39]   Lämmel, Ralf. "Google's MapReduce programming model—Revisited." Science
       of computer programming 70.1 (2008): 1-30.

[40]   Lemmer, Ryan. Haskell Design Patterns. Packt Publishing Ltd, 2015.

[41]   Lima, Luís Gabriel Nunes Ferreira. "Understanding the energy Behavior of
       concurrent haskell programs." (2016).

[42]   Lindley, Sam, and Conor McBride. "Hasochism: the pleasure and pain of
       dependently typed Haskell programming." ACM SIGPLAN Notices 48.12 (2014):
       81-92.

[43]   Lipovaca, Miran. Learn you a haskell for great good!: a beginner's guide. no
       starch press, 2011.

[44]   Liu, Lei, et al. "An abstract description method of map-reduce-merge using
       Haskell." Mathematical Problems in Engineering 2013 (2013).

[45]   Liu, Yu, Zhenjiang Hu, and Kiminori Matsuzaki. "Towards systematic parallel
       programming over mapreduce." Euro-Par 2011 Parallel Processing (2011): 39-50.

[46]   Lohr, Steve. "The age of big data." New York Times 11.2012 (2012).1

[47]   Logothetis, Dionysios, et al. "Stateful bulk processing for incremental analytics."
       Proceedings of the 1st ACM symposium on Cloud computing. ACM, 2010.

[48]   Low, Yucheng, et al. "Graphlab: A new framework for parallel machine learning."
       arXiv preprint arXiv:1408.2041 (2014).

[49]   Manyika, James, et al. "Big data: The next frontier for innovation, competition,
       and productivity." (2011).

[50]   Marin, Mircea. "Advanced features of Functional Programming (Haskell)."
       (2017).

[51]   Marlow, Simon. "Parallel and concurrent programming in Haskell." Central
       European Functional Programming School. Springer Berlin Heidelberg, 2012.
       339-401

[52]   Marlow, Simon. "Parallel and concurrent programming in Haskell: Techniques
       for multicore and multithreaded programming". " O'Reilly Media, Inc.", 2013.

[53]   Marlow, Simon, et al. "Asynchronous exceptions in Haskell." Acm sigplan
       notices. Vol. 36. No. 5. ACM, 2001.

[54]   Marlow, Simon, et al. "A lightweight interactive debugger for haskell."
        Proceedings of the ACM SIGPLAN workshop on Haskell workshop. ACM, 2007.

[55]   Maurer, Luke, et al. "Compiling without continuations." Proceedings of the
        38th ACM SIGPLAN Conference on Programming Language Design and
        Implementation. ACM, 2017.

[56]   Mazumder, Mark, and Timothy Braje. "Safe Client/Server Web Development with
        Haskell." Cybersecurity Development (SecDev), IEEE. IEEE, 2016.

[57]   McAfee, Andrew, and Erik Brynjolfsson. "Big data: the management revolution."
        Harvard business review 90.10 (2012): 60-68.

[58]   Mell, Peter, and Tim Grance. "The NIST definition of cloud computing." (2011).

[59]   Mena, Alejandro Serrano. "Time Traveling with Haskell." Beginning Haskell.
        Apress, 2014. 391-392.

[60]   Najd, Shayan, and Simon Peyton Jones. "Trees that Grow." J. UCS 23.1 (2017): 42-
        62.

[61]   O'Driscoll, Aisling, Jurate Daugelaite, and Roy D. Sleator. "'Big data,' Hadoop and
        cloud computing in genomics." Journal of biomedical informatics 46.5 (2013):
        774-781.

[62]   O'Sullivan, Bryan, John Goerzen, and Donald Bruce Stewart. Real world haskell:
        Code you can believe in. " O'Reilly Media, Inc.", 2008.

[63]   Paykin, Jennifer, and Steve Zdancewic. "The Linearity Monad." (2017).

[64]   Pelletier, Francis Jeffry. "The principle of semantic compositionality." Topoi 13.1
        (1994): 11-24.

[65]   Qian, Ling, et al. "Cloud computing: An overview." Cloud computing (2009): 626-
        631.

[66]   Ranger, Colby, et al. "Evaluating mapreduce for multi-core and multiprocessor
        systems." High Performance Computer Architecture, 2007. HPCA 2007. IEEE
        13th International Symposium on. Ieee, 2007.

[67]   Ribeiro, Rodrigo, et al. "Optional Type Classes for Haskell." Brazilian Symposium
        on Programming Languages. Springer International Publishing, 2016.

[68]   Ryzhov, Pavel. Haskell Financial Data Modeling and Predictive Analytics. Packt
        Publishing Ltd, 2013.

[69]   Rubio, Fernando, et al. "A Parallel Swarm Library Based on Functional
        Programming." International Work-Conference on Artificial Neural Networks.
        Springer, Cham, 2017.

[70]   Schlatt, S., et al. "The Holumbus distributed computing framework &
        MapReduce in Haskell." (2009).

[71]   Schmidt, Douglas C., and Tim Harrison. "Double-checked locking-an
        optimization pattern for efficiently initializing and accessing thread-safe objects."
        (1997).

[72]   Snoyman, Michael. Developing web applications with Haskell and Yesod. "
        O'Reilly Media, Inc.", 2012.

[73] Subashini, Subashini, and Veeraruna Kavitha. "A survey on security issues in service delivery models of cloud computing." Journal of network and computer applications 34.1 (2011): 1-11.

[74] Takuya, Matsumoto, and Matsuzaki Kiminori. "Evaluation of Libraries for Parallel Computing in Haskell—A Case Study with a Super-resolution Application." 情報処理学会論文誌プログラミング (PRO) 10.2 (2017).

[75] Tate, Bruce A. Seven languages in seven weeks: a pragmatic guide to learning programming languages. Pragmatic Bookshelf, 2010.

[76] Thompson, Martin, et al. Disruptor. Tech. Rep., May, 2011.

[77] Thomasson, Samuli. "Haskell High Performance Programming". Packt Publishing, 2016.

[78] Thompson, Martin, et al. "High performance alternative to bounded queues for exchanging data between concurrent threads." technical paper, LMAX Exchange (2011).

[79] Thompson, Martin, et al. "Disruptor: High performance alternative to bounded queues for exchanging data between concurrent threads." Technical paper. LMAX, May (2011): 206.

[80] Vasconcellos, Cristiano. "Optional Type Classes for Haskell." Programming Languages: 20th Brazilian Symposium, SBLP 2016, Maringá, Brazil, September 22-23, 2016, Proceedings. Vol. 9889. Springer, 2016.

[81] Vassena, Marco. "A Verified Information-Flow Control Library." (2017).

[82] Vassena, Marco, Joachim Breitner, and Alejandro Russo. "Securing Concurrent Lazy Programs." Security Principles and Trust Hotspot 2017 (2017).

[83] Vassena, Marco, Joachim Breitner, and Alejandro Russo. "Securing Concurrent Lazy Programs Against Information Leakage." Proceedings of the 30th IEEE Computer Security Foundations Symposium (CSF), 2017.

[84] Vazou, Niki, and Ranjit Jhala. "Refinement Reflection (or, how to turn your favorite language into a proof assistant using SMT)." arXiv preprint arXiv:1610.04641 (2016).

[85] Vlissides, John, et al. "Design patterns: Elements of reusable object-oriented software." Reading: Addison-Wesley 49.120 (1995): 11.

[86] Viera, Marcos, S. Doaitse Swierstra, and Wouter Swierstra. "Attribute grammars fly first-class: how to do aspect oriented programming in Haskell." ACM Sigplan Notices. Vol. 44. No. 9. ACM, 2009.

[87] Vollmer, Michael, et al. "SC-Haskell: Sequential Consistency in Languages That Minimize Mutable Shared Heap." Proceedings of the 22nd ACM SIGPLAN Symposium on Principles and Practice of Parallel Programming. ACM, 2017.

[88] Vossen, J. J. Offloading Haskell functions onto an FPGA. MS thesis. University of Twente, 2016.

[89] Winograd-Cort, D. A. N. I. E. L., Hengchu Zhang, and Benjamin C. Pierce. "Partial Evaluation for Typechecking."

[90]   Wu, Xindong, et al. "Data mining with big data." IEEE transactions on knowledge and data engineering 26.1 (2014): 97-107.

[91]   Yang, Hung-chih, et al. "Map-reduce-merge: simplified relational data processing on large clusters." Proceedings of the 2007 ACM SIGMOD international conference on Management of data. ACM, 2007.

[92]   Yates, Ryan, and Michael L. Scott. "Improving Haskell STM Performance."

[93]   Zhang, Qi, Lu Cheng, and Raouf Boutaba. "Cloud computing: state-of-the-art and research challenges." Journal of internet services and applications 1.1 (2010): 7-18.

[94]   Zhang, Yanfeng, et al. "I2mapreduce: Incremental mapreduce for mining evolving big data." *IEEE transactions on knowledge and data engineering* 27.7 (2015): 1906-1919.

[95]   Zikopoulos, Paul, and Chris Eaton. Understanding big data: Analytics for enterprise class hadoop and streaming data. McGraw-Hill Osborne Media, 2011.

[96]   Abrahamson, Joseph. "A Little Lens Starter Tutorial", https://www.schoolofhaskell.com/school/to-infinity-and-beyond/pick-of-the-week/a-little-lens-starter-tutorial

[97]   Andersson, Oscar and Jin, Yanling."A tutorial on Parallel Strategies in Haskell", http://www.cse.chalmers.se/edu/year/2014/course/DAT280_Parallel_Functional_Programming/Papers/strategies-tutorial-v2.pdf

[98]   Apfelmus, Heinrich. "How Lazy Evaluation Works in Haskell", https://hackhands.com/lazy-evaluation-works-haskell

[99]   Chiang, Derek. "Haskell-Page-Rank", https://github.com/derekchiang/Haskell-Page-Rank/blob/master/pagerank.hs

[100]   de Vries, Edsko. "Communication Patterns in Cloud Haskell (Part 3)"http://www.well-typed.com/blog/2012/10/communication-patterns-in-cloud-haskell-part-3/

[101]   de Vries, Edsko. "Communication Patterns in Cloud Haskell (Part 4)", http://www.well-typed.com/blog/many-10-74

[102]   Freeman, Phil. "Haskell on Azure", http://blog.functorial.com/posts/2012-04-29-Haskell-On-Azure.html

[103]   Goldberg, Drew. "Executive Summary: Balking Design Patterns", https://www.cs.colorado.edu/~kena/classes/5828/s12/presentation-materials/goldbergdrew.pdf

[104]   Marlow, Simon. "Sample geturls.hs", https://github.com/simonmar/parconc-examples/blob/master/geturlscancel.hs

[105]   Marlow, Simon. "Parallel and Concurrent Haskell Part II", http://slidegur.com/doc/3167714/parallel-and-concurrent-haskell-part-ii

[106]   Marlow, Simon, et al. "A lightweight interactive debugger for haskell." Proceedings of the ACM SIGPLAN workshop on Haskell workshop. ACM, 2007.

[107]   Marlow, Simon. "Parallel & Concurrent Haskell 3: Concurrent Haskell", http://community.haskell.org/~simonmar/slides/cadarache2012/3%20-%20concurrent%20haskell.pdf

[108]   Mestanogullari, Alp, and Boespflug, Mathieu. "Haskell meets large scale distributed analytics", http://www.tweag.io/posts/2016-02-25-hello-sparkle.html

[109]   Sakr, Majd F., Rehman, Suhail and Hammoud, Mohammad. "Dryad and GraphLab. Lecture 11"

[110]   Stewart, Don. "Haskell in the large". Google Tech Talks, 2015.

[111]   Tibell, Johan. "The design of the Strict Haskell pragma", http://blog.johantibell.com/2015/11/the-design-of-strict-haskell-pragma.html

[112]   Turoff, Adam. "Design Patterns in Haskell: bracket", 2007, http://notes-on-haskell.blogspot.ro/2007/03/design-patterns-in-haskell-bracket.html

[113]   "ACID (atomicity, consistency, isolation, and durability)", http://searchsqlserver.techtarget.com/definition/ACID

[114]   "Cloud Haskell", http://haskell-distributed.github.io

[115]   "Conquering Hadoop with Haskell and Ozgun Ataman", https://vimeo.com/90189610

[116]   "Control.Concurrent.Chan", https://hackage.haskell.org/package/base-4.9.1.0/docs/Control-Concurrent-Chan.html

[117]   "Data-parallel-Haskell", https://wiki.haskell.org/GHC/Data_Parallel_Haskell

[118]   "Design Patterns", https://en.wikipedia.org/wiki/Design_Patterns

[119]   "Evaluation Strategy", https://en.wikipedia.org/wiki/Evaluation_strategy

[120]   "GenBank Overview", https://www.ncbi.nlm.nih.gov/genbank

[121]   "GHC Language Features", https://downloads.haskell.org/~ghc/7.0.3/docs/html/users_guide/lang-parallel.html

[122]   "haskell-barrier/examples/MatrixMultiplication.hs", https://github.com/aartamonau/haskell-barrier/blob/master/examples/MatrixMultiplication.hs

[123]   "haskell-distributed/distributed-process", https://github.com/haskell-distributed/distributed-process

[124]   "Haskell-MapReduce",https://git://github.com/Julianporter/Haskell-MapReduce.git

[125]   "Introduction to optics: lenses and prisms", https://medium.com/@gcanti/introduction-to-optics-lenses-and-prisms-3230e73bfcfe

[126]   "haskell_hadoop", https://github.com/paulgb/haskell_hadoop

[127]   "Haskell Lenses Notes", https://rafal.io/posts/haskell-lenses-notes.html

[128]   "Haskell-page-rank", https://github.com/derekchiang/Haskell-Page-Rank/blob/master/pagerank.hs

[129]   "krapsh/kraps-haskell", https://github.com/krapsh/kraps-haskell

[130]   "Performance/Data types", https://wiki.haskell.org/Performance/Data_types

[131]   "simonmar/parconc-examples", https://github.com/simonmar/parconc-examples/blob/master/geturlscancel.hs

[132]   "Soostone/hadron", https://github.com/Soostone/hadron

[133]   "Testing Haskell with QuickCheck", http://jasani.org/2008/01/03/testing-haskell-with-quickcheck

[134]   "The network-transport package", http://hackage.haskell.org/package/network-transport

[135]   "ThreadPool.hs", https://gist.github.com/NicolasT/4163407

[136]   "Types of Program Errors", http://www.inf.unibz.it/~calvanese/teaching/ip/lecture-notes/uni10/node2.html

[137]   "xmonad", http://xmonad.org

[138]   "zeromq-haskell", https://gitlab.com/twittner/zeromq-haskell

Index

© Stefania Loredana Nita and Marius Mihailescu 2017

S. L. Nita and M. Mihailescu, *Practical Concurrent Haskell*, DOI 10.1007/978-1-4842-2781-7

Get the eBook for only $5!

Why limit yourself?

With most of our titles available in both PDF and ePUB format, you can access your content wherever and however you wish—on your PC, phone, tablet, or reader.

Since you've purchased this print book, we are happy to offer you the eBook for just $5.

To learn more, go to http://www.apress.com/companion or contact support@apress.com.

Apress®

Printed in the United States
By Bookmasters